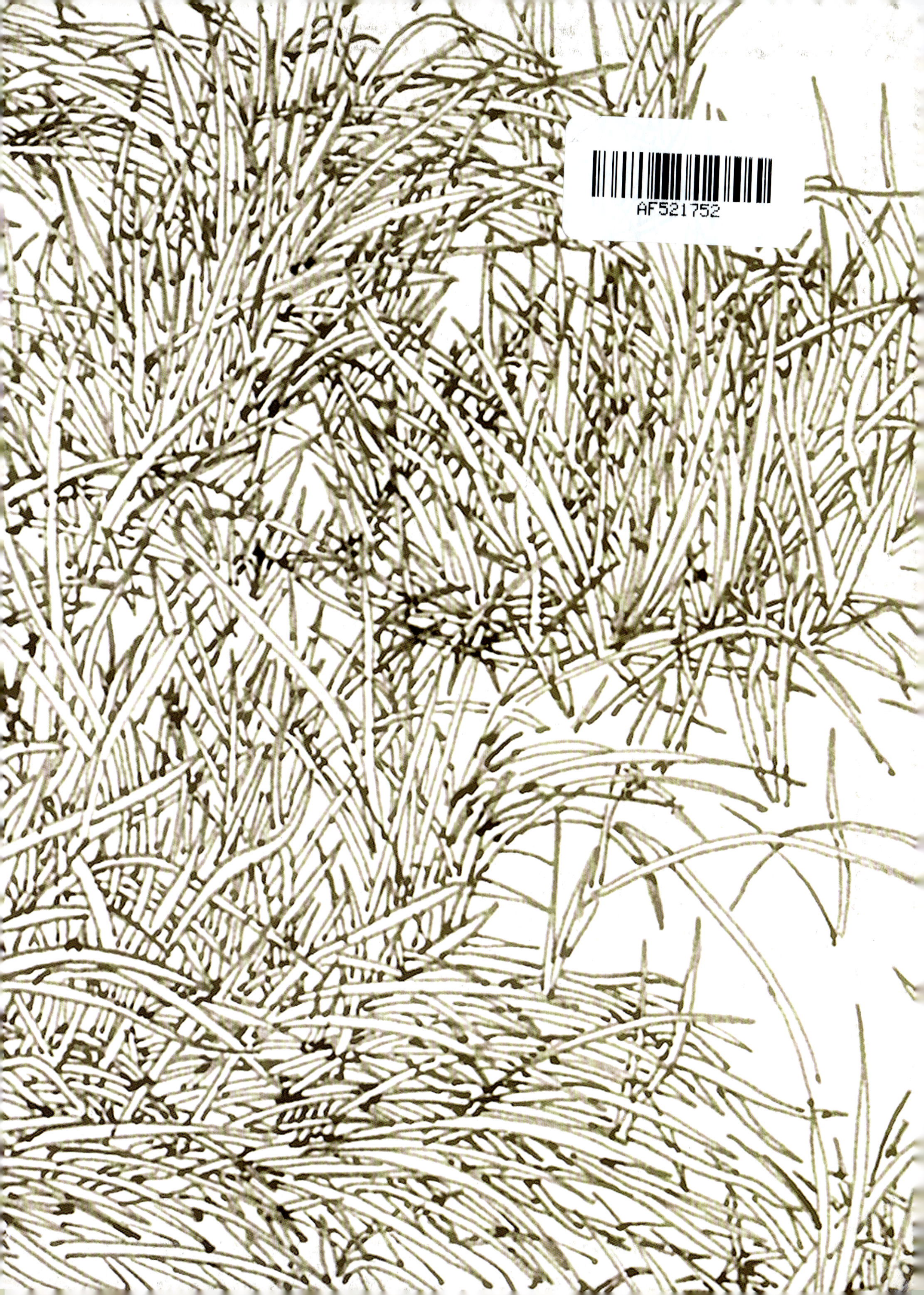

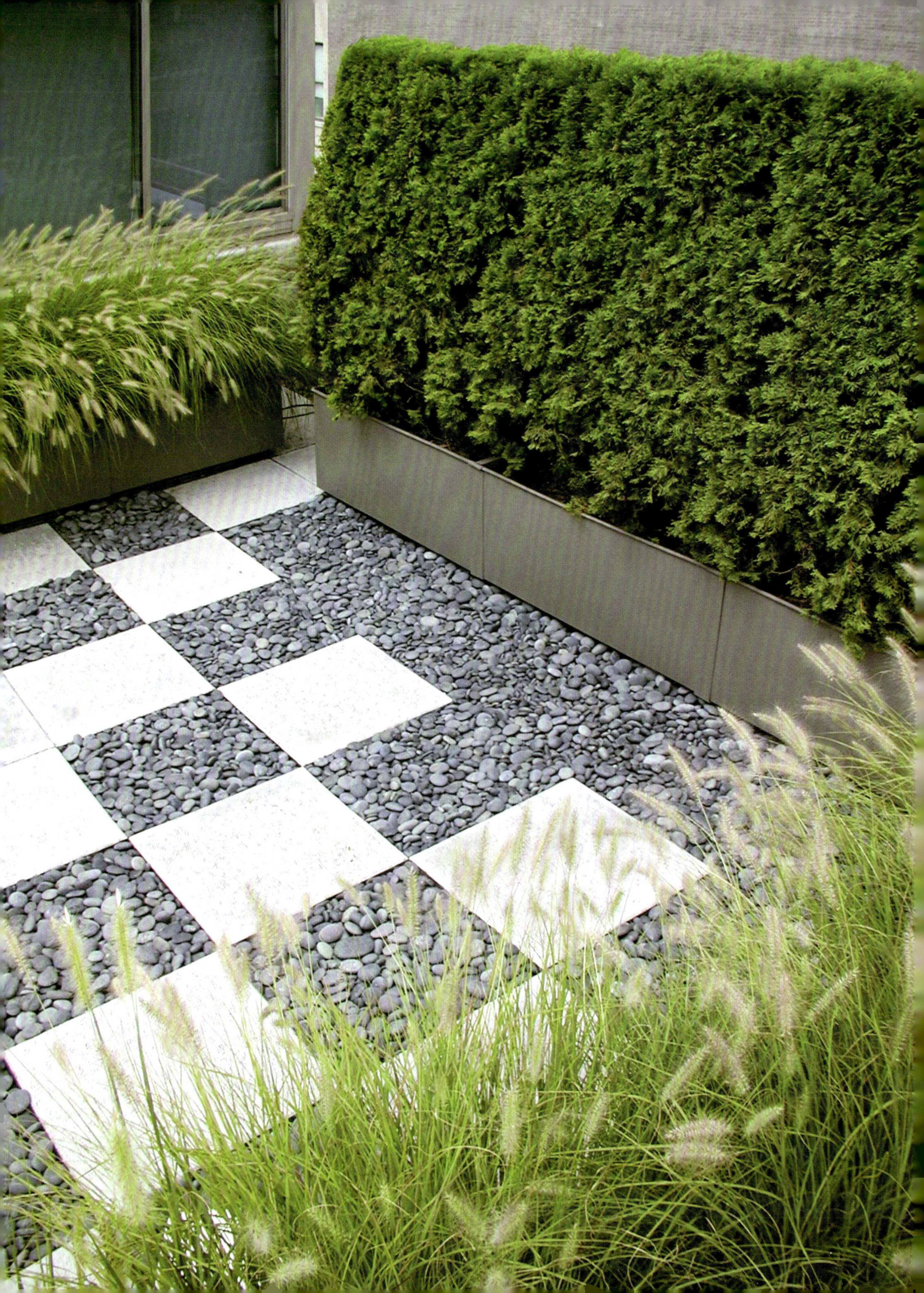

ARTIFACT

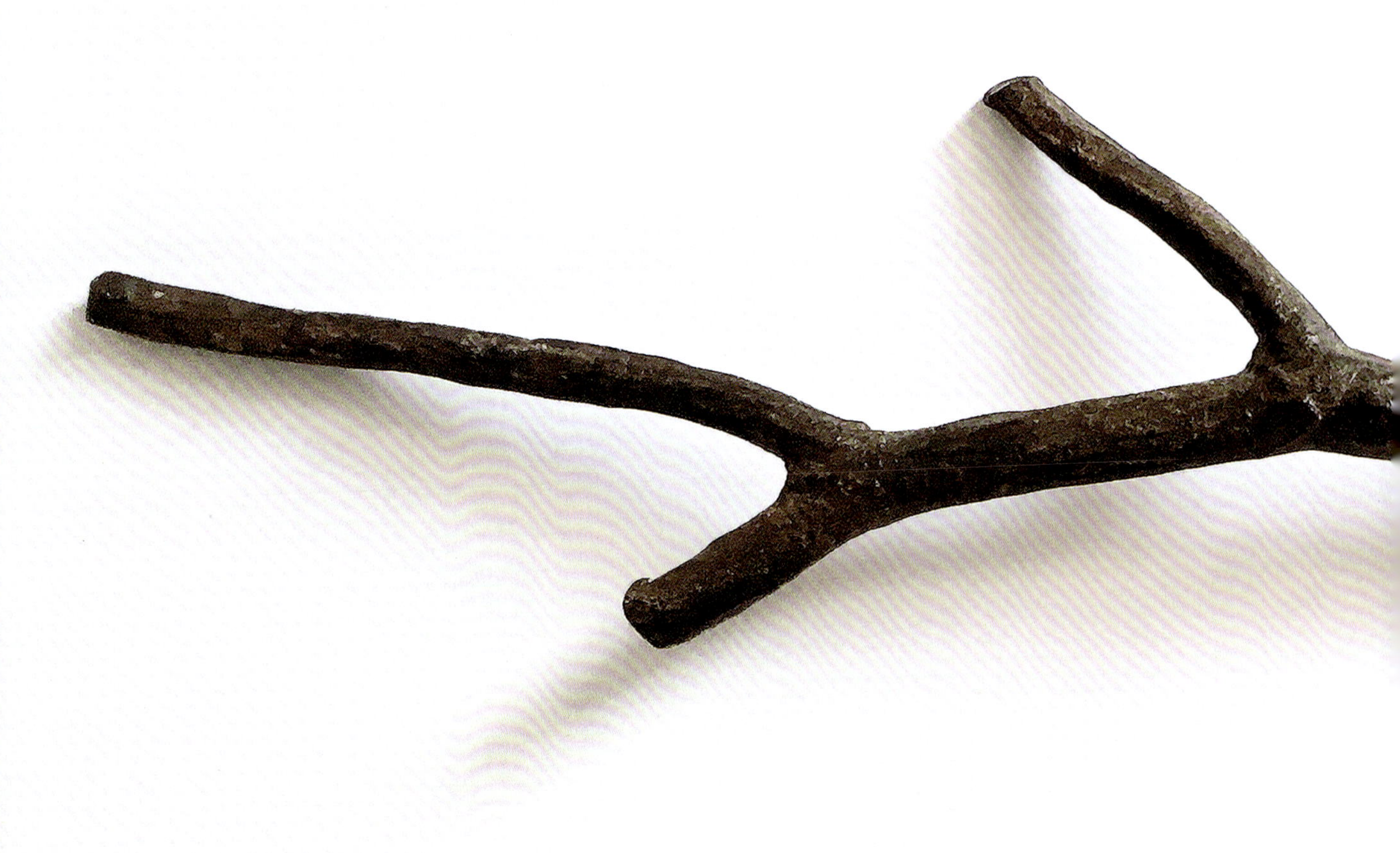

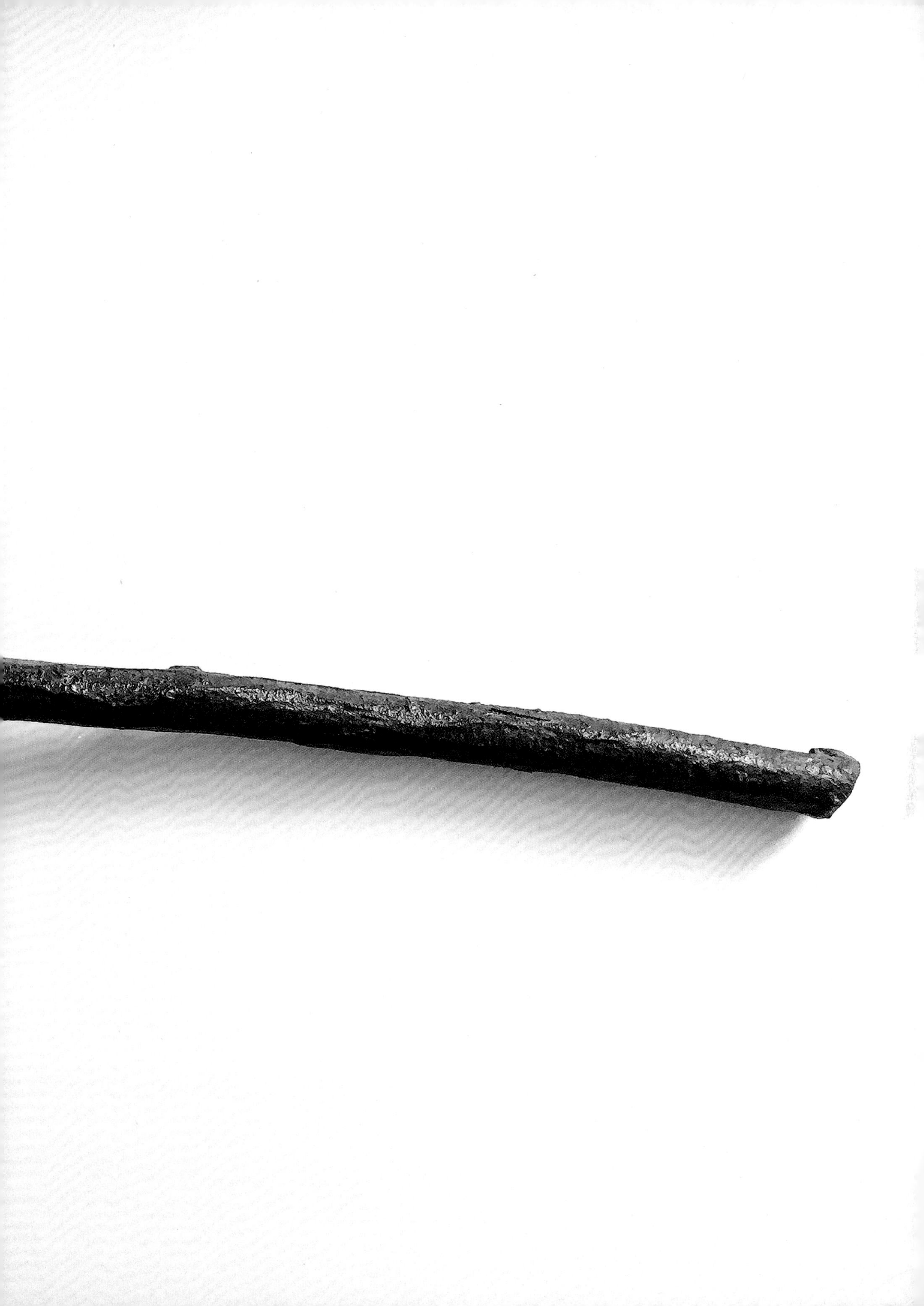

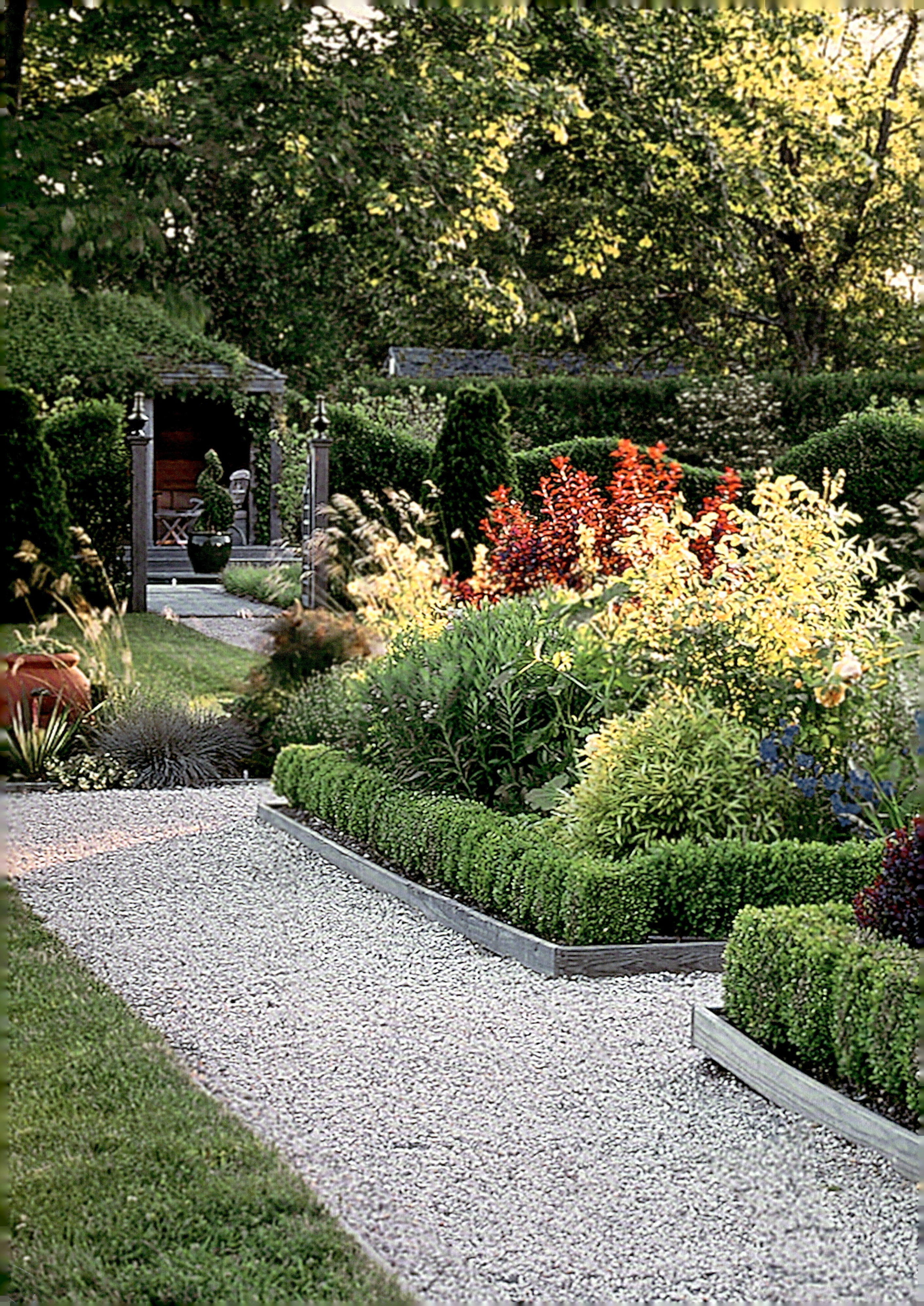

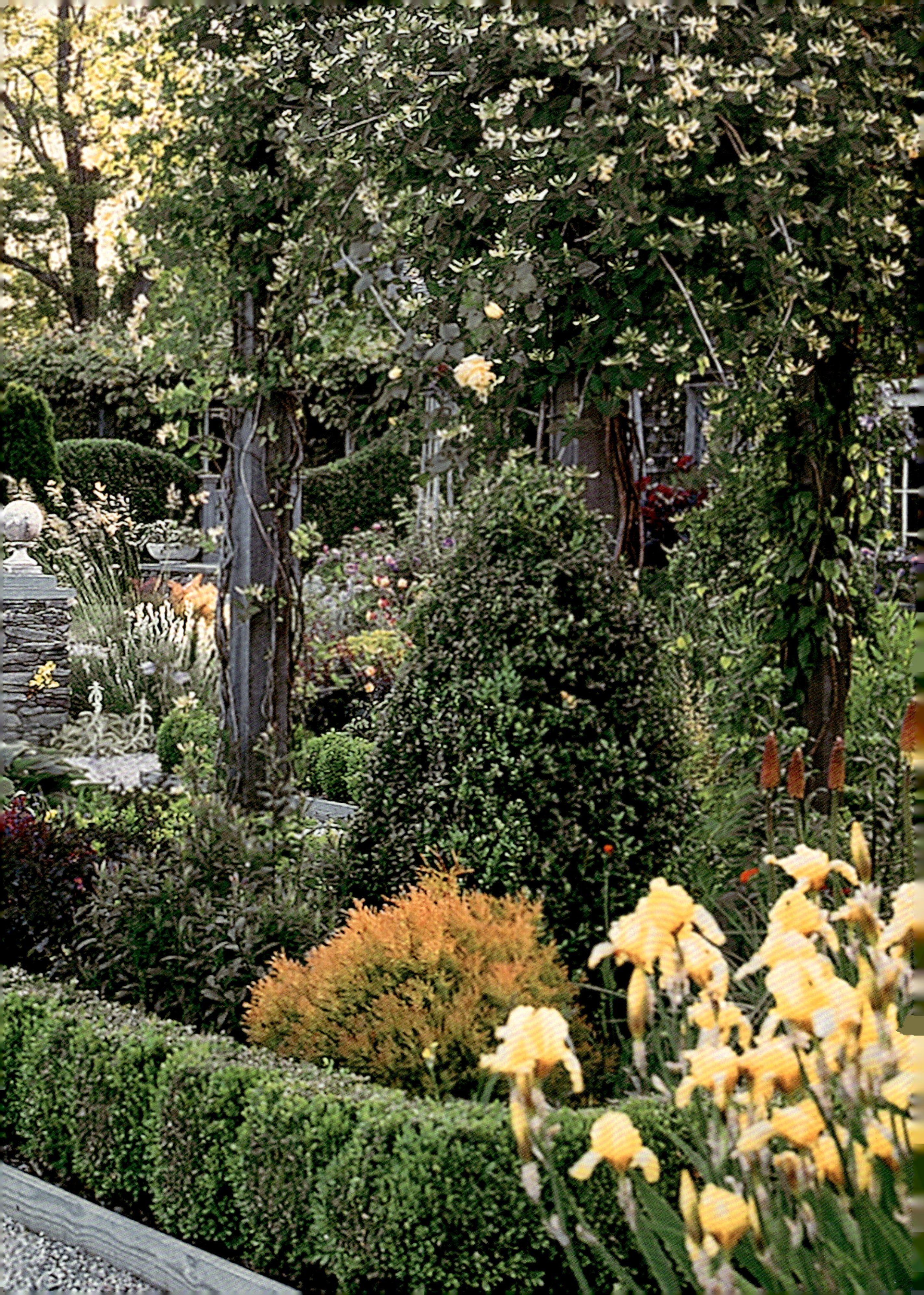

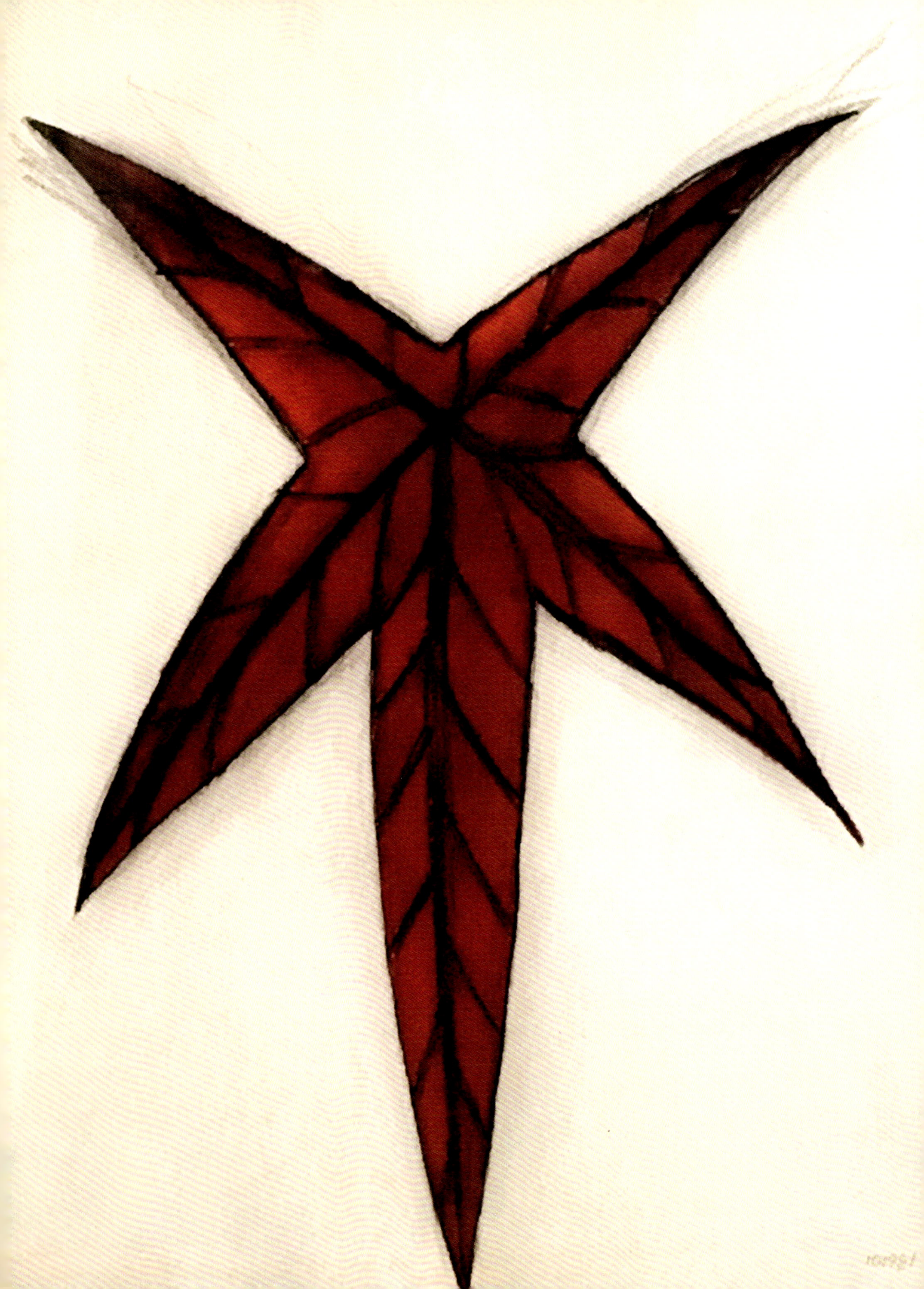

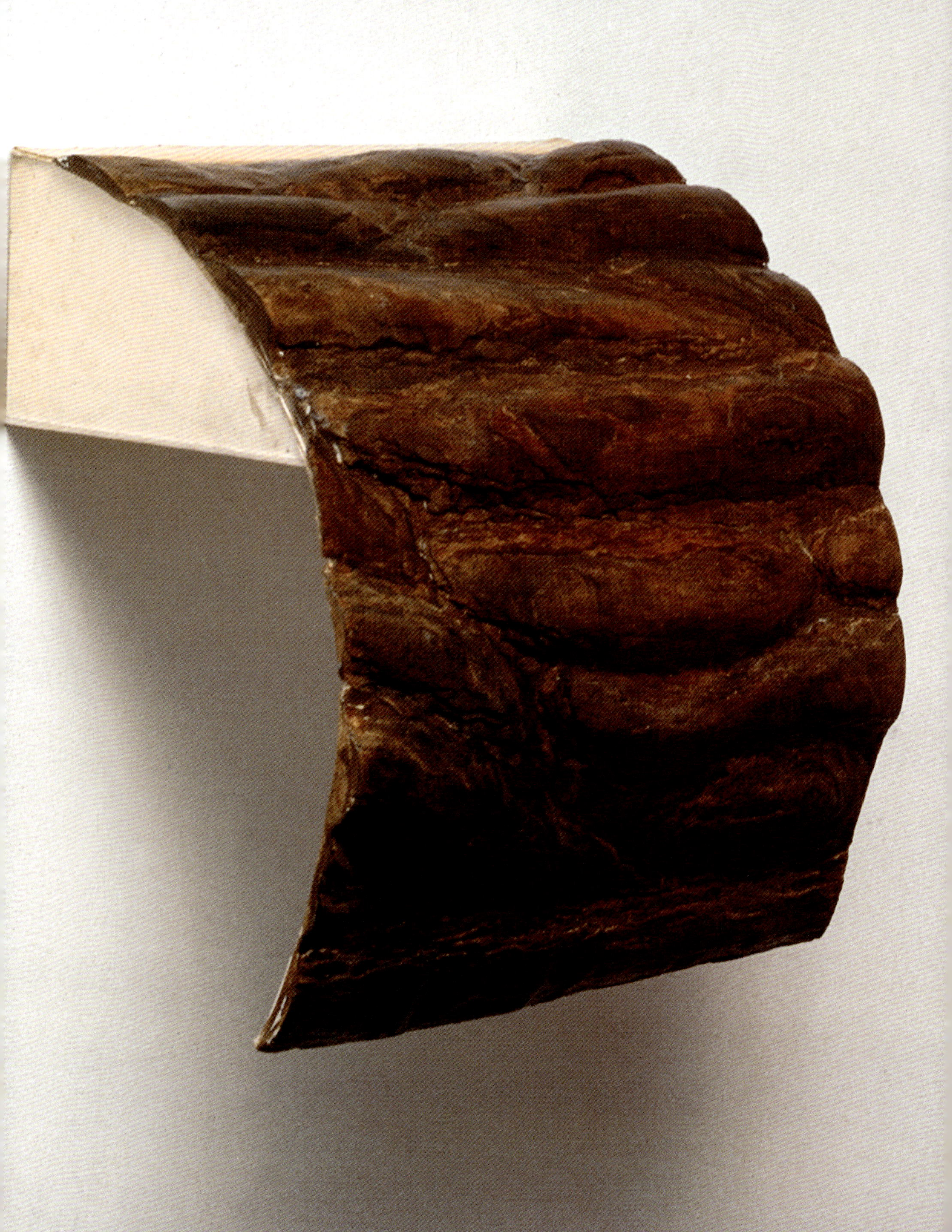

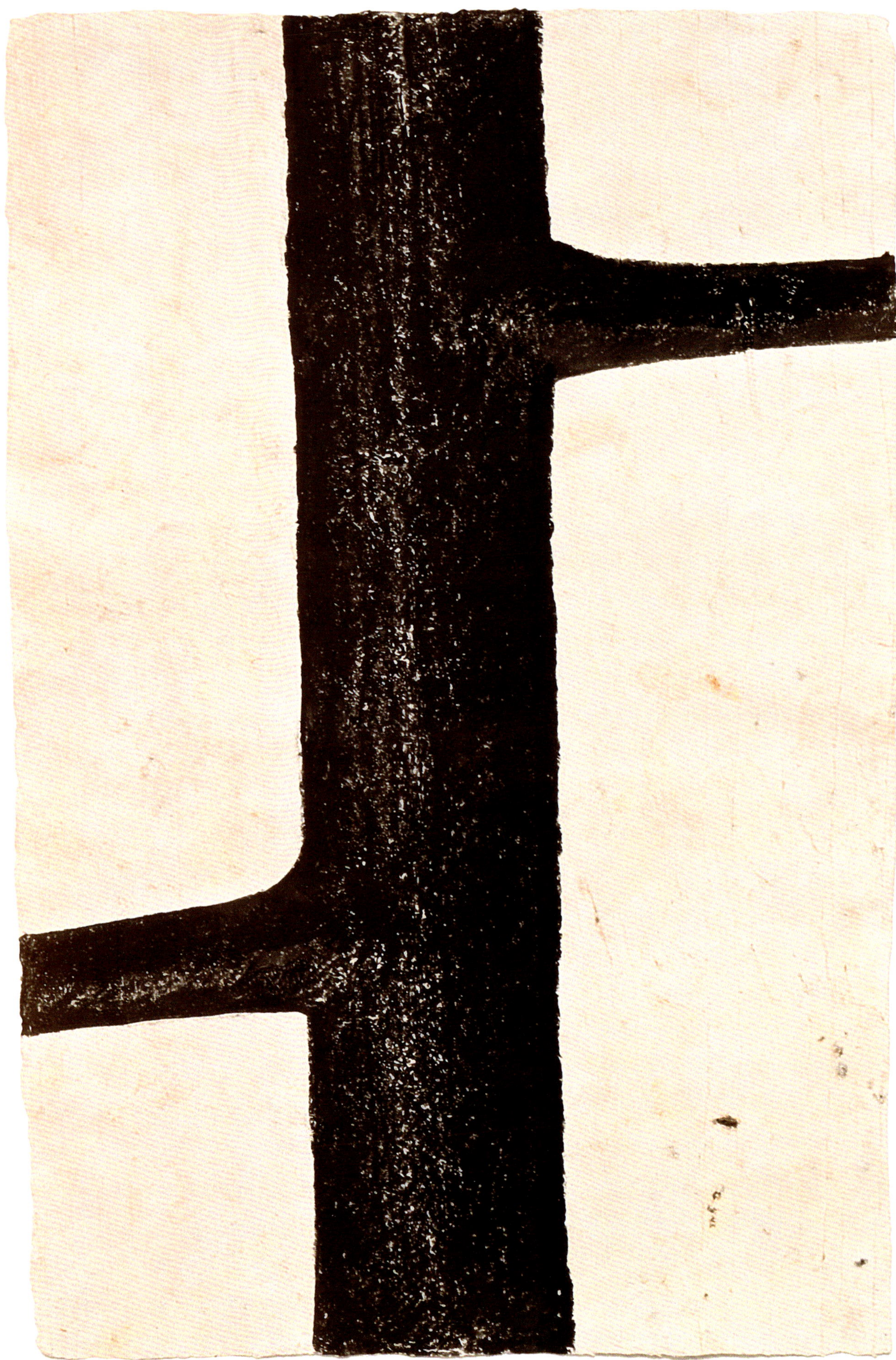

ARTIFACT

THE ART AND GARDENS OF JEFF MENDOZA

TEXT AND PHOTOGRAPHS BY JEFF MENDOZA

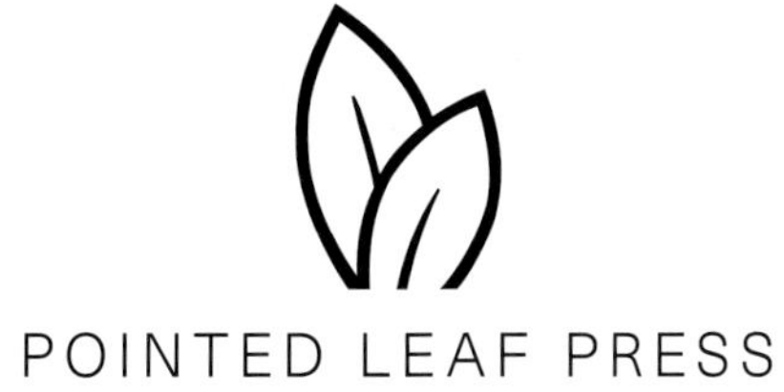

POINTED LEAF PRESS

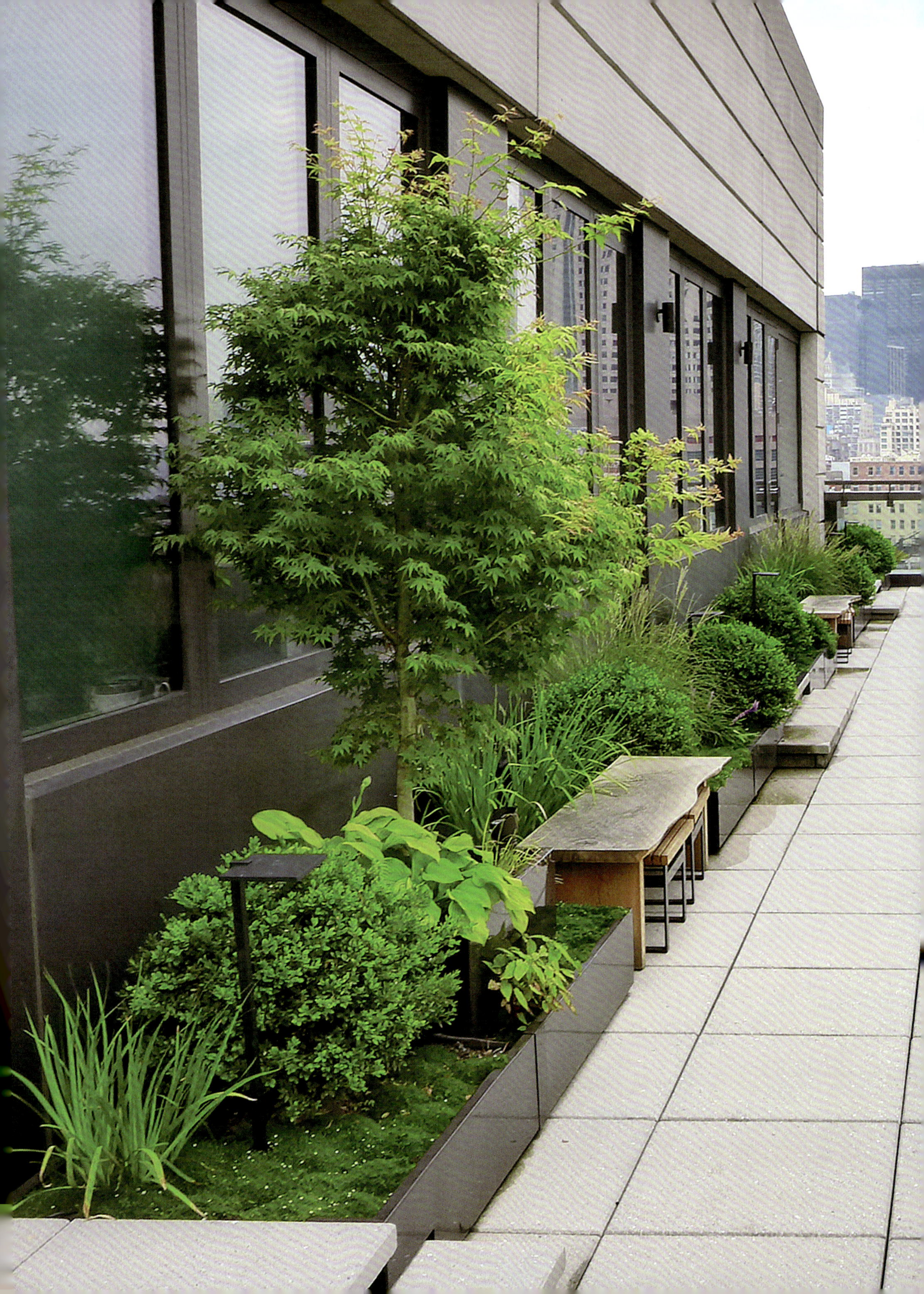

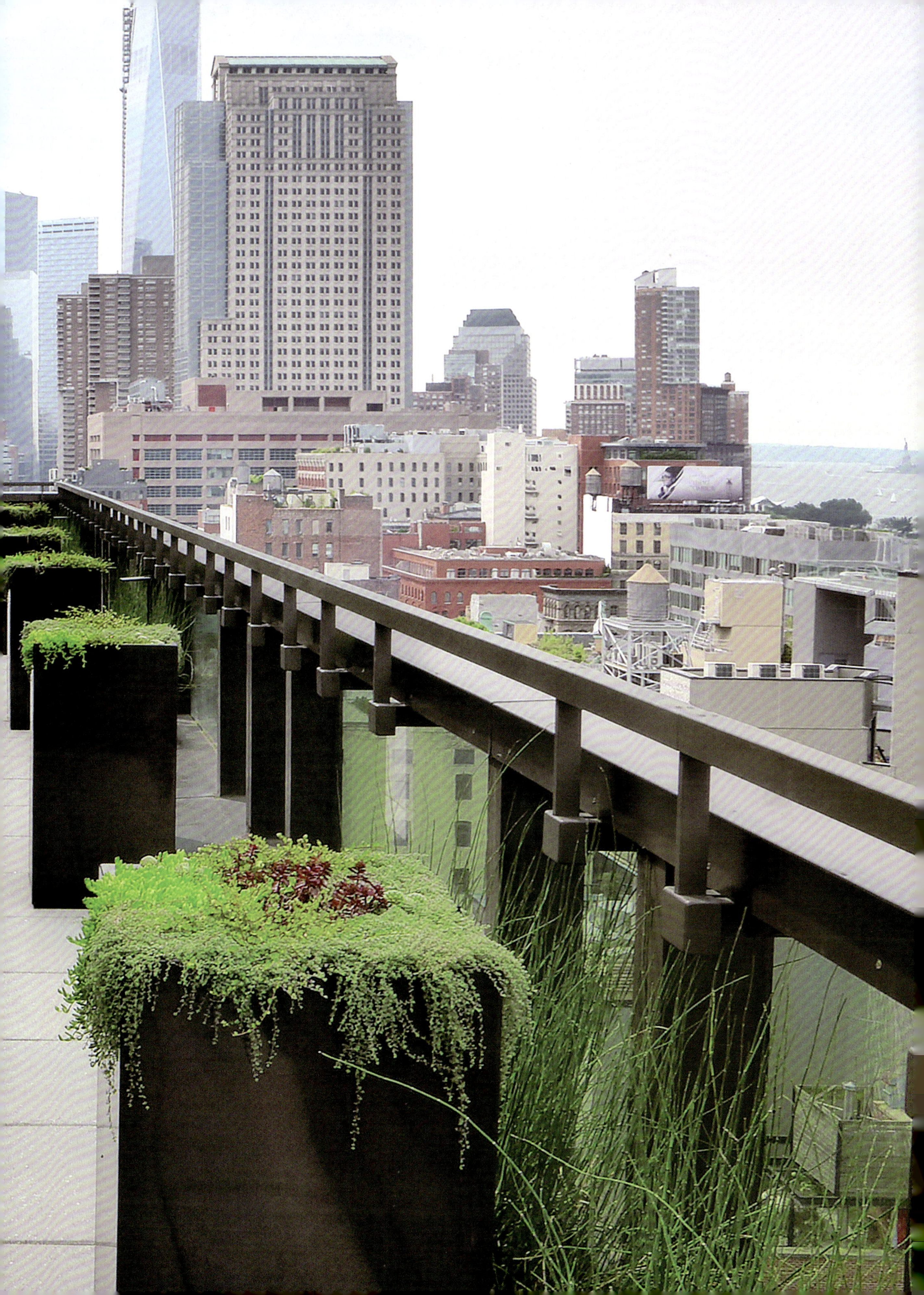

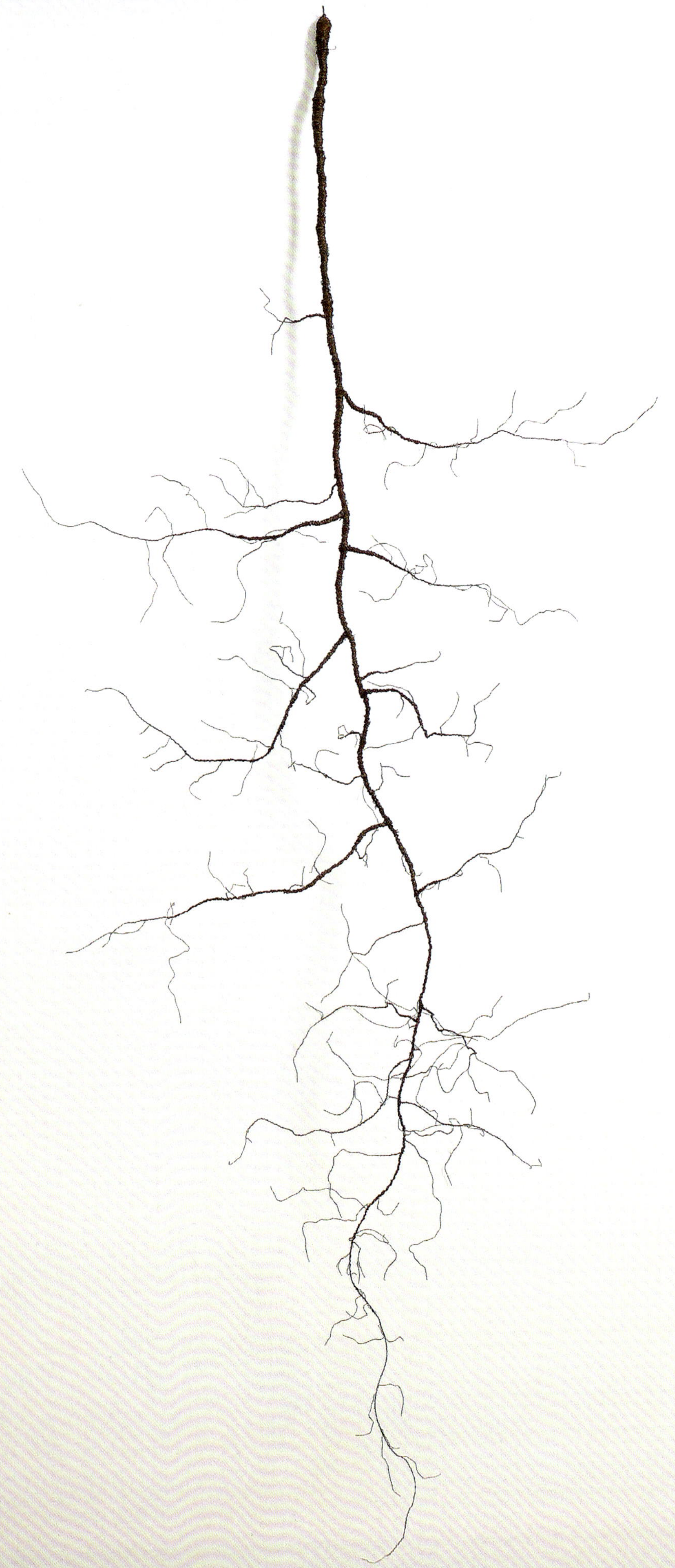

CONTENTS

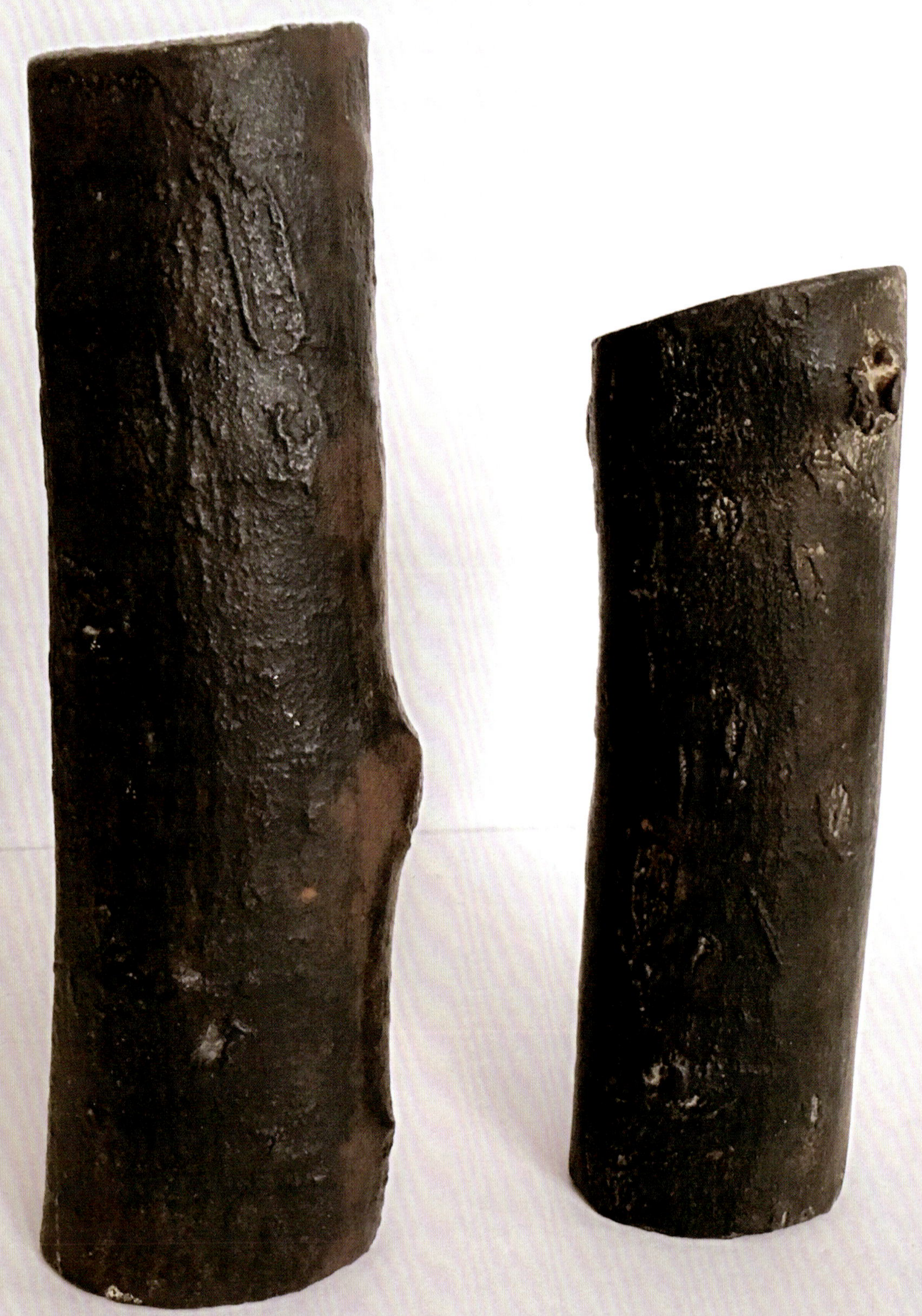

INTRODUCTION JEFF MENDOZA

I've lived in an apartment all of my life. As a kid growing up in working class neighborhoods in Chicago, when I looked outside our apartment windows, there was nothing to see but streets, cars, and brick buildings. My only escape from this monotonous urban landscape was my imagination. The vehicle for my escape was drawing. My father was born in the Philippines, and as a child I remember drawing palm trees. Looking back now, I realize palm trees fascinated me both as part of my heritage and because they represented an escape to a landscape very different from what I saw outside my window.

As I got older I knew I wanted to be an artist. I went to art school and then studied art history in college. In the 1970s, I moved to New York as an artist. I had an apartment and a separate small studio. To support myself I had several jobs. One was with a friend who had a landscaping company. I loved plants and liked working with my hands, so it seemed like a good fit. I installed gardens and made drawings for my friend's landscape business.

In my studio at the time, I made sculptures and drawings of elements of the natural world such as leaves, roots, trees, branches, mesas, mountains, and water. Botanical forms had interested me since I was a child. The simple beauty of an avocado pit growing a stem and leaves fascinated me. Seeds of any kind slowly sprouting tender shoots continue to amaze me.

I worked with my friend for several years. In 1987, I decided to strike out on my own and opened J. Mendoza Gardens. After a few years, I realized the objects I made in my studio and the landscapes I created as a garden designer were closely related. It seems obvious in retrospect, but back then,

OPPOSITE When removed from their source, tree parts often take on a life of their own, and can be functional, like a post for fencing or a cane for walking. When isolated without a function, they have their own integrity. This piece, entitled *Limb*, was created in 1986 as part of a series of cast-iron tree sculptures.

OVERLEAF LEFT Traveling through the Southwest in the 1970s, I witnessed a mesa at sunset. The dramatic silhouette of its hard, flat, horizontal top and sloping sides contrasted sharply with the thin, wispy sky, producing a lasting image for me. In 1983, I created a series of *Mesa* wall pieces. This 30 x 20 x 1½-inch wood piece, painted with acrylic, was one of the earliest in the series.

OVERLEAF RIGHT This is a detail of a Japanese-inspired garden I created in 2012. For a number of years I have tested the ability of plants to survive on harsh Manhattan rooftops in only four or five inches of soil. Here, moss *Minuartia verna*, iris *Iris tectorum* and bergenia *Bergenia cordifolia* are thriving.

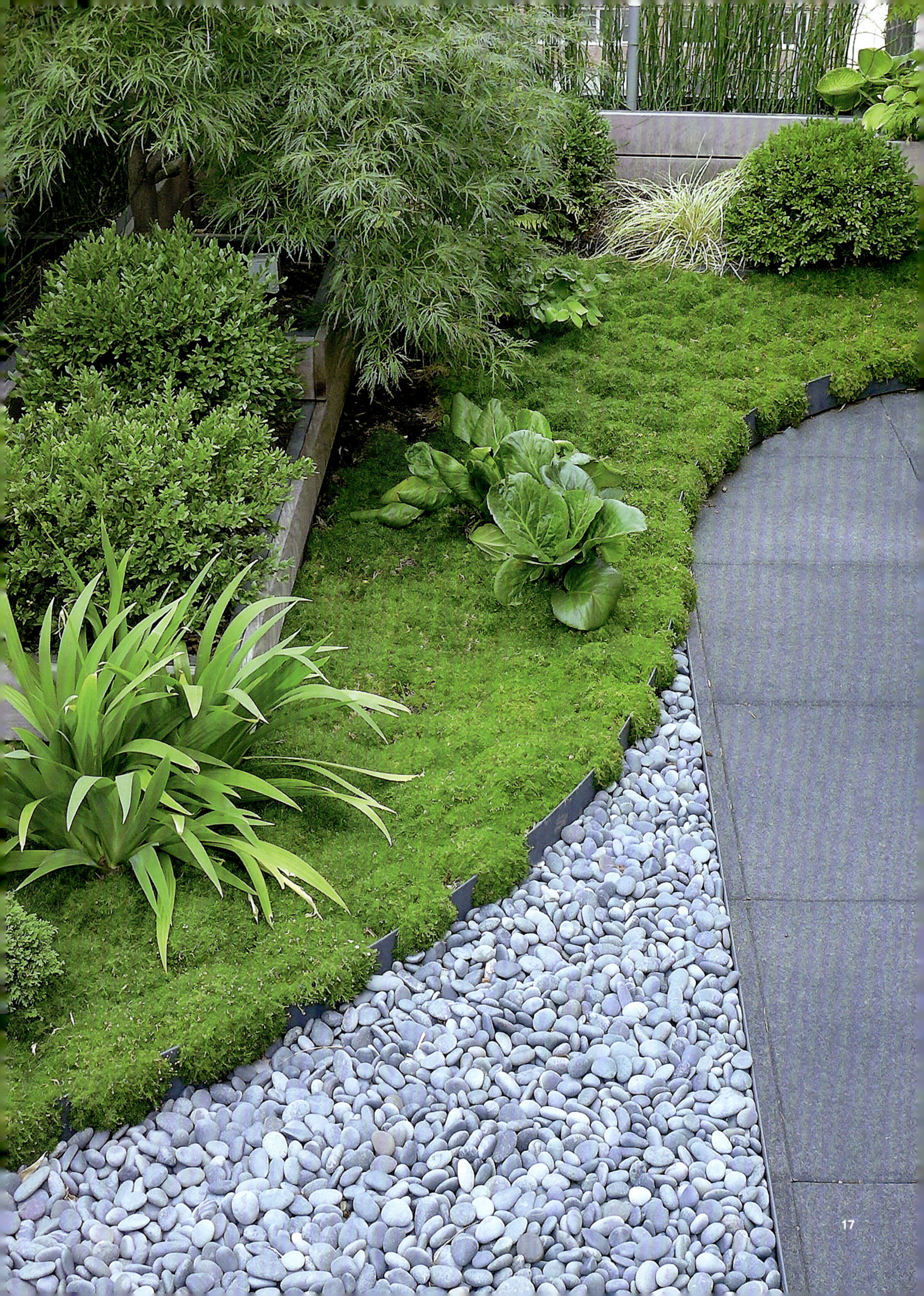

I kept each in its own compartment. Eventually, I realized the formal concerns and subjects of my art were now translated into my gardens. As an artist I was primarily interested in sculptural form and color. In the garden, the sculptural form of an individual plant or a group of plants is what interests me to this day. As a sculptor, pencil, paper, paint, and metal were my media. As a garden designer, pencil, paper, and plants—an endless variety of plants—were my media.

All man-made gardens and landscapes are artifacts of the natural world. We try to reproduce, however humbly, the effect of abundance, quiet, mystery or beauty that we experience in natural landscapes. Plants are chosen with a curatorial eye for their form, color, texture or scale, as part of a composition of plants or as specimens in larger designed landscapes. The juxtaposition of these groups of plants creates a botanical mosaic of ephemeral beauty. That beauty changes with the seasons as a progression of plants bloom, recede, and are succeeded by other plants. This happens throughout the growing season. In a good garden, that progression can be either subtle or dramatic. And sometimes even both.

My landscape designs have been greatly influenced by English and Japanese gardens. Both cultures have a long history and reverence for the natural world in both art and literature. I admire English gardens for their highly orchestrated abundance of color and form. Japanese gardens, on the other hand, are the finest examples of artistic restraint with the use of a single color: Green. The gardens I've created are not literally English or Japanese but rather a synthesis of English and Japanese elements as interpreted by an American.

As an artist and plantsman, the polarity between English gardens and Japanese gardens interests me. Abundance or restraint; the objects and gardens I've created lie somewhere between. This book illustrates a body of work that explores both extremes and some grey, or should I say green, areas in between.

OPPOSITE The pronounced vein pattern in some leaves provides added interest and beauty. This 1981 13¾ x 10⅞-inch colored pencil leaf drawing was part of a series.

OVERLEAF LEFT This highly stylized leaf from the 1981 *Leaf* drawing series is reminiscent of decorative motifs from the Art Nouveau movement.

OVERLEAF RIGHT I purchased a single bromeliad *Aechmea blanchetiana* as one of the first plants for my garden in Vieques, Puerto Rico, in 2008. It has continuously produced numerous offshoots. Nine years later, from that single parent plant, I have seven very large 4 x 6-foot clumps of bromeliad—a plant that keeps on giving and is striking, even when not in bloom—distributed throughout the garden.

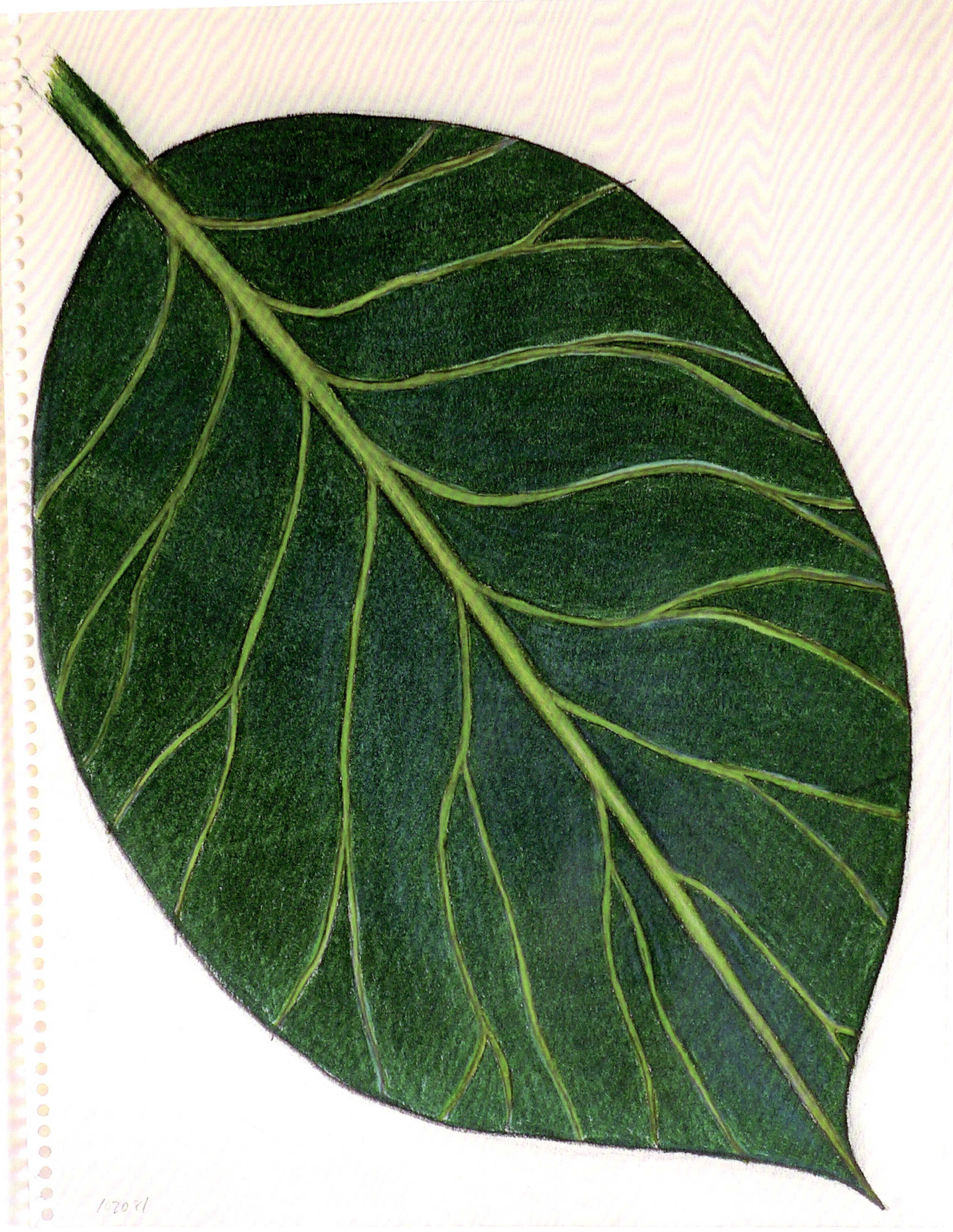

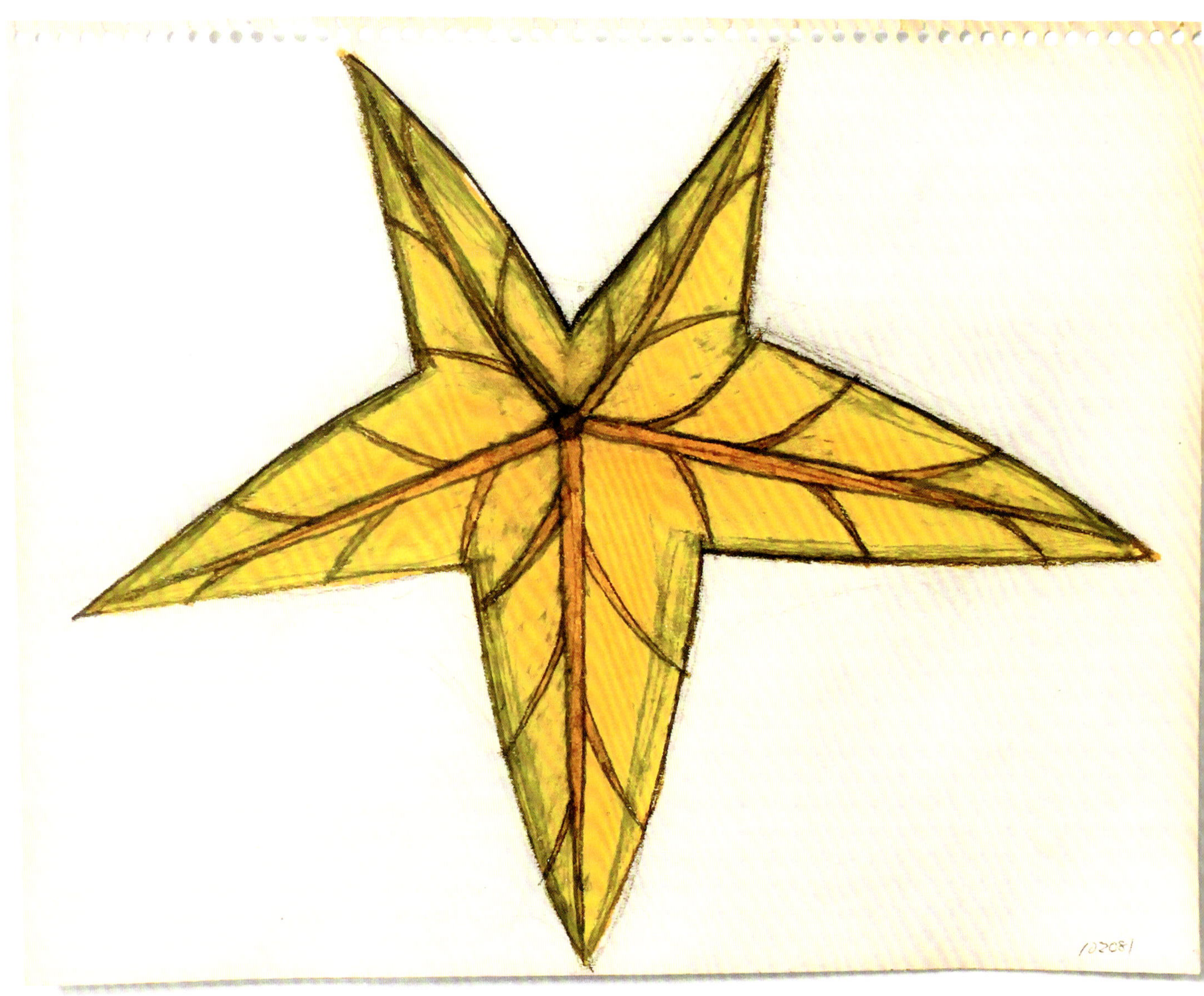

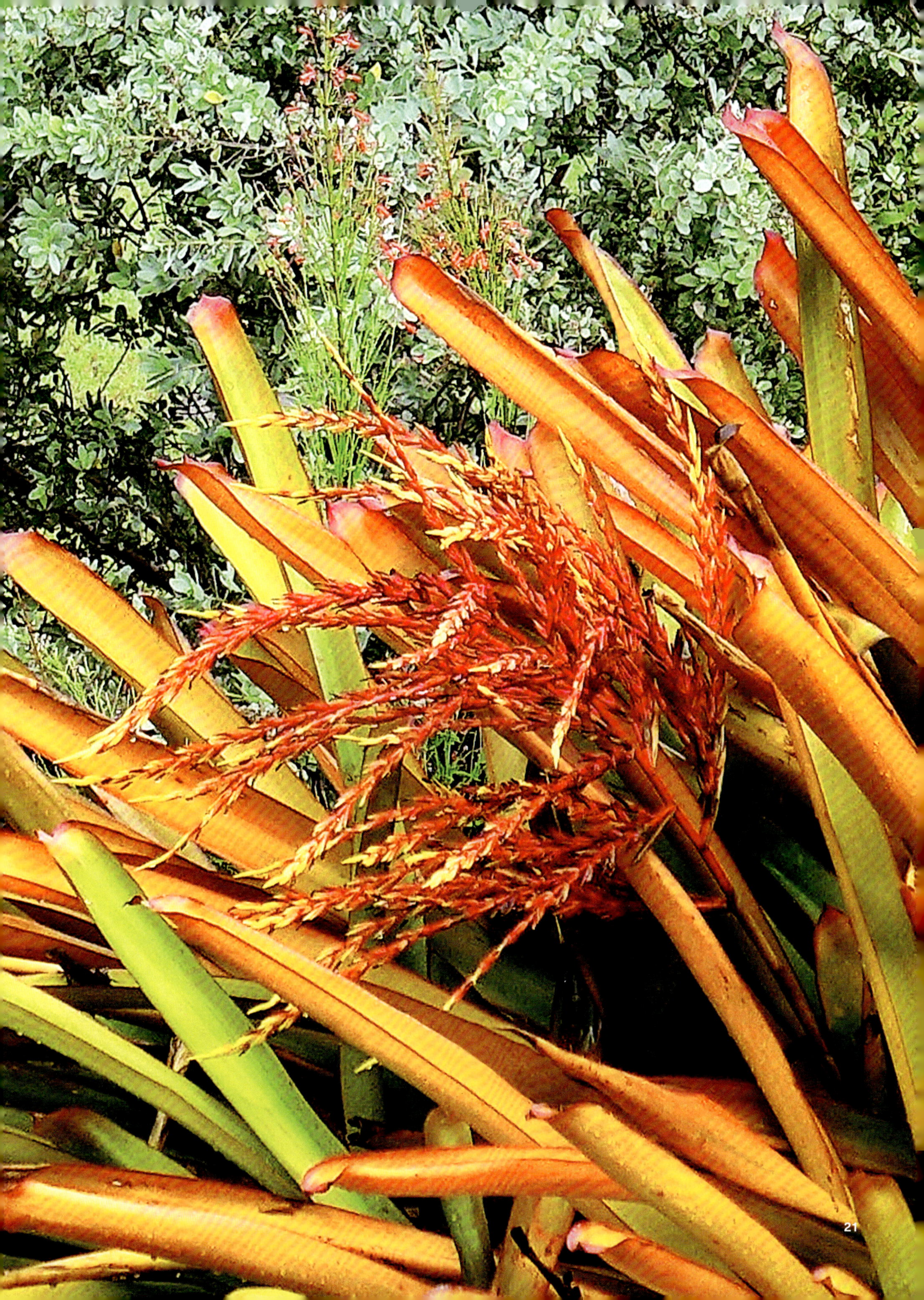

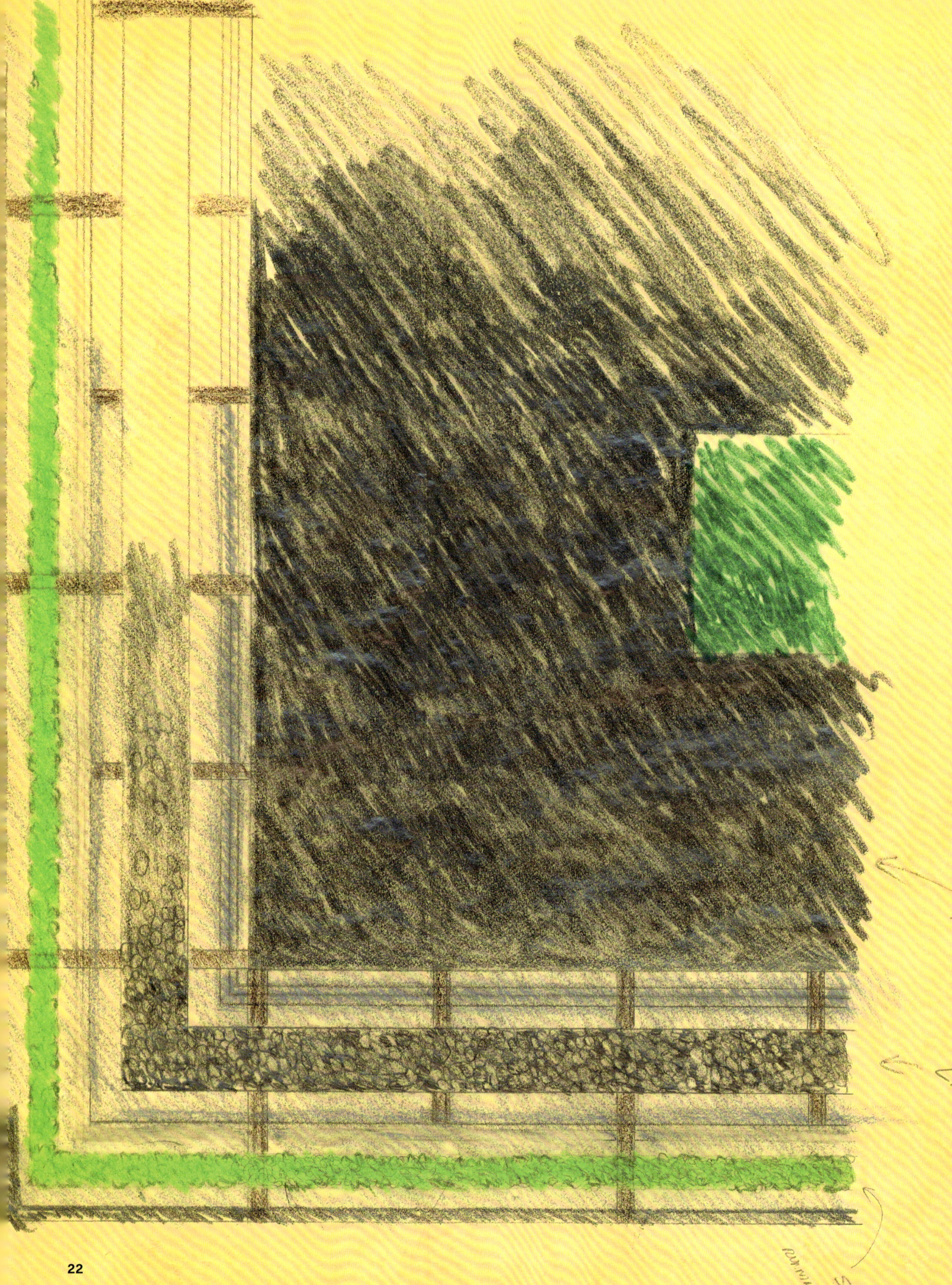

CONTINUUM JUDITH RUSSI KIRSHNER

OPPOSITE This 13 x 10-inch pencil sketch on tracing paper from 1985 was a preliminary concept for one of my first garden designs. It was inspired by photographs of the famous Zen garden Ryōan-ji in Kyoto, Japan. Years later, I was able to go there and saw the difference between my idea of it and the actual garden. As with many people, my inspirations for objects and gardens have come from photographs. I've often found that actually seeing an art object or experiencing a garden can be illuminating in subtle and surprising ways, and that unexpected dimensions of which one hadn't been aware before become apparent.

Like many young artists of his generation, Jeff Mendoza left Chicago, where he was born, raised, and educated, for New York, making the big move in 1975. Also like many others, his earliest years as an artist were consumed with settling in and getting by, working jobs in social service, pursuing graduate studies in art history, and traveling to the American Southwest and Mexico. A participant in the lively SoHo art world and galleries, Mendoza enjoyed friendships with other Chicagoans such as Lynn Blumenthal and Michael Hurson, and the painters Hermine Ford and Robert Moskowitz.

But what makes Mendoza's career exceptional, beginning in 1979, is his fusion of studio art with landscape design, so that the two overlap and interlock like braided strands. Surveying his history in this book, we discover shared principles, purposes, and geometry, and acknowledge how fluidly Mendoza translates from artifact to garden and vice versa. Among the constant concerns in his practice is an emphasis on scale, simultaneously small and large, and sight lines, simultaneously near and far; his tools, both lens and telescope, invite our visual and physical engagement in environments recalling and rivaling the picturesque wonder of painted landscapes or the serenity of a Japanese garden. Indeed, Mendoza's strong foundations in art history have served him in good stead, with his sensitivity to classical systems of proportions from the Italian Renaissance, as well as flowering English gardens, resonating in his designs.

Happily, such learned references never appear as quotations but are calibrated to the specific requirements of each project, whether rooftop or waterfront. Detailed measurements of plan and section, height and breadth, texture and hue of each individual element are reconciled with the proportions of the entire scheme, in a nod to the classical theory of consistent relationships and, more informally, to an organic interrelationship of part to whole. Mendoza has a particular talent for finding exceptional plant materials and juxtaposing colors that defy chromatic definition, neither matching nor clashing with each other.

Mendoza based his artistic practice on earlier strategies derived from Minimalism, conceptual foundations, and rational design, often anchored by a modernist grid. Geometrical formulae establish ideal compositions and allow for dynamic variables that can be altered over time. Grids frequently underlie Mendoza's urban and country landscapes, organizing contrasts in surface effects, distinct volumes, and collections of color; some of these gardens suggest a meeting or even a collision between Gertrude Jekyll and Carl Andre. Another contemporary context was the emergence of giant land–art projects like those by James Turrell and Robert Smithson in the West, and the politics of site-specific art, actively debated during the 1970s and 1980s. Less about public interventions, these examples of Mendoza's gardens nevertheless incorporate and visually toggle between the spiky edges of an exotic succulent and the sprawling perspective of a seemingly endless lawn. Commissioned by patrons whose private wish might be an attempt to revive a bit of the wilderness or a memory of a dream, Mendoza's imaginative sites surround and augment their residences with unexpected, visually stimulating settings.

The early drawings of Mendoza, a gifted draftsman, are contemplative, close-up observations of nature: fragments of tree bark, details of branches or leaves. According to the artist David Hockney, "Being able to draw means being able to put things in believable space. People who don't draw very well can't do that." In miniature sculptural dioramas, Mendoza invented gigantic, believable landscapes, modeling mountains on a tabletop from humble materials like those used for train sets, where a small stack of glass rectangles implies a waterfall. Similarly, he would twist and weave multiple strands of copper wire to evoke networks of roots, which, when suspended on the wall at eye level, evoke corporeal references such as arteries. Also installed on a wall, a dark, linear fragment from 1986–87 at first resembles a slender twig but on closer inspection reveals itself to be a meticulously crafted cast-iron sculpture. The parallels in appearance of image and referent in Mendoza's work are never mere re-creations but rather produce uncanny artifacts drawn from the poetics of nature, then subtly altered.

"Every garden-maker should be an artist along his own lines. That is the only possible way to create a garden, irrespective of size or wealth," noted the British writer and garden designer Vita Sackville-West. To be sure, the synthesis of art and garden is hardly novel; one famous example is Monet's gardens, in which the artist created ponds for his self-reflections, rendered into mural paintings. Yet that pairing can become a cliché in the hands of the less talented. Mendoza prefers the title of "plantsman" to "horticulturalist." His technical knowledge and rigorous procedures are fused with his subjective gaze alongside the "ambition" of land art, which reinforces the modernist scope of his expansive environments. At the same time, Mendoza's refinement also nurtures the soft composition of mosses, the exacting placement of stepping stones and the tight framing of pebble margins, all elements inspired by his stated preference for Japanese aesthetics. Amid the continual flux of media-driven culture, fortunate are those who find a place where they might flourish like a plant, tall or short, wide or thin, in the landscape.

A remarkable orchestration of dimensions and perspectives—a recurrent theme in Mendoza's work—is adjusted to the site and conditions of each of his gardens; they subtly offer orientation and sequential encounters. Think of a procession of plinths echoing skyscrapers in the distance, but whose surfaces, festooned with dripping vines, look as if they might have softened and melted. Overlapping pine fronds and ferns disturb the stacked stone layers, while gently trickling water amplifies the cracks and marks that time and weather inscribe in a nod to the Japanese aesthetic tradition of wabi-sabi. In some immense lawns, Mendoza solves an artistic problem with a

OPPOSITE This is one of the moments I look forward to in the garden, when blue globe thistle *Echinops bannaticus 'Blue Glow'* is in bloom behind pale yellow Yucca *filamentosa 'Color Guard.'*

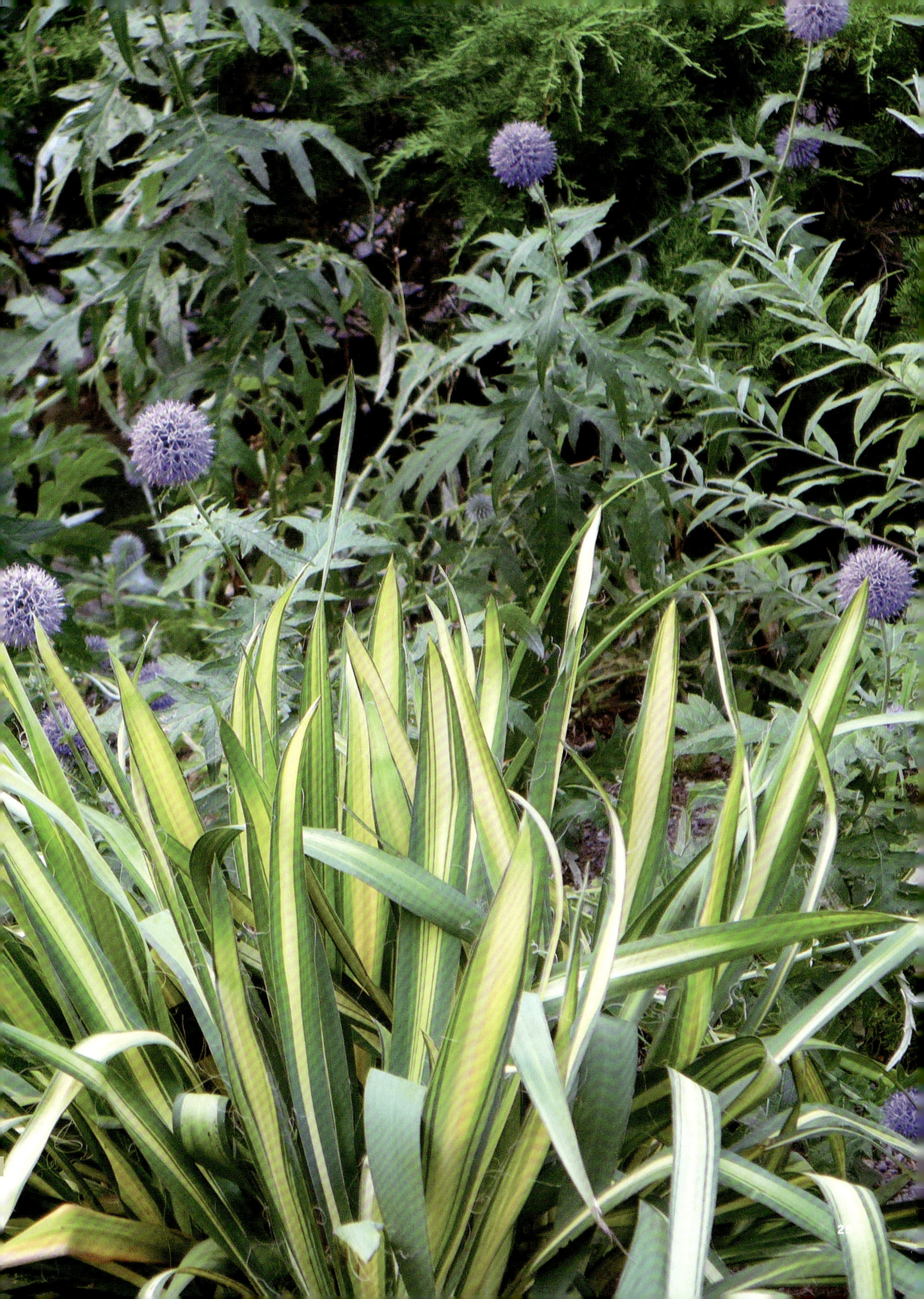

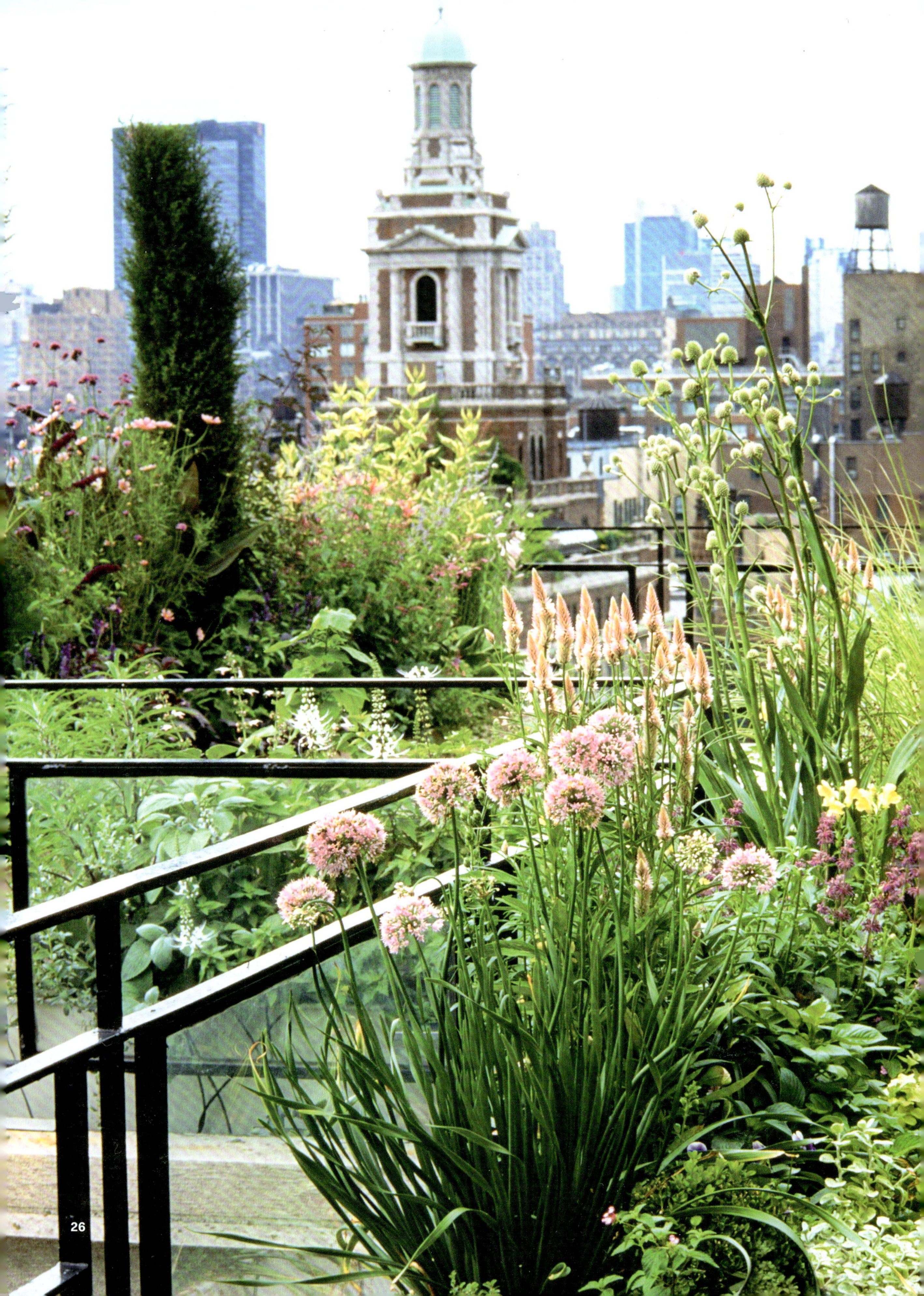

OPPOSITE This view, looking north from a terrace in downtown New York City, shows the garden in mid-summer, in full bloom.

OVERLEAF LEFT This tree drawing from 1985 is on Japanese bark paper, with embedded bark shavings. Black oil- stick is used to cover the background, creating an almost birch tree-like illusion from the paper itself.

OVERLEAF RIGHT The client for this 2001 project asked if he could have a fountain on his terrace as part of the garden design. Thin pieces of stone were applied to a marine plywood base to give the illusion of a 50 x 60 x 12-inch stone wall. Water flowed into a copper basin and was re-circulated. The sound of falling water on an urban terrace is calming in the city.

repeating square pattern defined by a geometry of trimmed hedges and distant vistas. An abundance of fanciful planting and luxurious foliage, ordered and interrupted by large trees, creates islands of shade before revealing strong axial planes. Coupled with his autonomous objects and drawings, Mendoza's visionary potential extends beyond depiction to translate concepts from the realm of representation into material realities and the experience of generous landscapes. Out of doors, the designer must plan for and contend with fleeting temporal and climatic conditions—the hourly shifting of light and atmosphere, and the unexpected variety of changing seasons. The visitor, stepping into these purposeful amalgams of artificial and natural places, park and wilderness, albeit fixed in time, is also affected by Mendoza's exhilarating compositions. Color fluctuations, myriad surfaces and shapes create exuberant patterns, punctuated by perfectly installed urns and garden furniture. Mendoza encourages a spiraling mass that envelops small microcosms of blossoms and tall grasses that dramatically magnify and make real the experimental task he earlier set himself: namely drawing grasses. Out of doors, thick, undulating waves of foliage impart texture and unexpected color; succulent forms in an exotic setting, perhaps the most vivid example of Mendoza's orchestration of fragment to whole, provide surreal interruptions to the narrative flow. In some projects, the perspective shifts suddenly from a horizontal to a vertical plane, moving from close to distant, in wandering paths that introduce extravagant clusters of tiny blooms and giant boxwood spheres as if one were encountering the flats in an opera where the garden is a stage set and the visitor has become the performer.

According to Roberto Burle Marx, the legendary Brazilian artist/designer, "A garden is a complex of aesthetic and plastic intentions; and the plant is, to a landscape artist, not only a plant—rare, unusual, ordinary or doomed to disappearance—but it is also a color, a shape, a volume or an arabesque in itself." In his prolific career, Mendoza has invented his own lexicon to narrate landscapes that range in character from baroque to minimal, from classic idioms to cubist rigor, creating spaces that reinforce the value of direct engagement and allude to the very meaning of place. Scientific warnings of "climate change" and industrial sprawl have caused many to re- examine the significance, history, and heritage of gardens, and of green space as cultural expression. This volume celebrates and attempts to understand how Mendoza's unique artifacts and aesthetic gardens converge, and how these gardens will endure to become artifacts themselves. Aware of the historical sources that precede him, Mendoza has never let those conventions impede his creativity; not only do these brilliant gardens appear of the moment, they also contribute significantly to those that follow. Unrepeatable but permanently installed in our memory, Mendoza's landscapes offer havens for refuge, and promises for natural renewal.

JUDITH RUSSI KIRSHNER IS A CRITIC, CURATOR, AND EDUCATOR WHO LIVES IN CHICAGO, ILLINOIS.

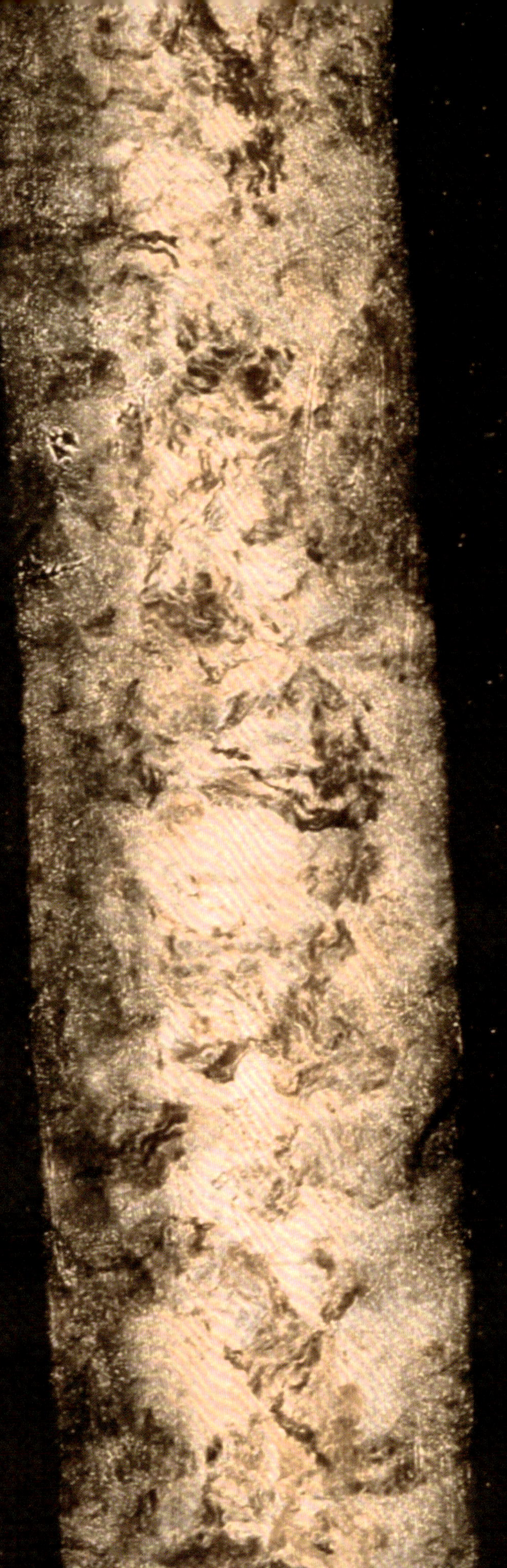

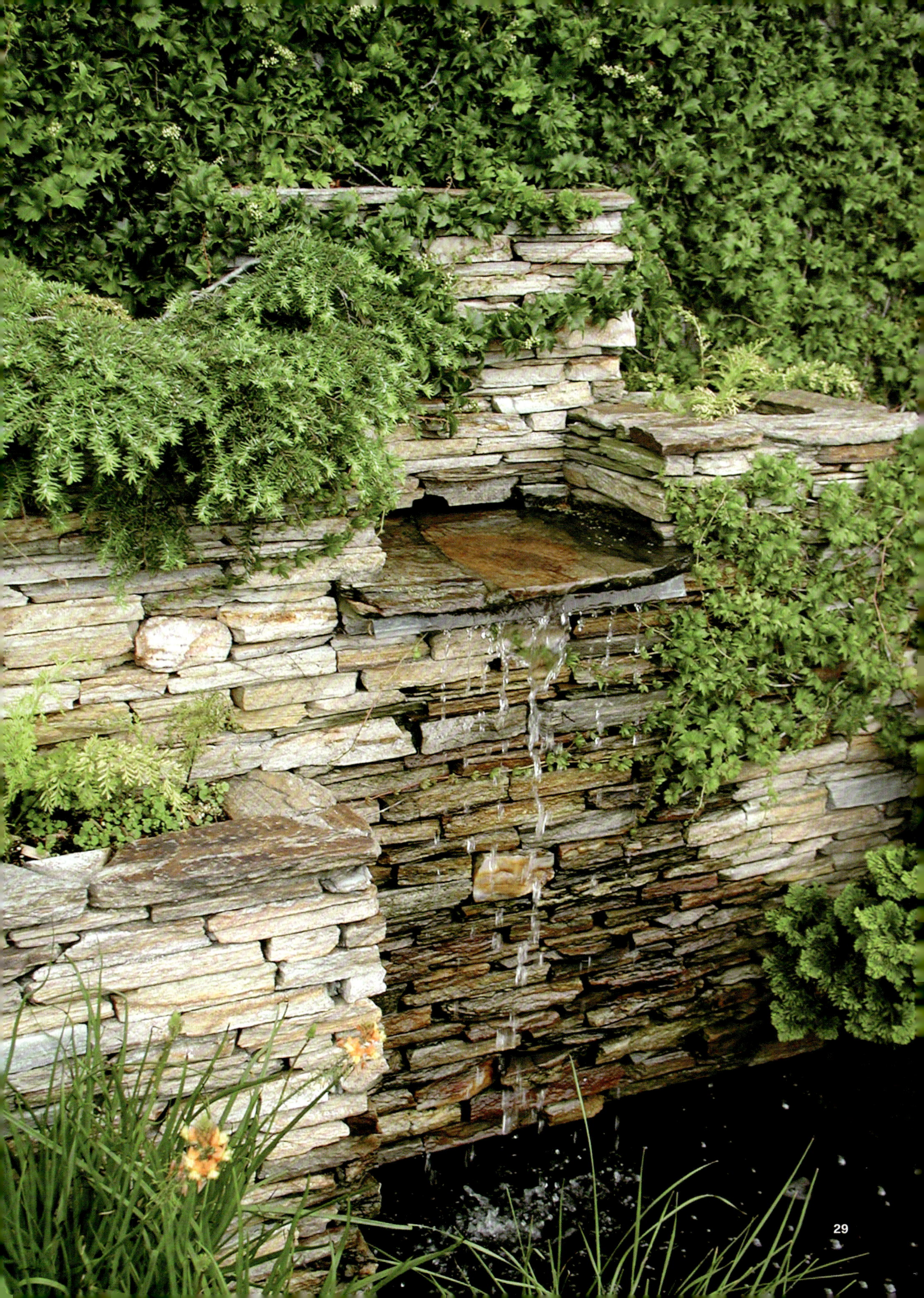

NOT FORGOTTEN BARBARA TOLL

OPPOSITE I created a writhing octopus bed with herbs in each of its eight red *Berberis* "arms" that we happily used to prepare wonderful meals throughout the summer.

Some paintings make sense from a distance, but dissolve into bland clichés up close. Others have fascinating detail, but lose all focus from far away. Jeff Mendoza treats gardens as paintings, which work both at a distance and close-up. His interest in form, volume, and color provides both intimate detail and high impact.

I first met Jeff in his studio in 1985, when several artist friends of his suggested I go see his work. When I arrived, I saw pieces unlike anything I had seen before: strange sculptures of plants and branches, in materials that looked mysteriously real. They were delicate, but sturdy at the same time. I was particularly taken with a water lily that projected out from the wall on a long, curved stem. I included it in a three-person show at my gallery in SoHo later that spring. The following year, I bought a house in Sag Harbor, New York. Having immediate buyer's remorse, I remembered that Jeff had worked for a landscaper. I asked him if he would come out to move some hydrangeas to help camouflage the ugly steps to the house. Jeff arrived, but his first words were: "Forget the hydrangeas; move the driveway." He said this with such authority that I immediately knew that he was right. From then on, Jeff was always right. We moved the driveway and created the first of six different gardens on my property over the next 30 years.

When I sold my house three years ago, the new owners gradually erased the garden. However, in my memory, that garden is still flourishing. I remember arriving on a Friday night in May, opening the gate and smelling the Styrax, the Daphne 'Carol Mackie' (my favorite), and the Viburnum. When we first planted the garden, Jeff asked me what colors I was thinking of. I responded, "Pastels, pale pinks, and blues. And lots of Delphinium," I added. But the Delphiniums never worked, romantic Foxglove finally naturalized, but, being used to looking at bold forms in contemporary art, I realized that Jeff's propensity for strong color, volume, and leaf forms was far more effective and pleasing than the blowsy romanticism I had envisioned.

Jeff really taught me everything I know about gardens. Mac Griswold, the garden historian, would say, when showing people my garden, "Barbara doesn't know names of plants." Jeff knew them all, as well as the characteristics of the plants. My garden was his personal experiment. Pots of Canna lilies that I had mocked before became dark punctuations in my beds. The only thing we didn't agree on was roses. But with the advent of long-blooming, mold-resistant roses, Jeff finally granted me some in the mixed beds. When Jeff told me he wanted to retire, I realized I would have to sell the house: The garden could never survive with another master; it was his complex combination of form and color. Hoping the new owners would keep at least some of the beds, I walked through what remained on a frigid winter day, telling the sleeping plants that all would be fine in the spring. Of course, it wasn't. The garden is gone, but Jeff and I had the very great pleasure of living deep in its green. BARBARA TOLL IS A NEW YORK-BASED ART DEALER AND CURATOR.

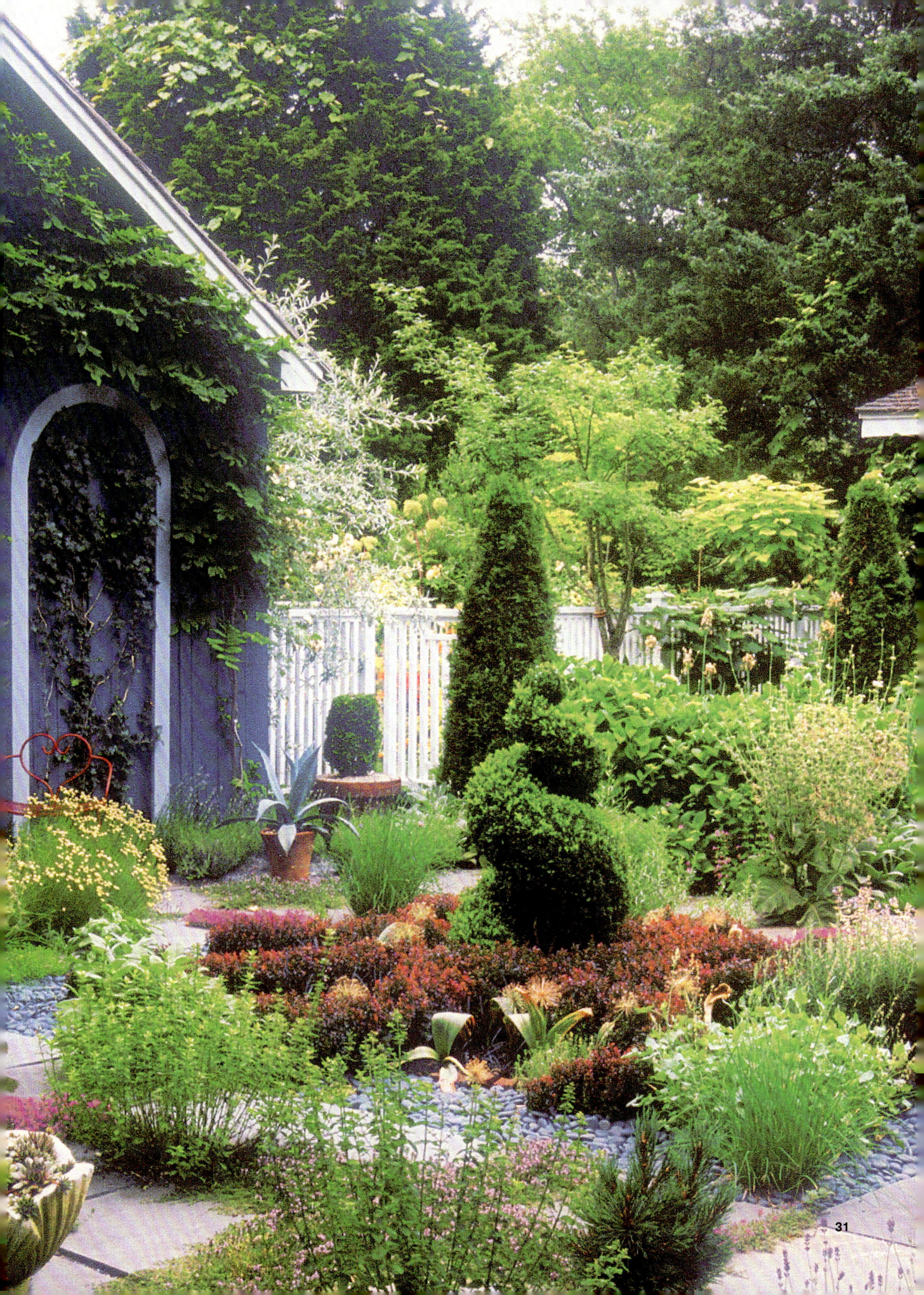

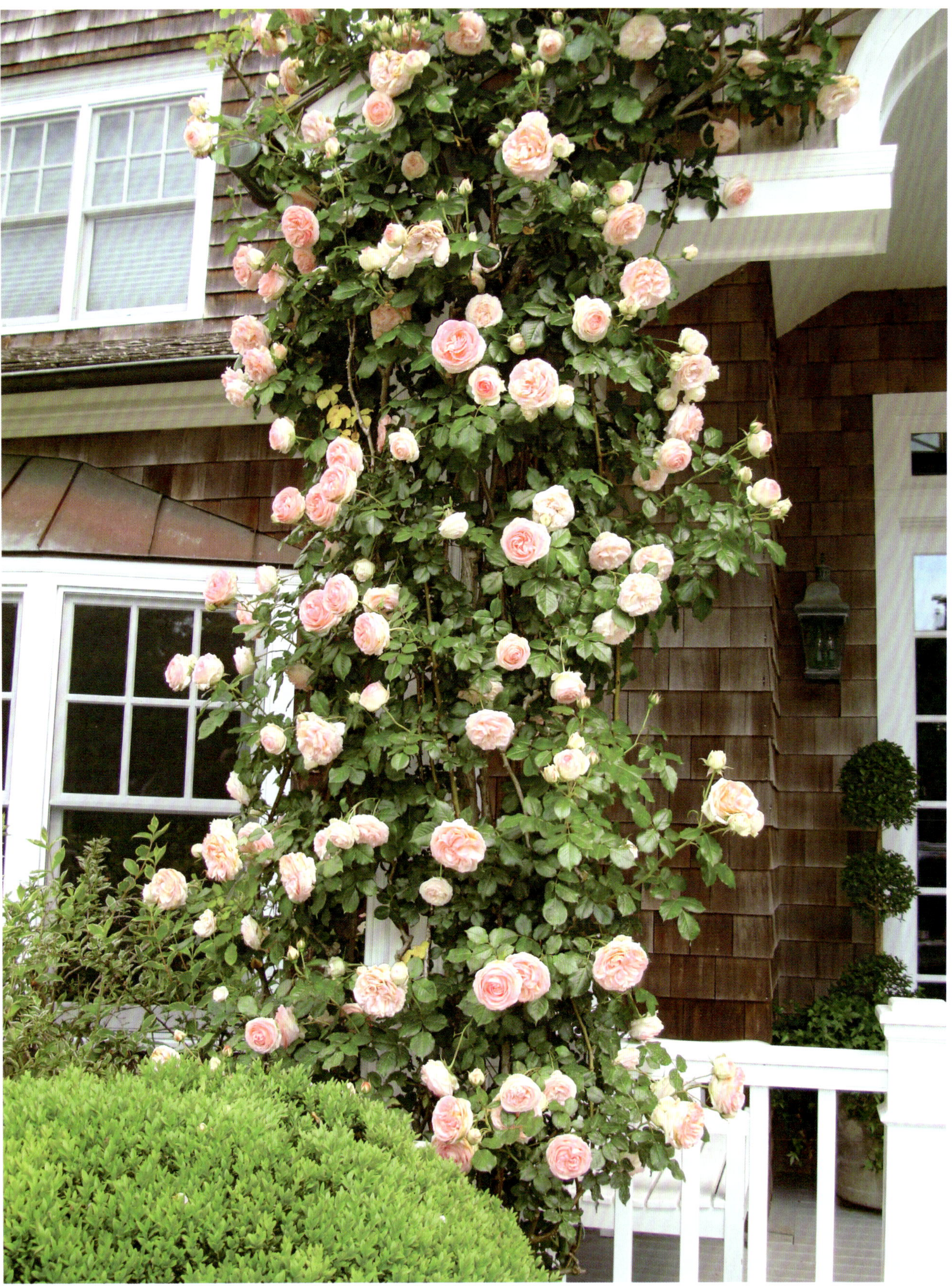

ROMANTIC

OPPOSITE A profusion of *Rosa 'Eden'* greets visitors at the entrance to this house on Long Island, New York.

Not all projects are a blank canvas where one can design a garden for a completely empty or new space. Some design projects are based on improving an existing garden by addition or subtraction. The owner of this two-and-a-quarter-acre property in Southampton, New York, was unhappy with her garden, which was full of plants including numerous perennials, annuals, shrubs, and roses. The layout of the plants was disorganized and confusing.

In 2001, I began reorganizing the beds. My associate, Paul Herkovic, and I dug up all the plants, removed unwanted ones, and reassembled the remaining ones in front of the existing dogwoods, *Cornus kousa*, creating harmonious compositions of color and form. We also added new plants to fill out the groups we created.

My relationship with this garden spanned more than 10 years. During that time, we added more beds, plants, and trees, moved existing trees, and created stone patios—all to improve the spatial flow and beauty of the property.

In 2011, the client decided she wanted a less complicated garden. She had admired photographs of the Dutch plantsman, Piet Oudolf's garden, with its clipped hedges offsetting masses of perennials, and asked if she could have something similar. Our first decision was to move the existing dogwoods out of the beds and relocate them to the rear of the property. This provided more space and sun in the 20-foot-deep beds. For the main architecture of the garden, I designed a group of juxtaposing convex and concave-shaped boxwood *Buxus Green Mountain* hedges, flanked by tall, clipped vertical *arborvitae Thuja occidentalis 'Smaragd.'* Drifts of fine-textured perennials were chosen and planted to complement the clipped shapes.

As in many cases, collaborating with a plant-loving client was hard work but fun—the best combination a designer can wish for. The deep satisfaction of developing a garden over many years and seeing the fruits of one's labor grow is an unmatched personal pleasure.

RIGHT Dogwoods, *Cornus kousa*, were photographed in bloom in the original design of the planting bed with its mixed perennials, roses, and tuteurs for climbing roses and clematis.

OVERLEAF In the new design of the garden, the dogwoods were removed from the perennial bed and relocated. They now frame the view of the house from the west.

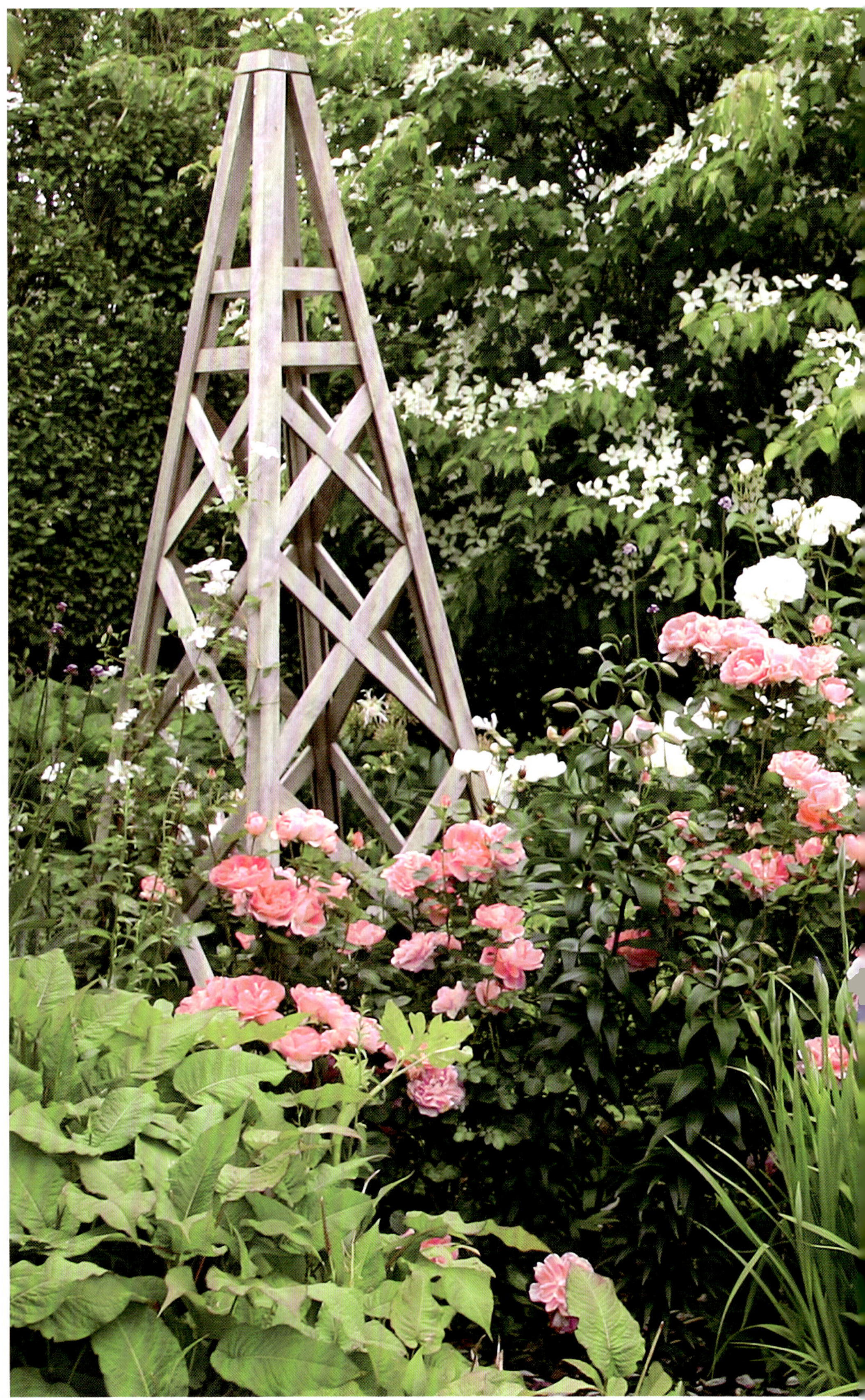

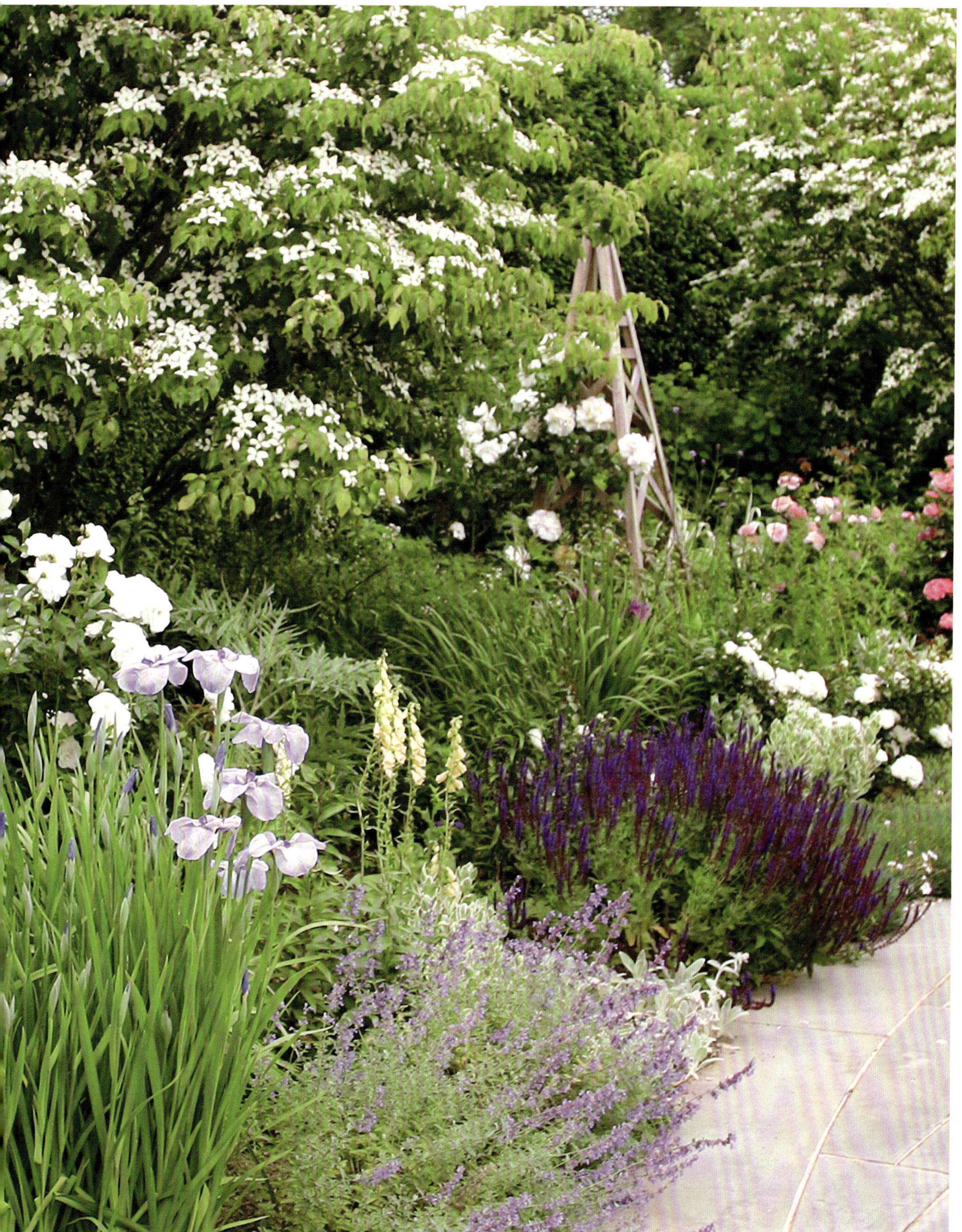

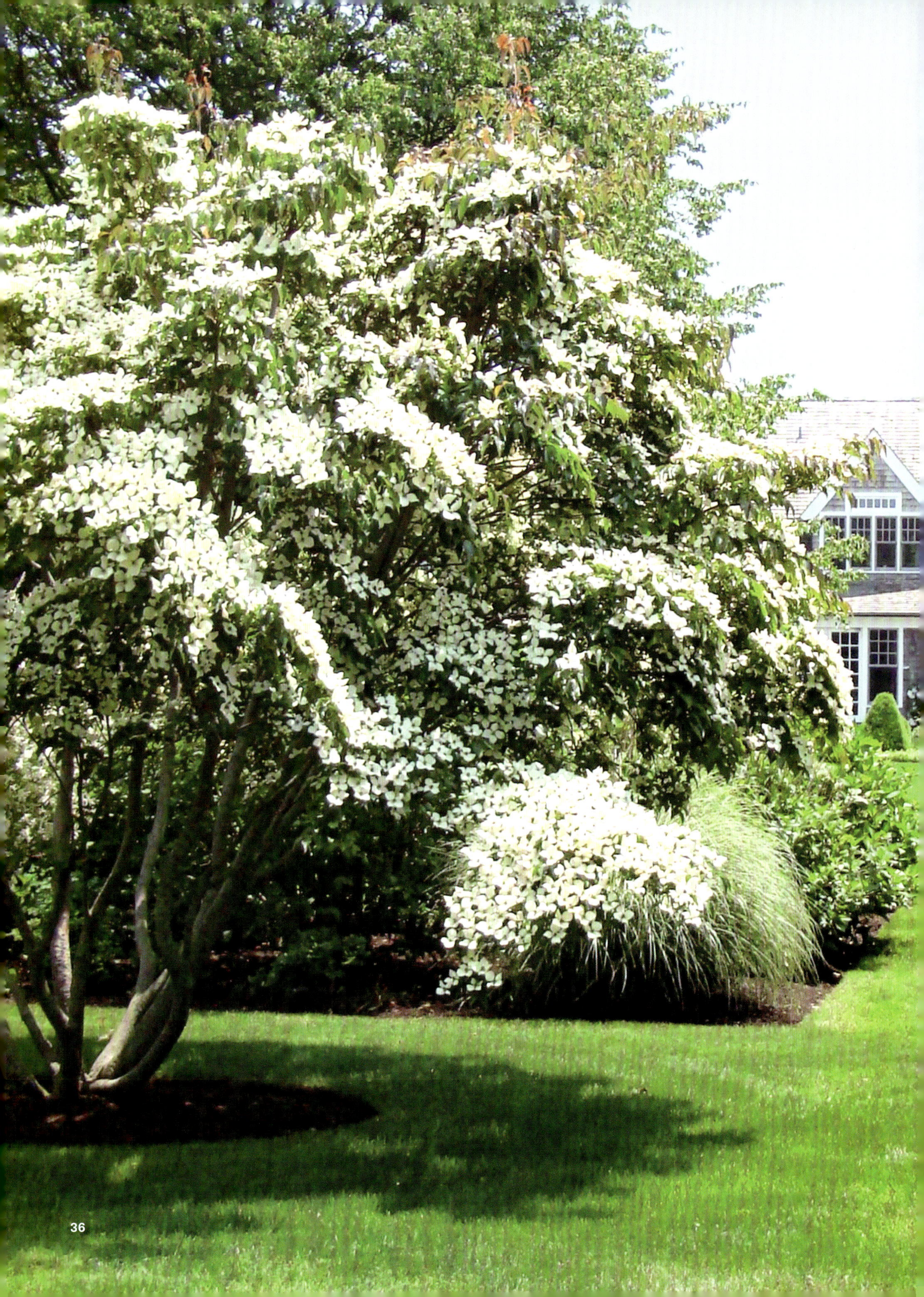

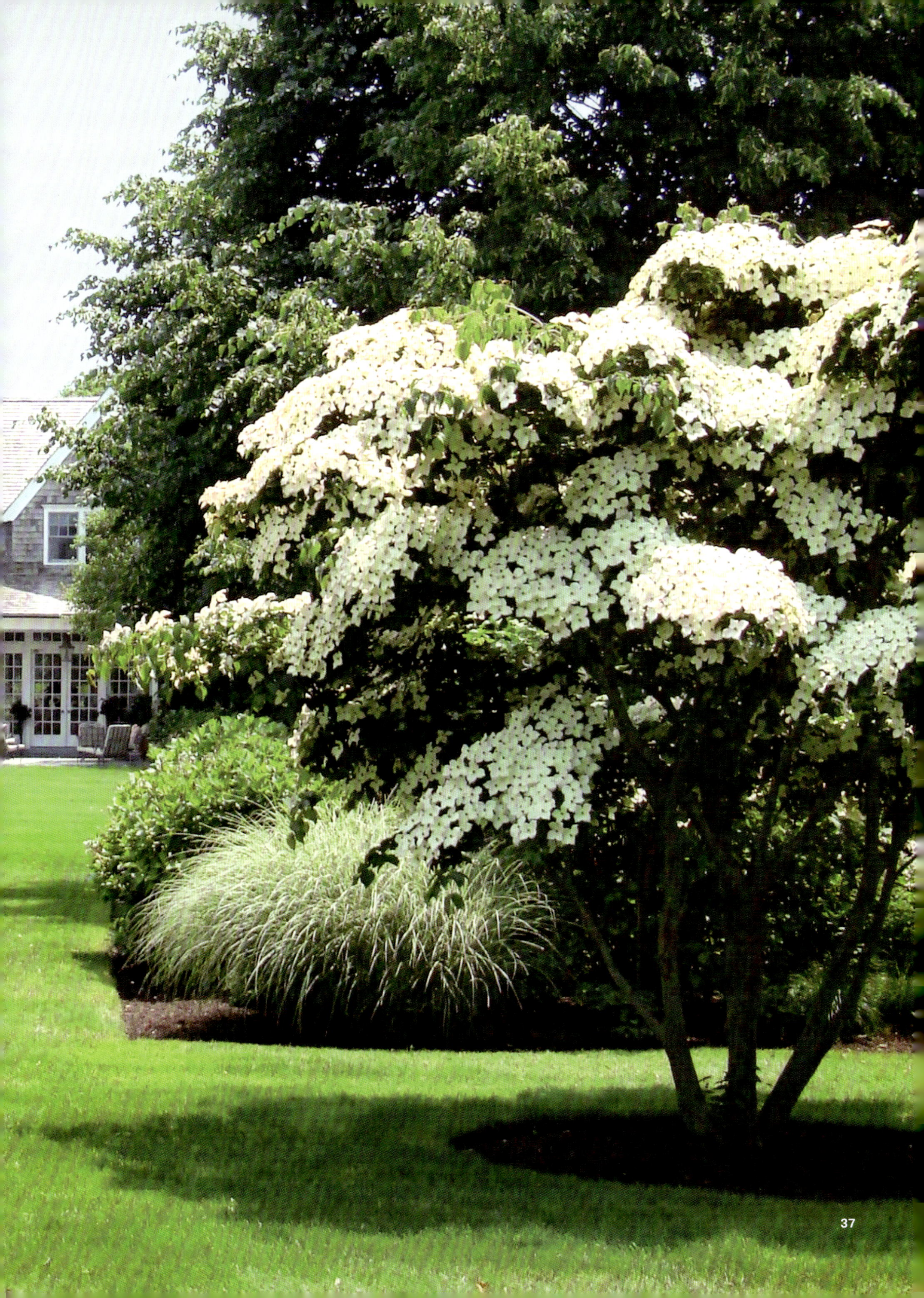

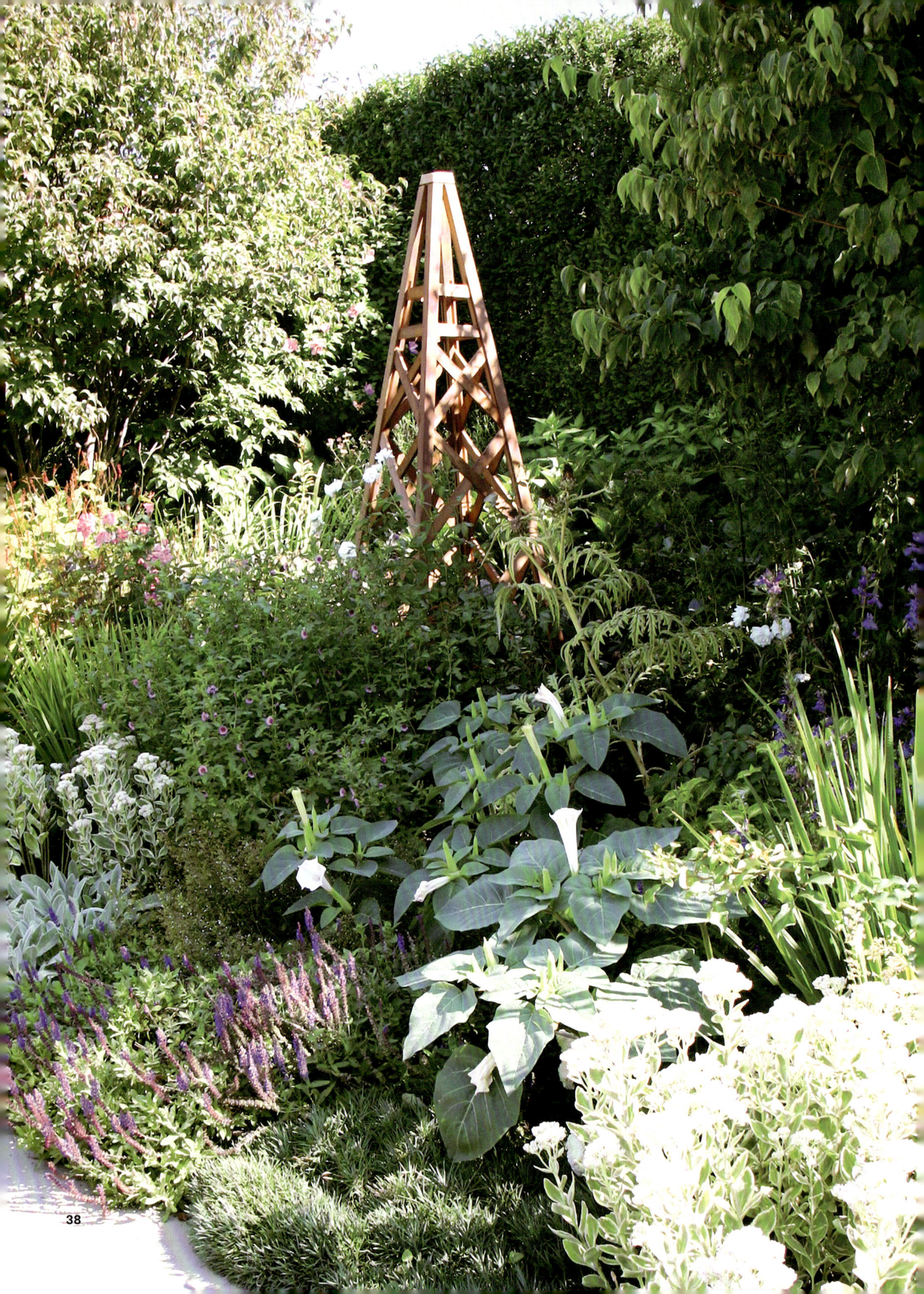

OPPOSITE Angel's trumpet, *Datura metel*, blooms in the original perennial bed design.

RIGHT Plant combinations based on color themes are an element in all my work. Here, purple and white perennials were combined in the shade garden under a linden *Tillia americana*. White flowers brighten shady areas.

OVERLEAF Rosa *'New Dawn'* covers the folly and adds a wonderful fragrance to the garden.

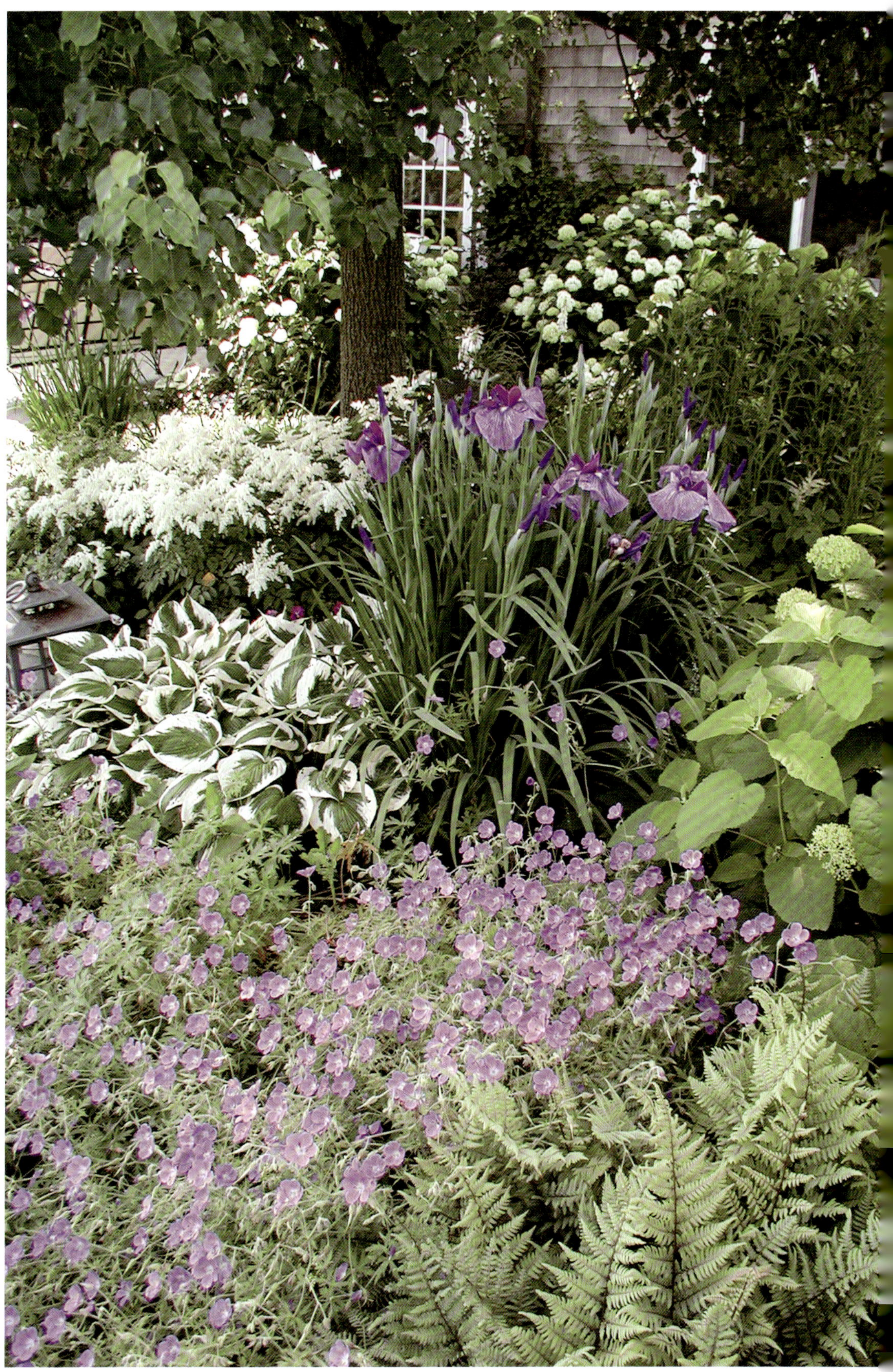

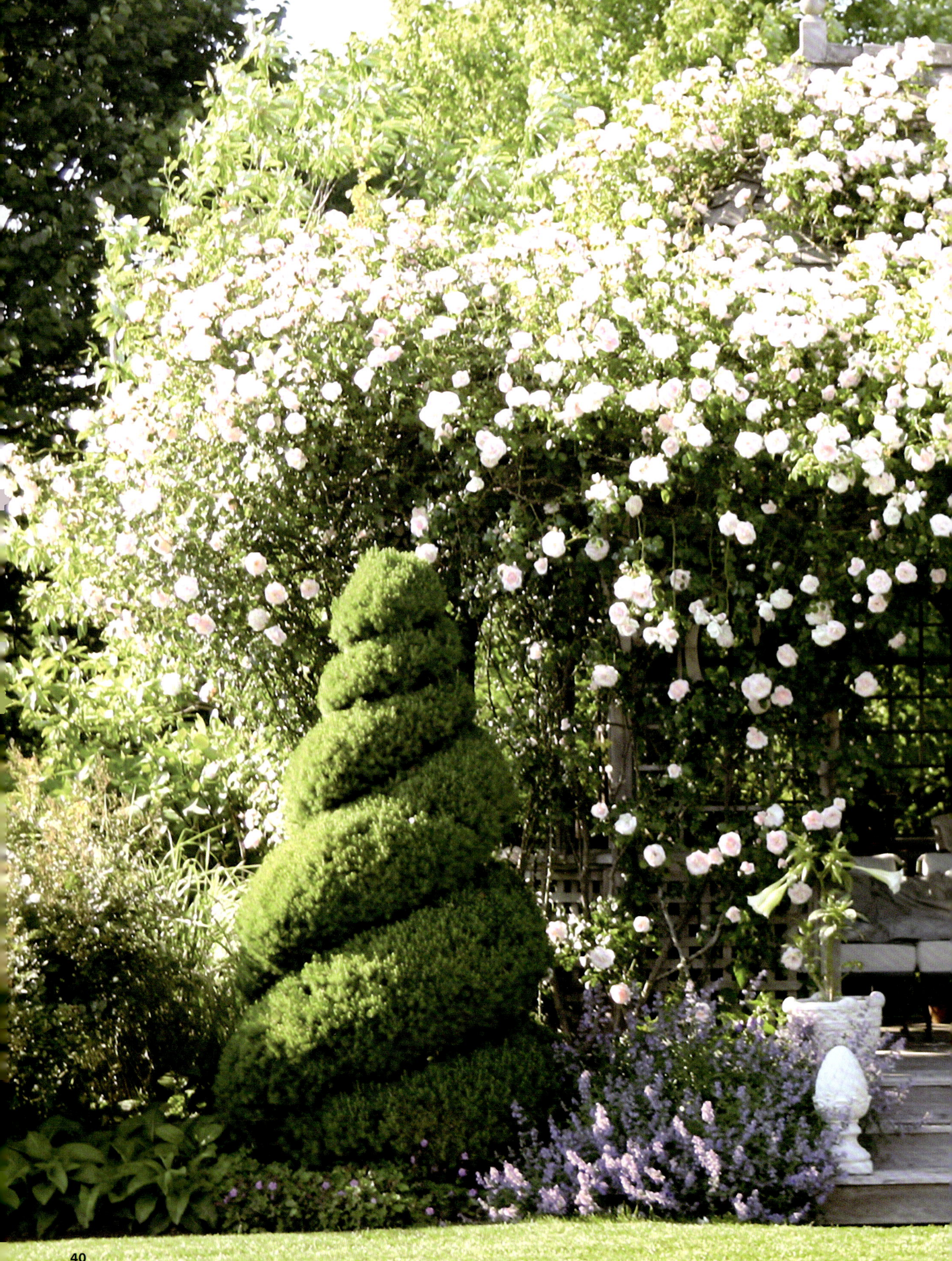

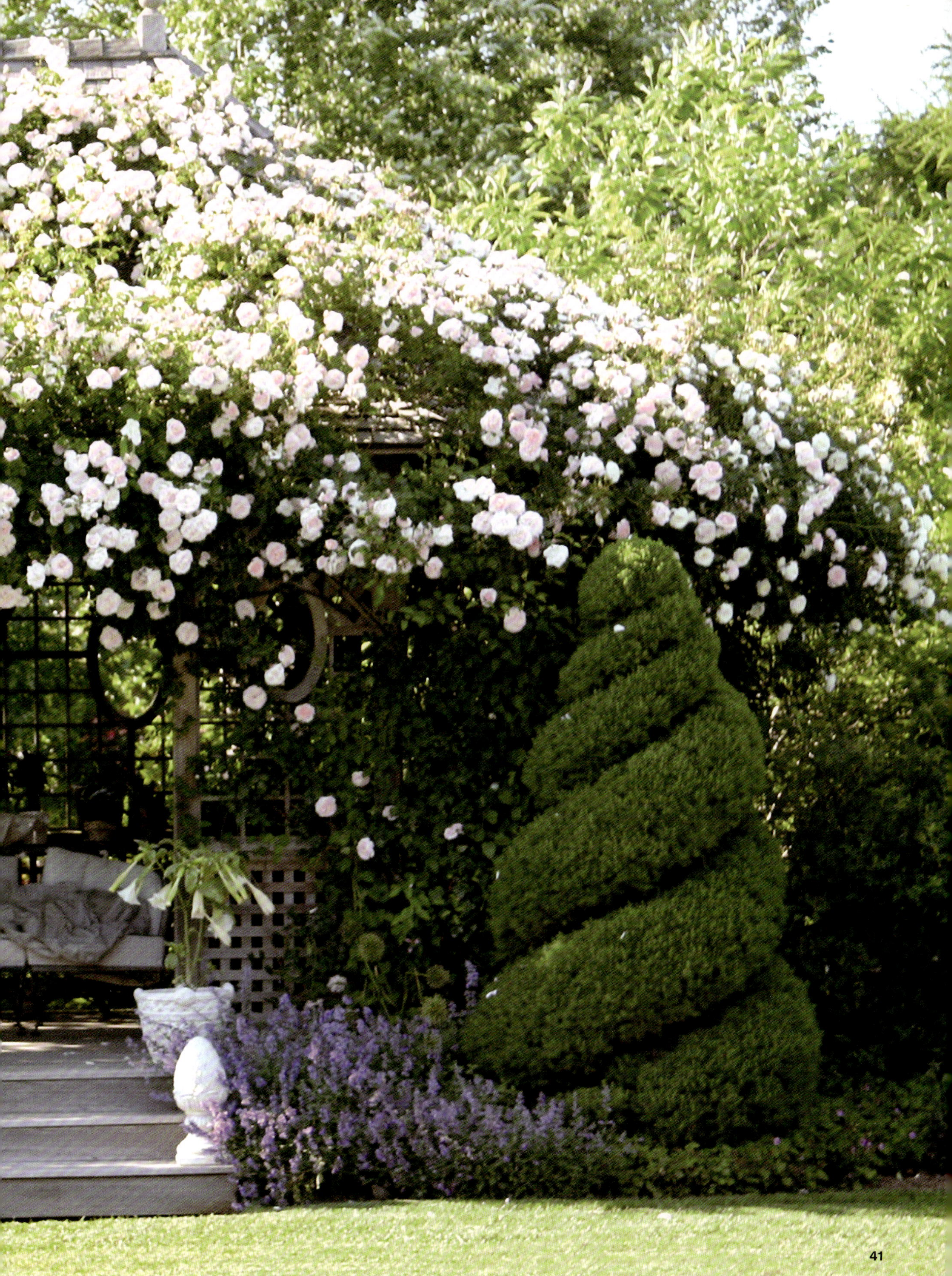

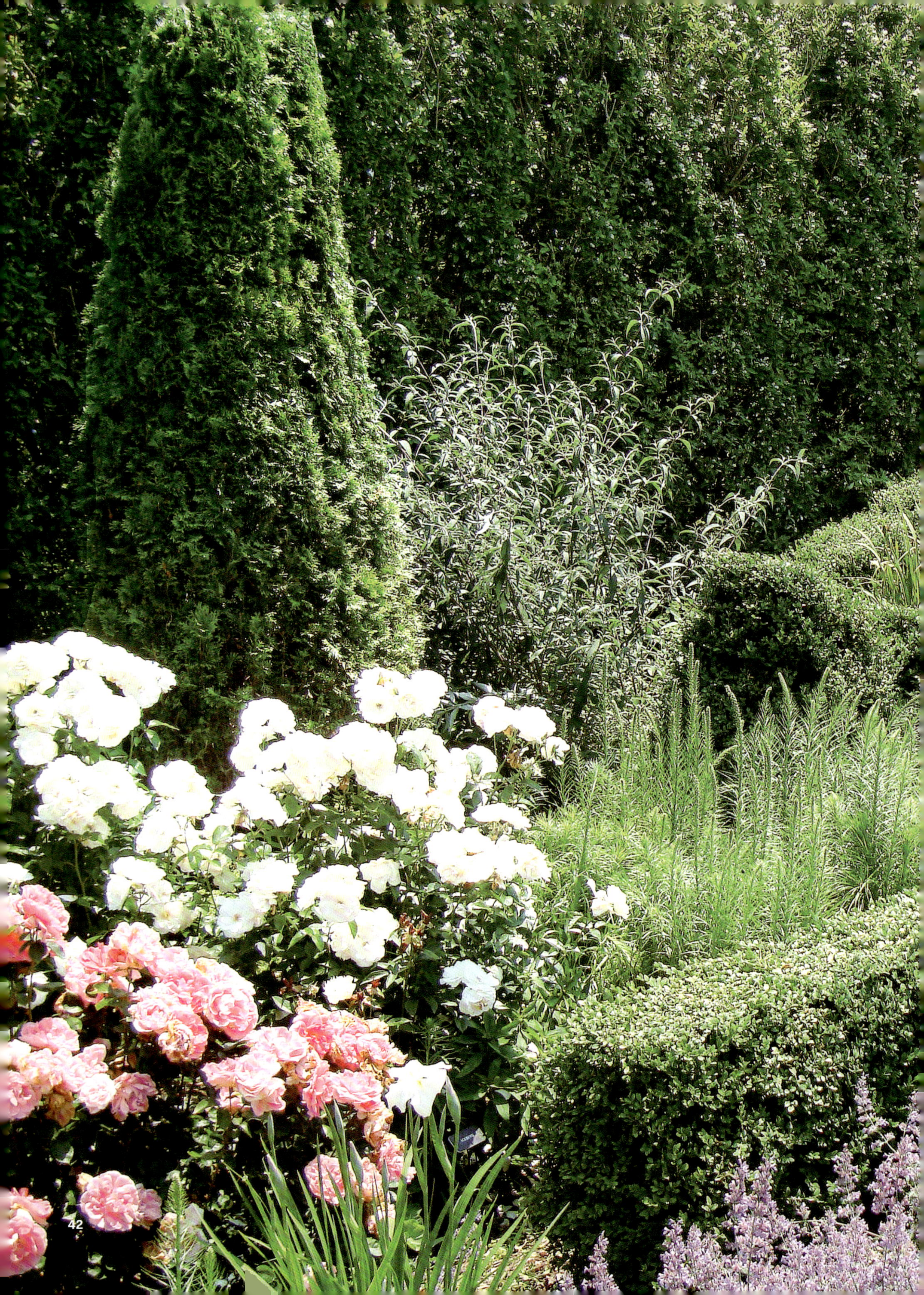

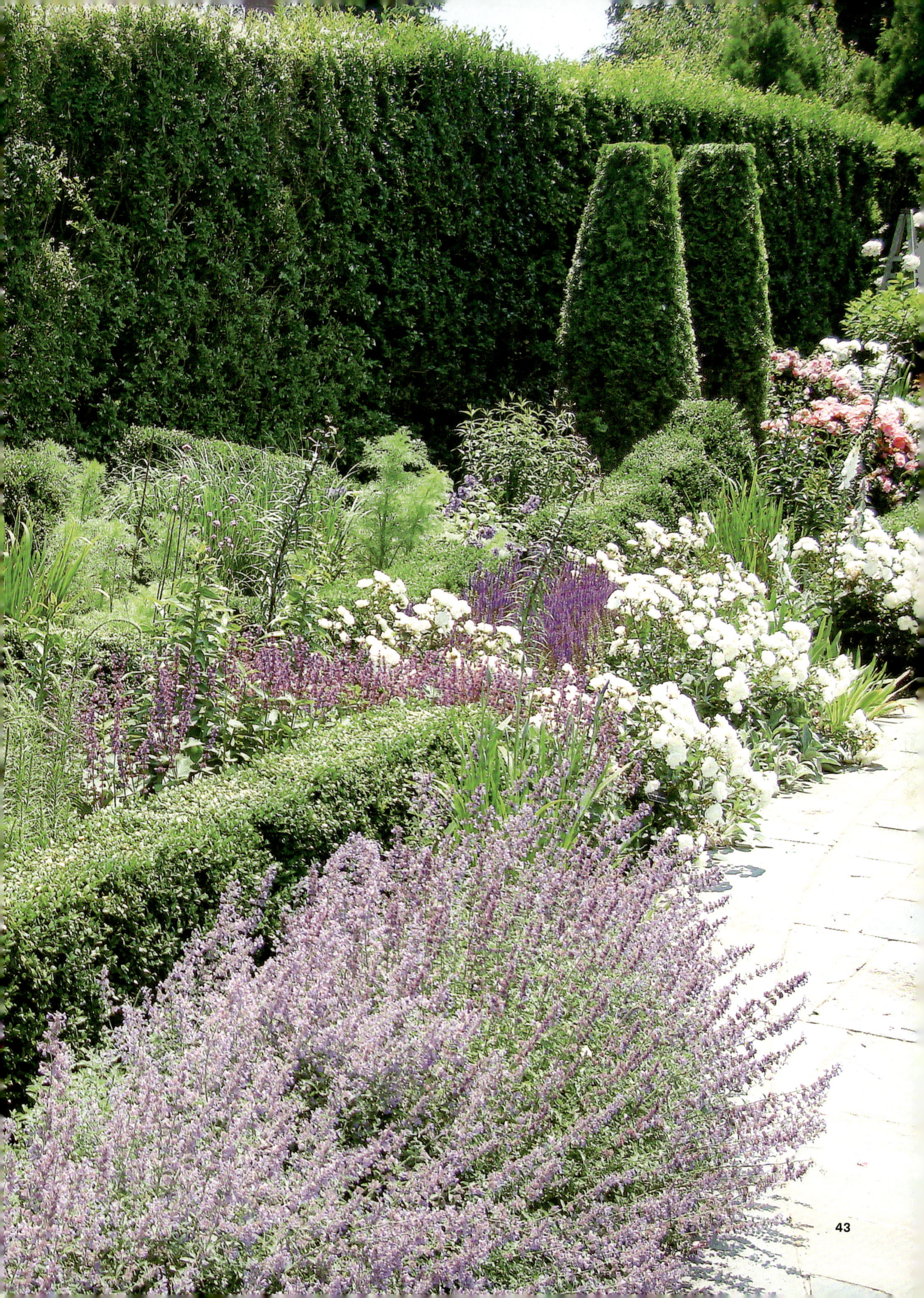

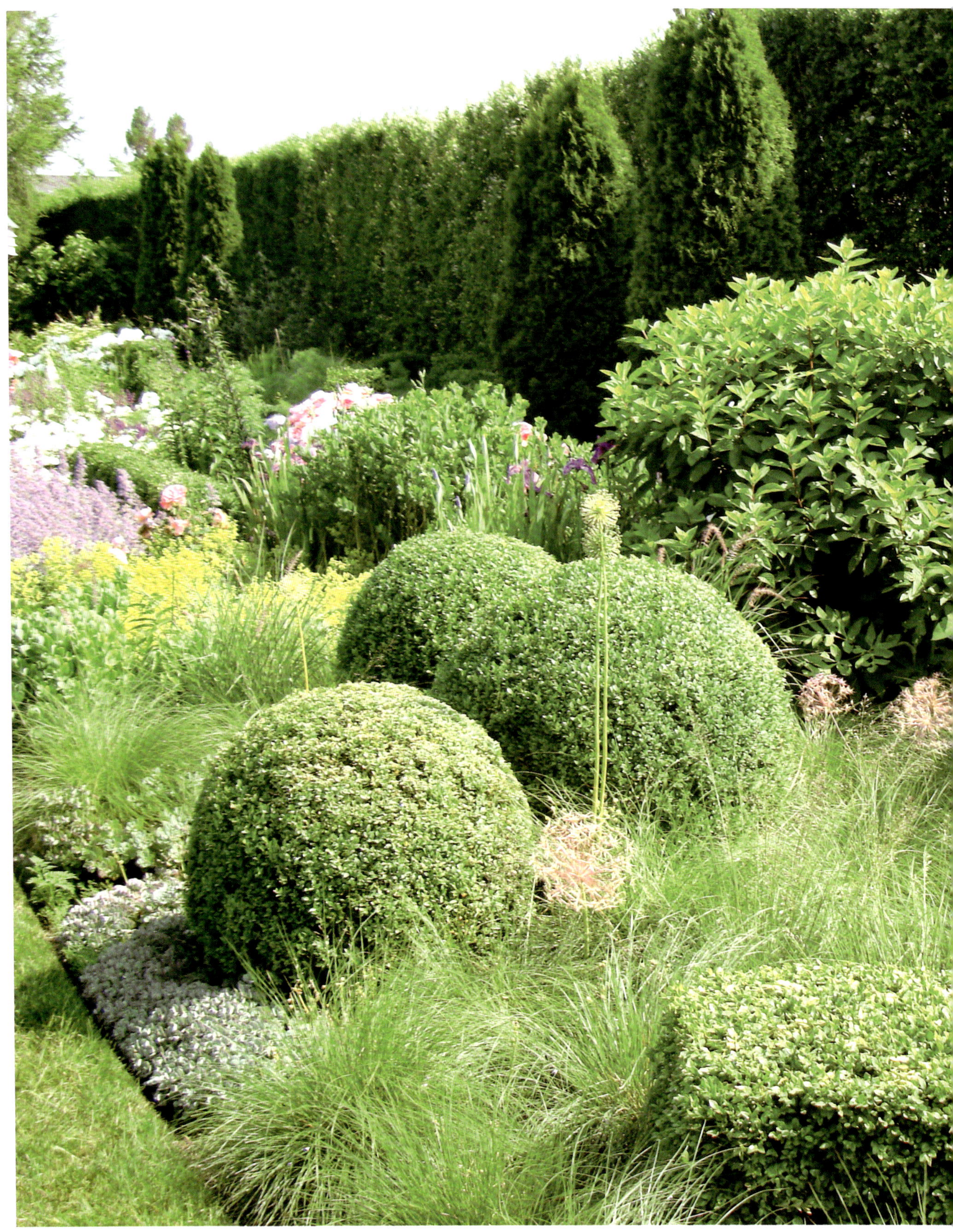

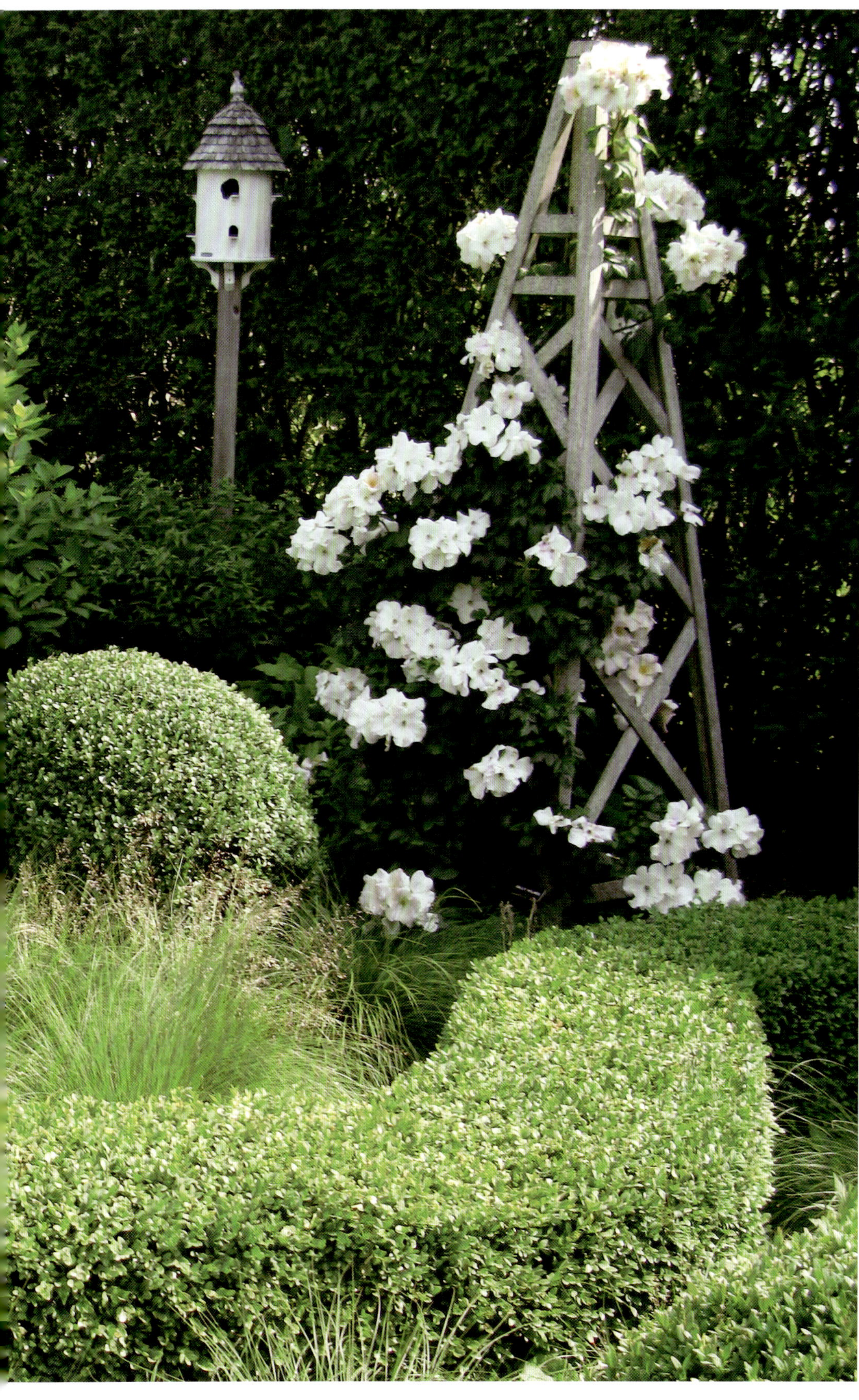

PREVIOUS PAGES In the redesigned perennial bed, curved clipped boxwood hedges are flanked by *arborvitae* columns *Thuja occidentalis 'Smaragd.'* Fine, textured perennials and roses in a pastel theme complement the tightly clipped boxwood and arborvitae.

LEFT At the east end of the main bed, an "S"-shaped boxwood hedge with box balls planted on both sides are surrounded by prairie dropseed *Sporobolus heterolepsis*. Tuteurs were moved there to provide vertical accents.

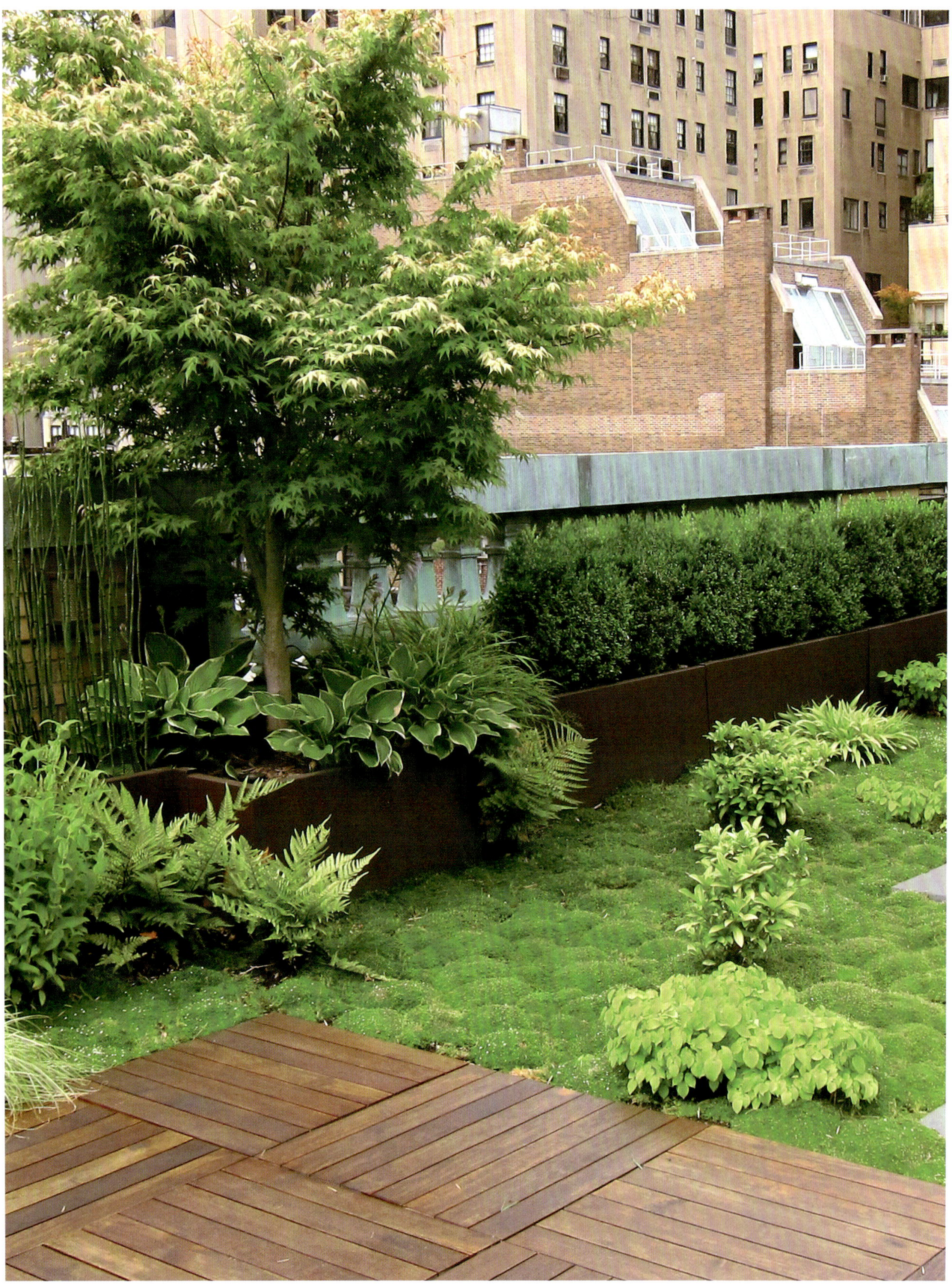

STYLIZED

Urban rooftop gardens not only have to survive the elements but have to counter the sounds and sights of hurried urban life. The challenge in these gardens is to create a serene, natural environment that is a refuge from the city.

In the natural world, the ground supporting plants and trees is an essential element of our experience in nature. When traveling through a landscape, we look around, including at the ground on which we are walking, with its plants, twigs, and rocks. I try to capture that effect on city rooftops by using the ground plane as part of the garden design.

In shallow four- to five-inch planters spread out over an area to maximize planting and minimize weight, I plant groundcovers and perennials to create a living ground plane. The secret is finding plants that will tolerate the conditions—with irrigation, of course. Fortunately, I have found many. In addition to the ground plane, taller side-by-side planters along the perimeter of the space were planted with shrubs and trees to provide a sense of enclosure and to keep the eye within the space.

Together, the groundcovers, trees, and shrubs create the feeling of a natural environment on a rooftop above the city. In this 1,200-square-foot Japanese-inspired corporate garden created in 2010, a carpet of moss *Minuartia verna*, punctuated by ferns and perennials, covers the ground to provide a calming effect, while trees, shrubs, grasses, and bamboo create a sense of enclosure. Experiencing the garden, your eye goes from the moss to the shrubs and trees, and back to the moss, as if you were taking a walk in nature.

OPPOSITE A Japanese Maple *Acer palmatum 'Katsura'* and a boxwood hedge sit in front of the parapet. Moss *Minuartia verna* and assorted perennials planted in shallow five-inch deep trays cover the floor.

OVERLEAF The long view of the garden looking west shows the moss carpet, benches, and stone pavers. In all green gardens, a plant's placement is determined by the size of its leaf—fine, medium, or bold—as either a contrast or a complement to neighboring plants. Here, medium-textured plants were placed in the fine moss to provide small accents along the length of the garden.

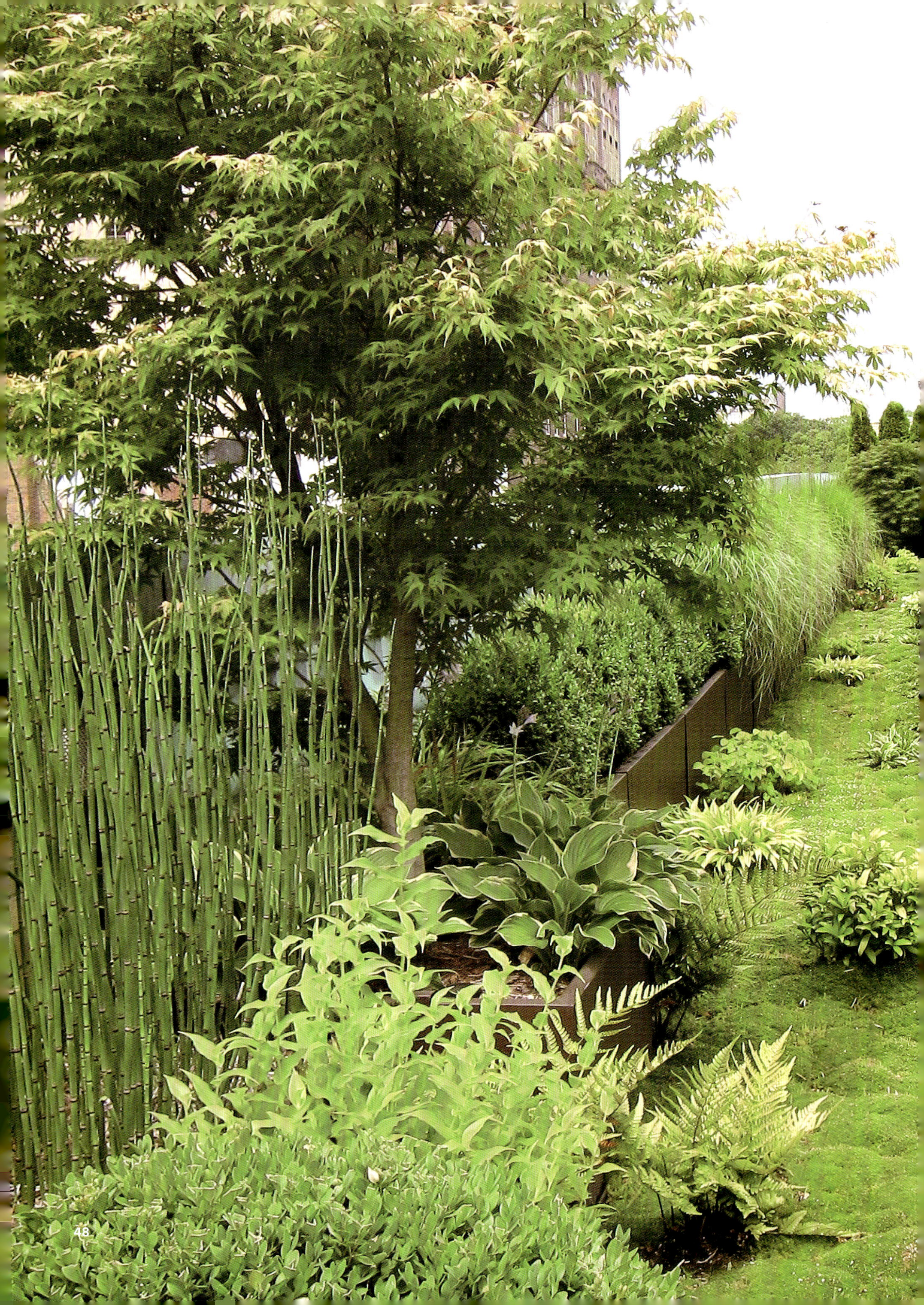

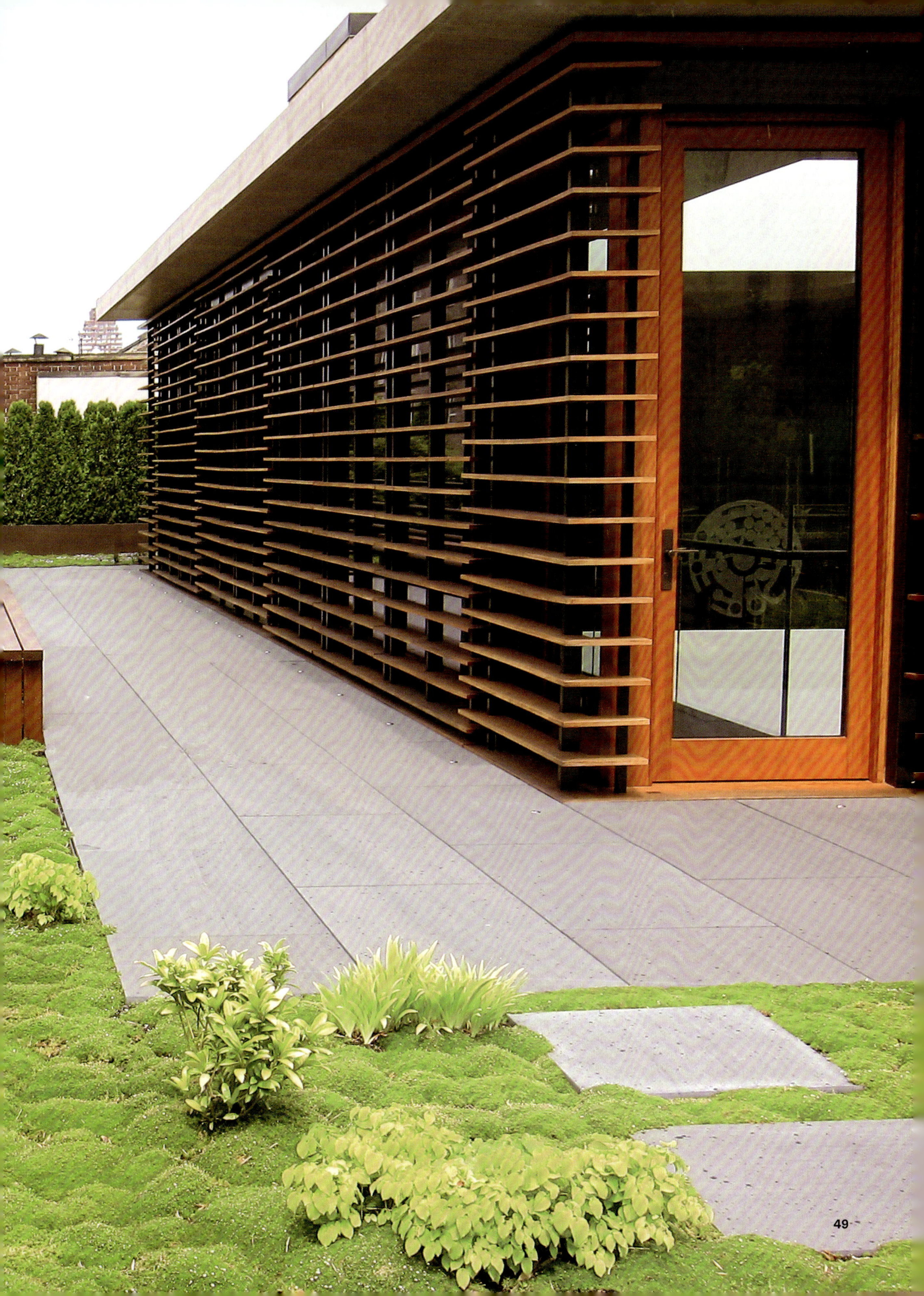

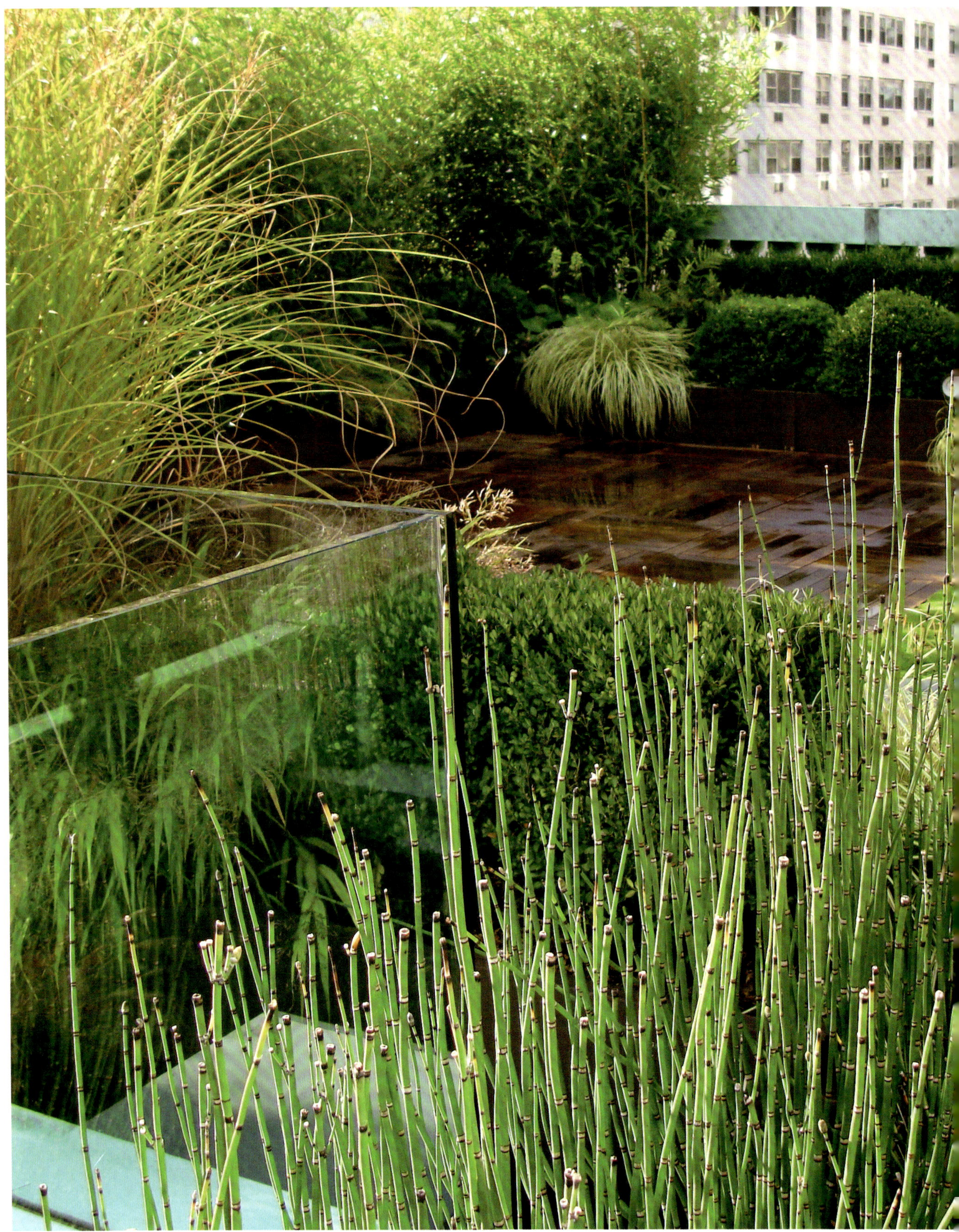

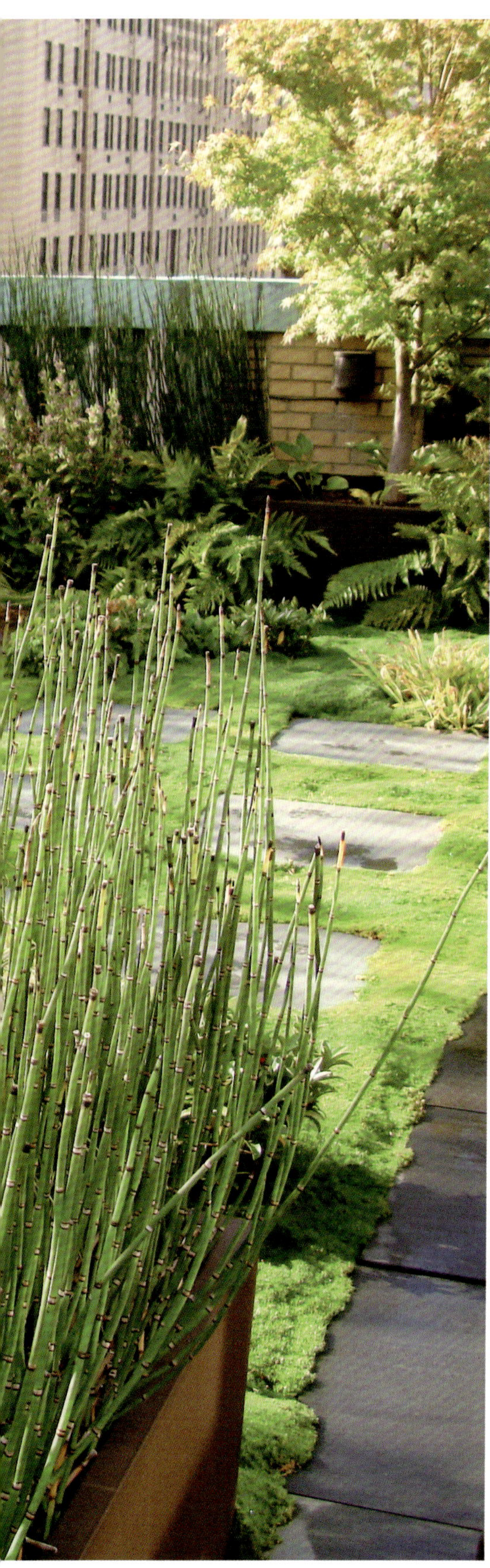

LEFT At the east end of the garden, a deck for seating was backed by bamboo *Phyllostachys bissetii*. In the foreground, the reed *Equisetum hymale*, and maiden grass *Miscanthus sinensis 'Morning Light,'* add textural interest.

OVERLEAF LEFT In another section of the garden, stepping stones allow walking over the moss *Minuartia verna* that is accented with sedge *Carex oshimensis 'Evergold'* and bergenia. The flat stones sit like islands in the fine moss.

OVERLEAF RIGHT In front of the seating deck, the moss was planted with iris *Iris cristata*, Japanese skimmia *Skimmia japonica*, barrenwort *Epimedium x versicolor*, Autumn fern *Dryopteris erythrosora*, and toad lily *Tricyrtis hirta*—all of which add interest to the moss carpet.

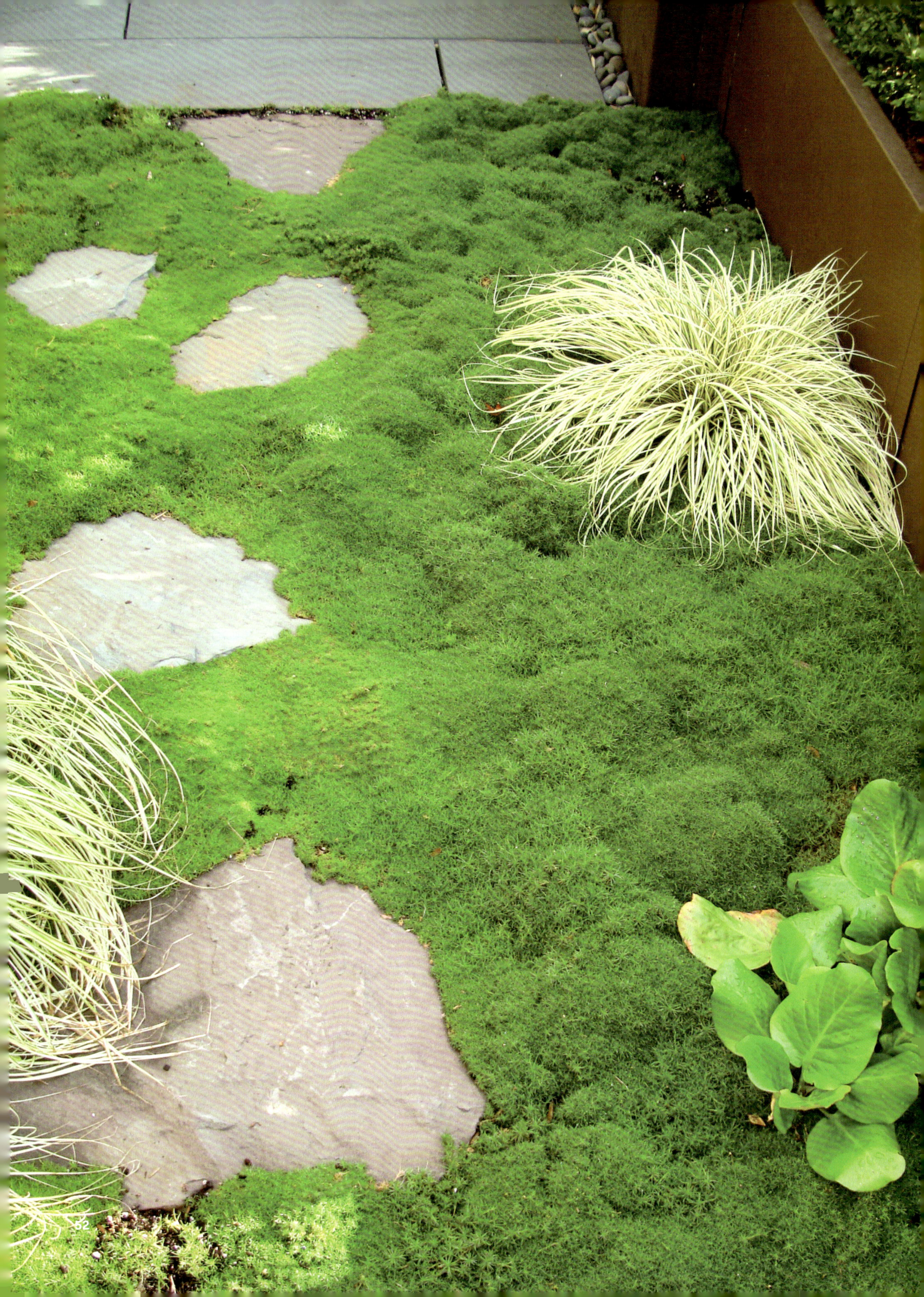

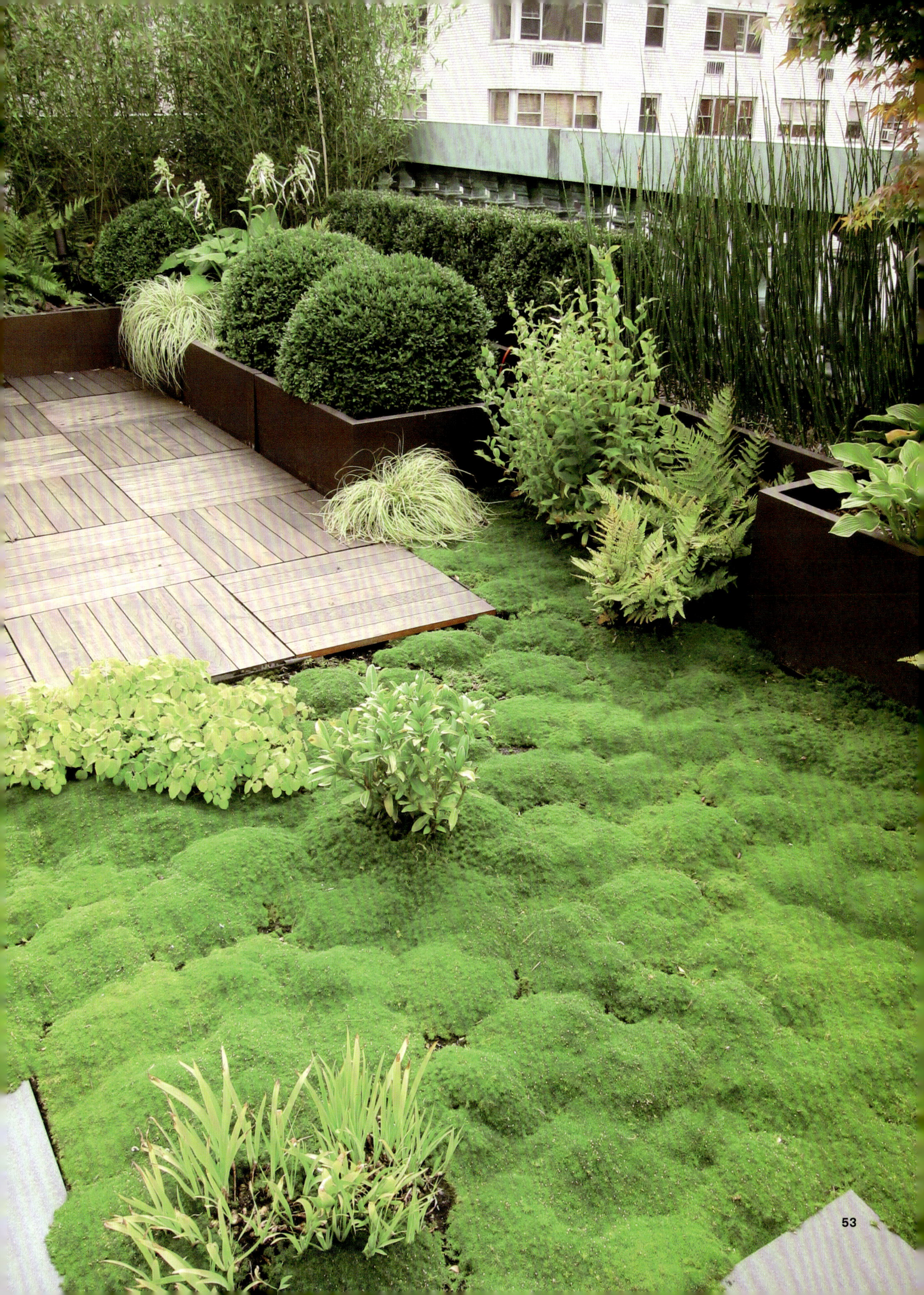

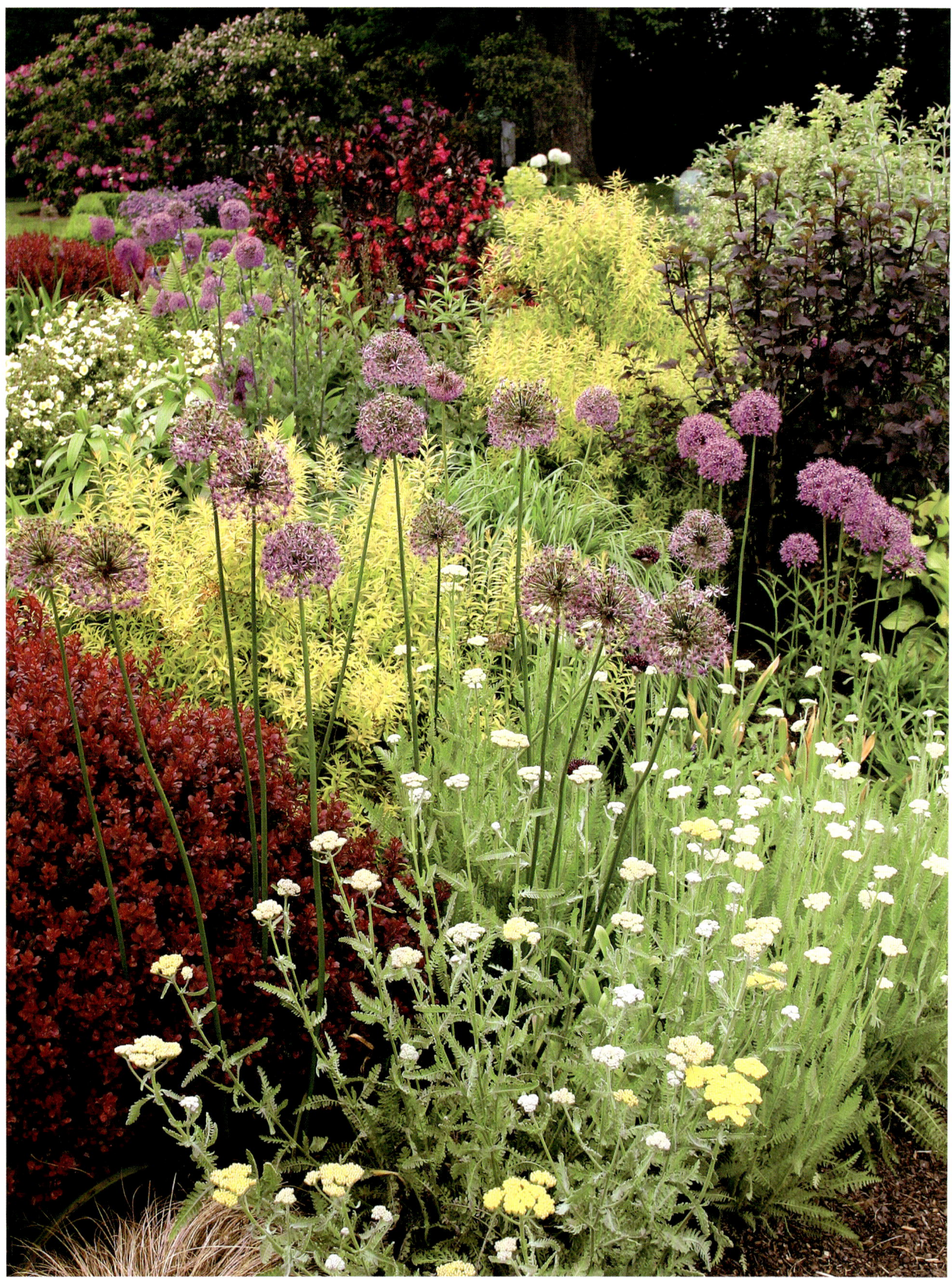

PICTORIAL

When I design a landscape or garden, I work with photographs of the site and draw directly on the photos. I was told Capability Brown, the 18th-century English landscape designer whose work I admire, did something similar. Though the photograph is a two-dimensional object, it flattens the space and helps me "see" it without distractions. The resulting sketch is a picture of the possible.

In 2000, I visited this park-like setting with mature trees in Bridgehampton, New York. At the rear of the house, a formal perennial garden and a rose garden with a tall Yew hedge sat near the house in a deep lawn. The client requested that the perennial and rose garden be left in their present location to preserve a part of the landscape's history. The preliminary sketch I produced on photographs showed the addition of a new, long shrub border at the end of the property, island beds, and specimen trees, to soften and articulate the empty lawn.

The existing perennial bed was filled with unattractive plants. Paul Herkovic and I removed most of the plants and replanted the area with perennials, shrubs, and bulbs in different color combinations. Next we addressed the heavy Yew hedge around the rose garden. In the 1990s, I visited the 18th century Villa Gamberaia outside of Florence, Italy, with its architectural hedges that beautifully animate the garden. With that in mind, I changed the top of the Yew hedge from a single flat surface to a stepped top, giving the hedge a more interesting architectural profile. Over the next several years, we continued to improve the property, adding an herb garden, stone patios, and more plantings to make the property more interesting and inviting.

OPPOSITE In this yellow- and red-themed section of the perennial garden, *Allium afflatuense* floats above yarrow *Achillea 'Moonshine,'* with Japanese barberry *Berberis thunbergii 'Crimson Queen,'* and yellow spiraea *Spiraea thunbergii 'Ogon'* behind.

OVERLEAF An overview of the property at the rear of the house shows the location of the perennial and rose gardens, as well as the specimen trees on the lawn, and the shrub border at the end of the property.

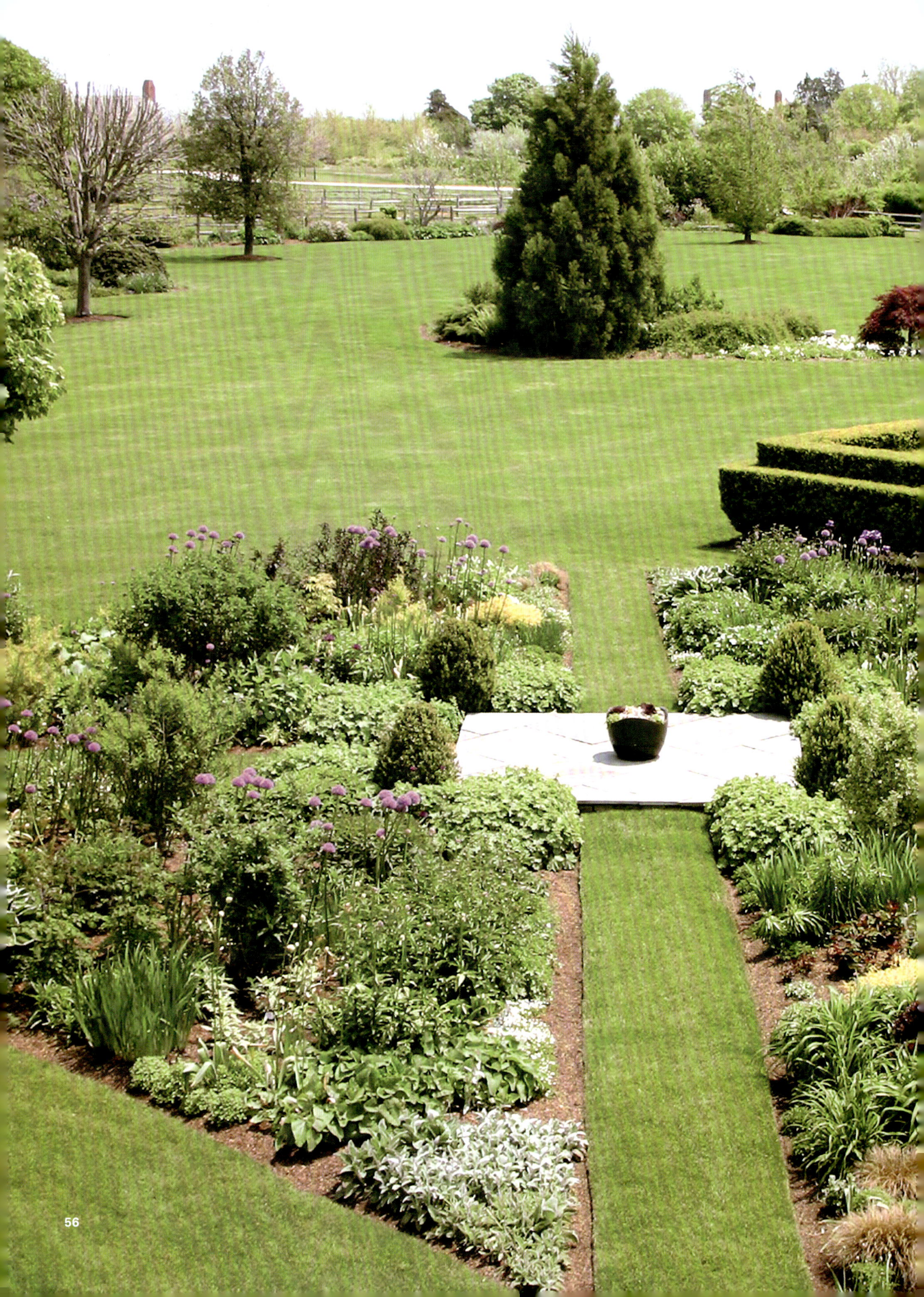

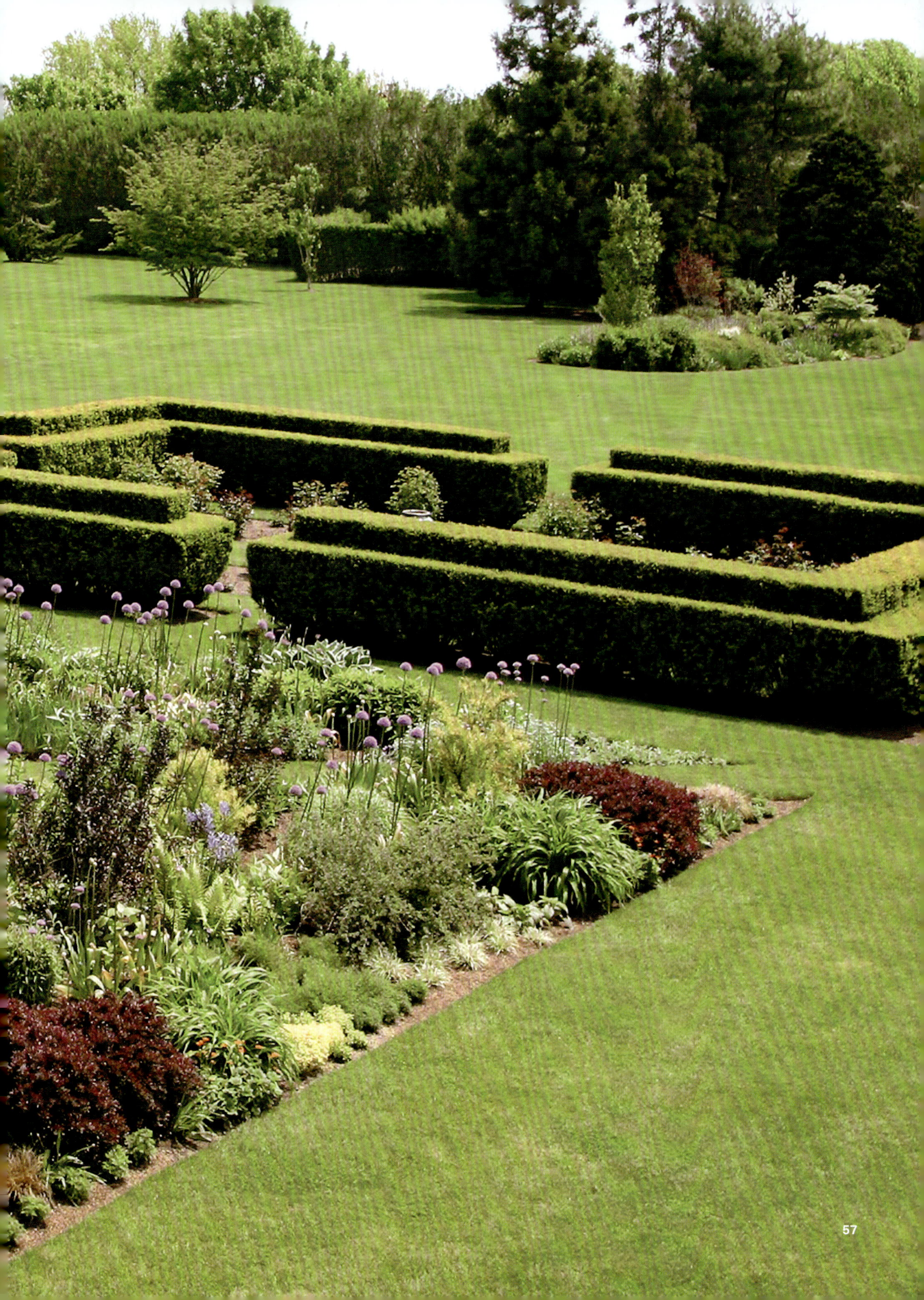

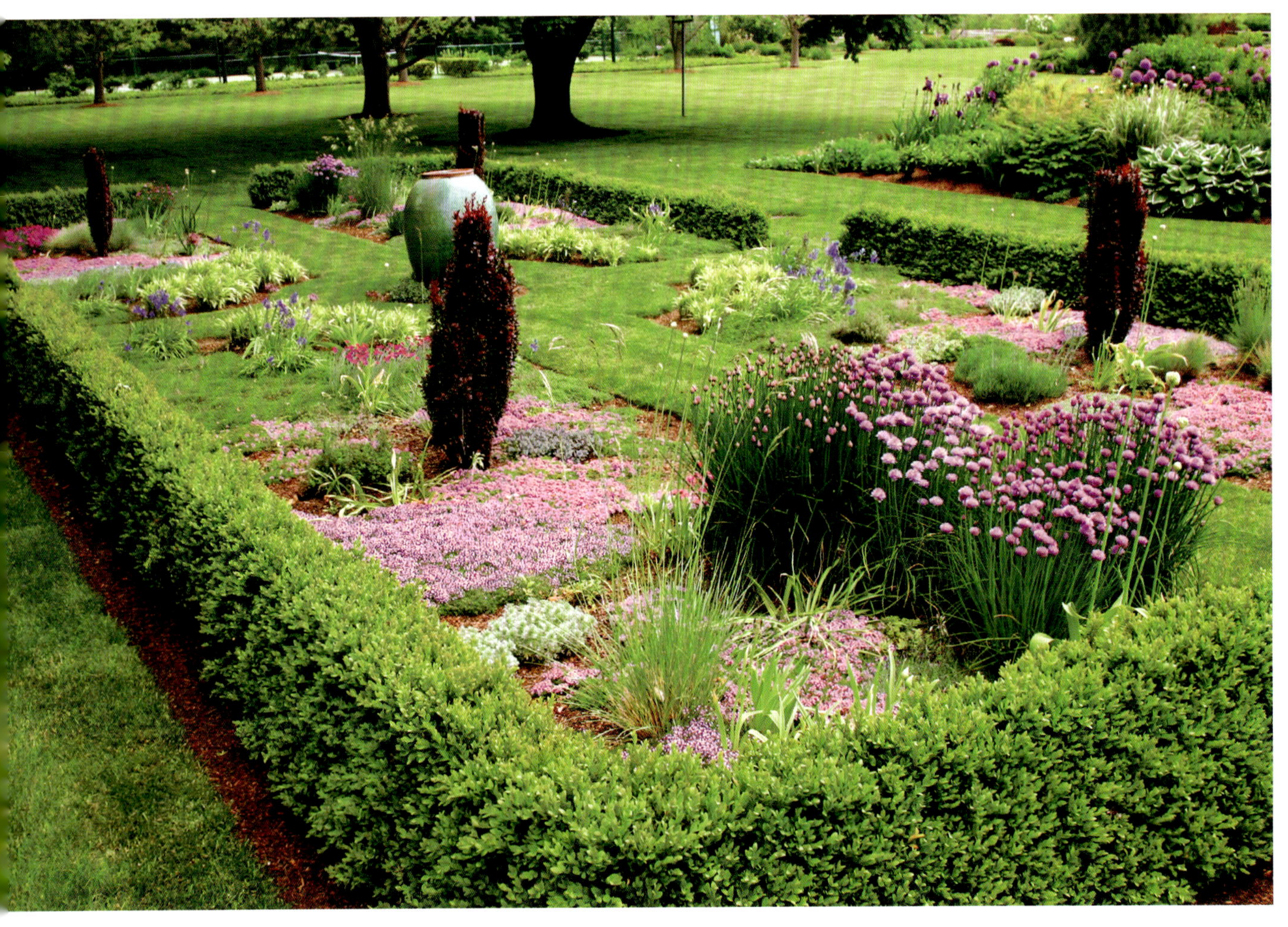

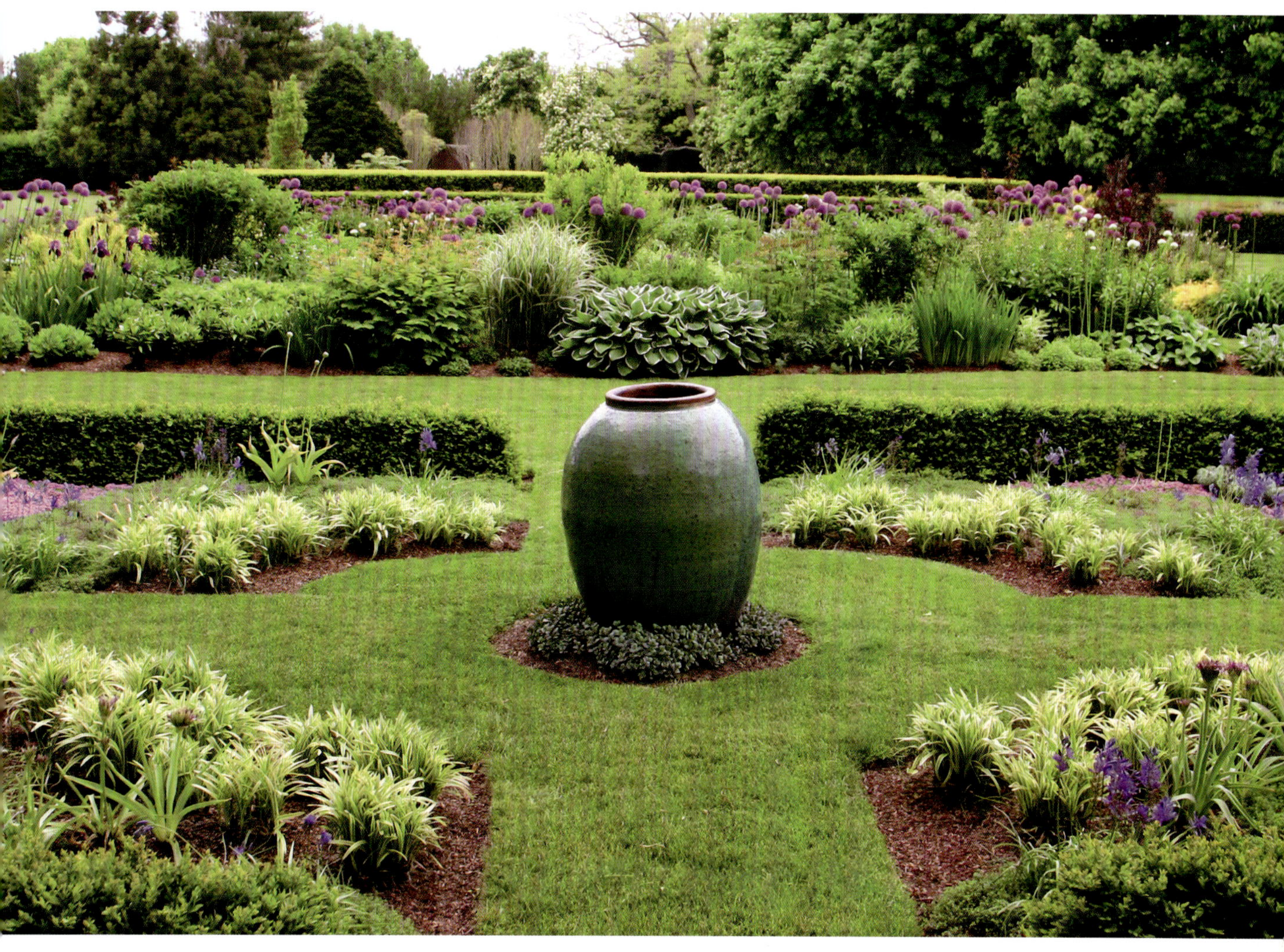

OPPOSITE The herb garden is a carpet of color, with various thymes and allium in bloom, and is punctuated with columnar bayberry *Berberis 'Helmond Pillar.'*

ABOVE In the herb garden, an overscale blue urn is circled by yellow lily turf *Liriope muscari 'Variegata.'*

OVERLEAF LEFT TOP A Japanese cedar *Cryptomeria japonica 'Yoshino'* frames the Shingle-style house. The rose garden hedge with its stepped top is in the background.

OVERLEAF LEFT BOTTOM In June, the perennial garden is viewed on an axis against a group of mature maple trees.

OVERLEAF RIGHT TOP The patio has been planted with angled boxwood hedges and maidenhair grass accents. The swimming pool is in the distance.

OVERLEAF RIGHT BOTTOM One of the quadrants of the multi-colored perennial garden is seen with the rose garden hedge behind.

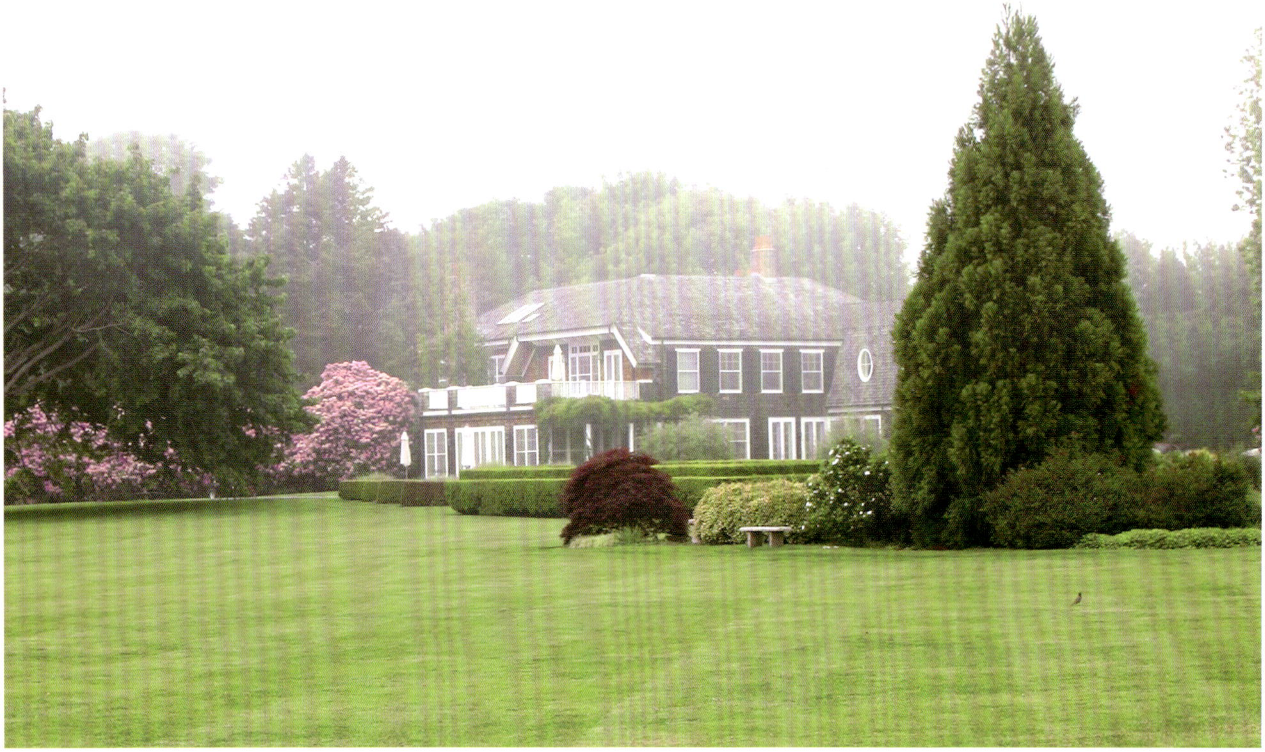

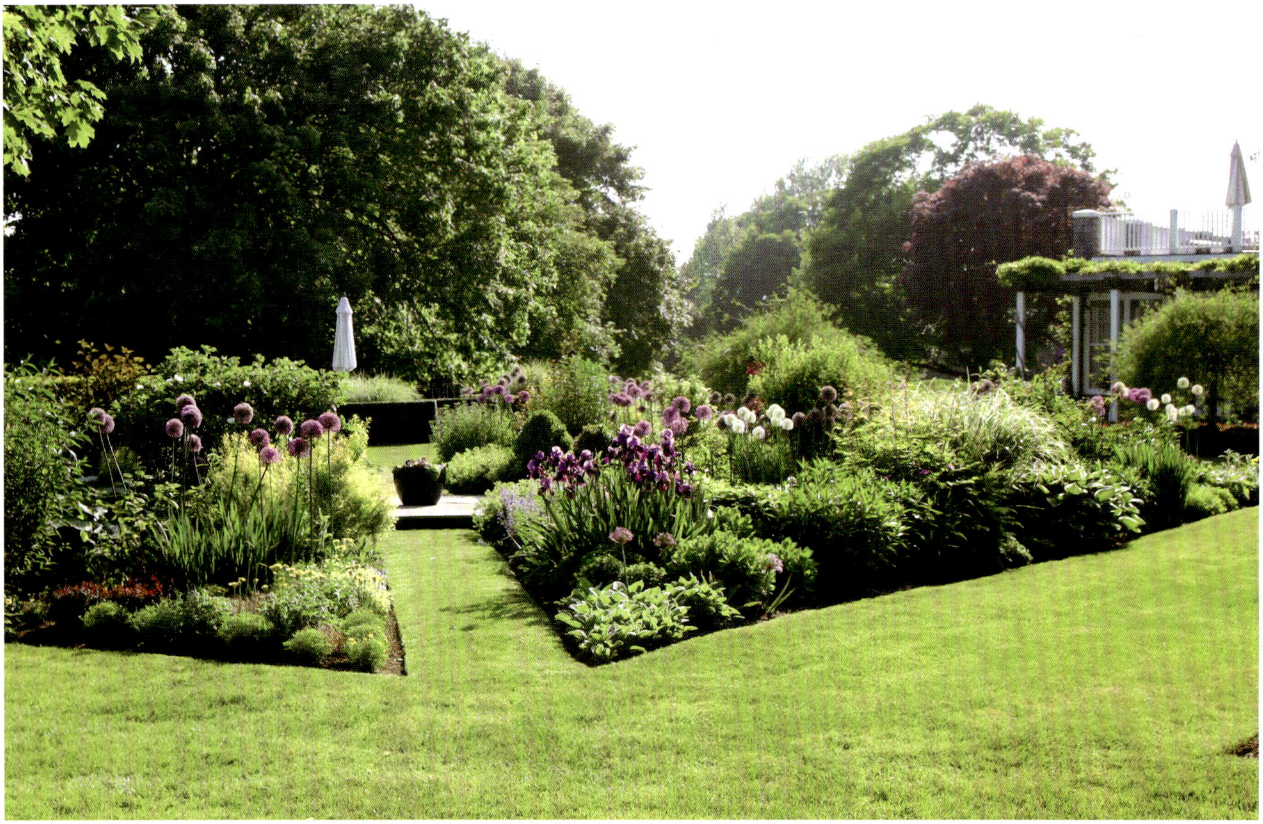

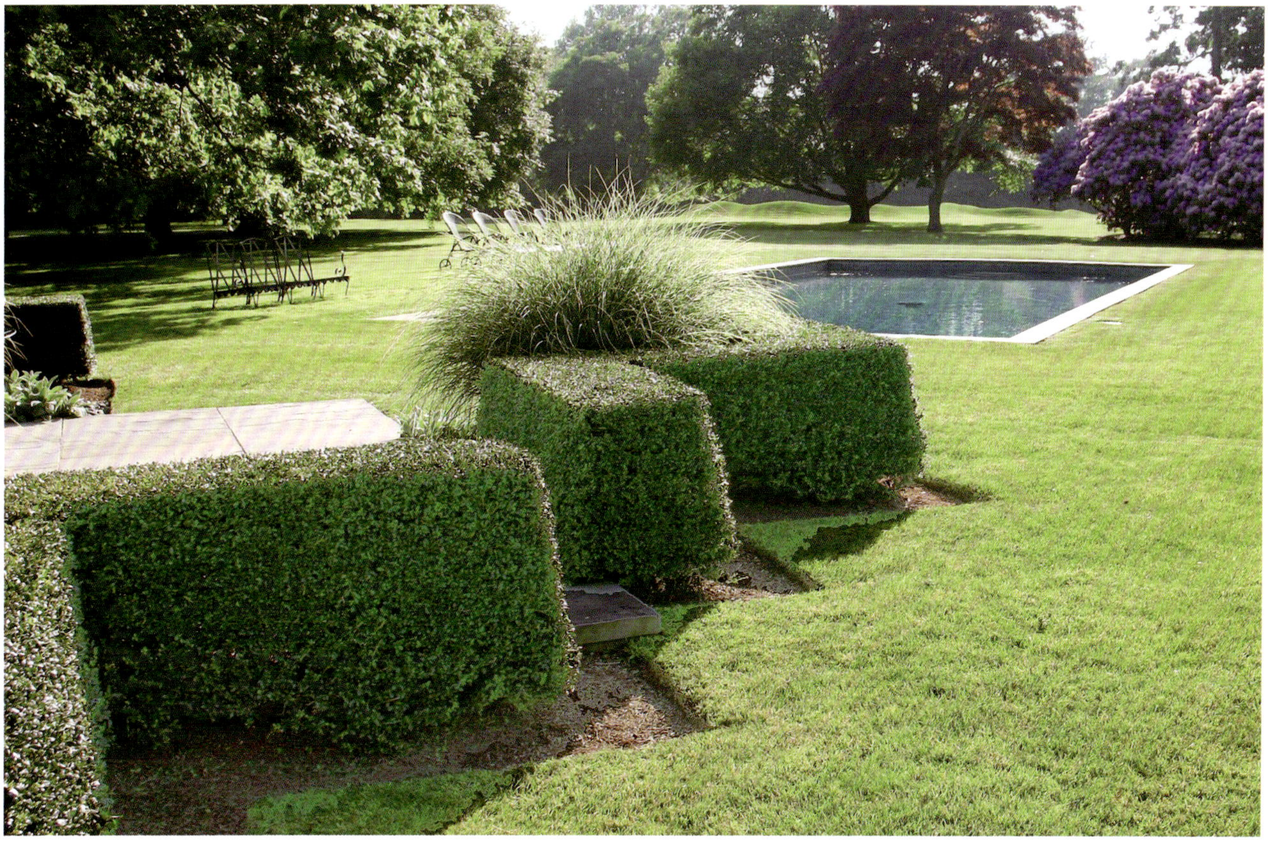

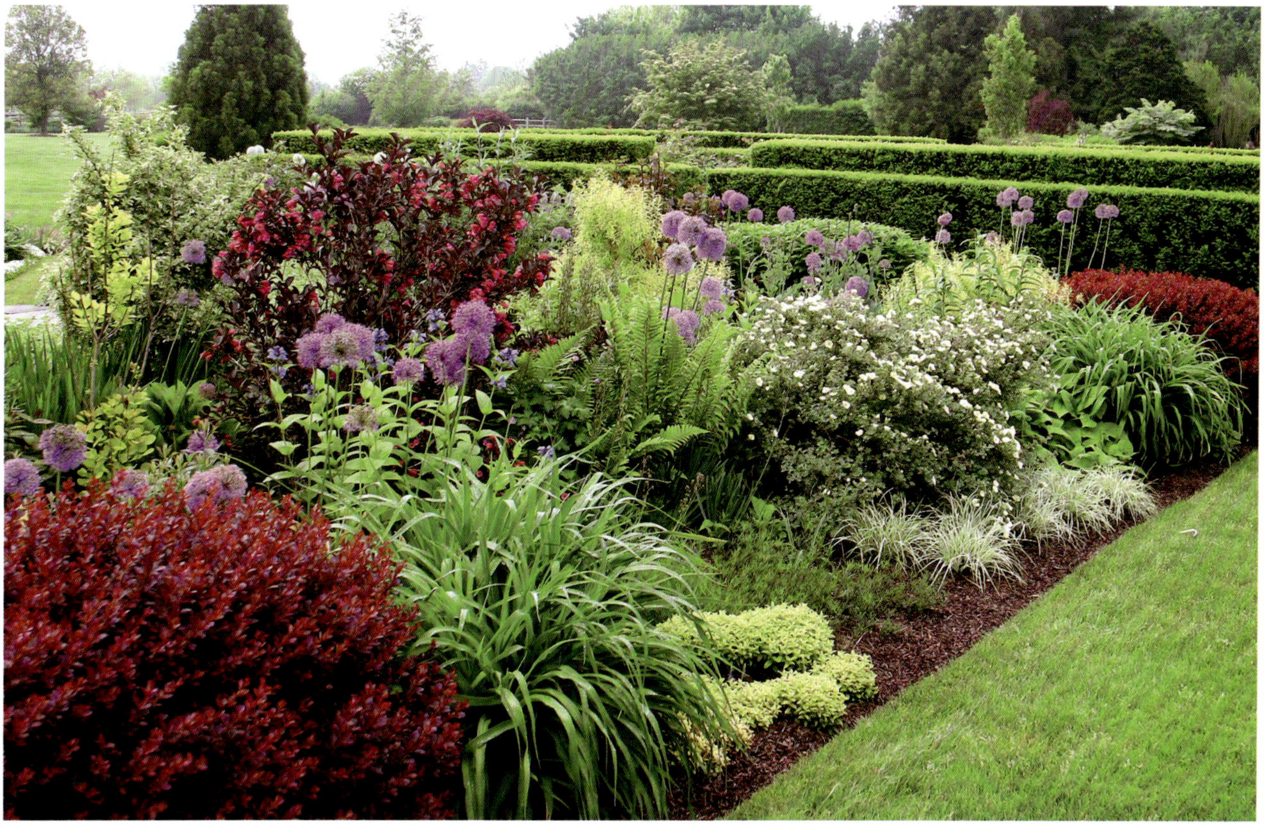

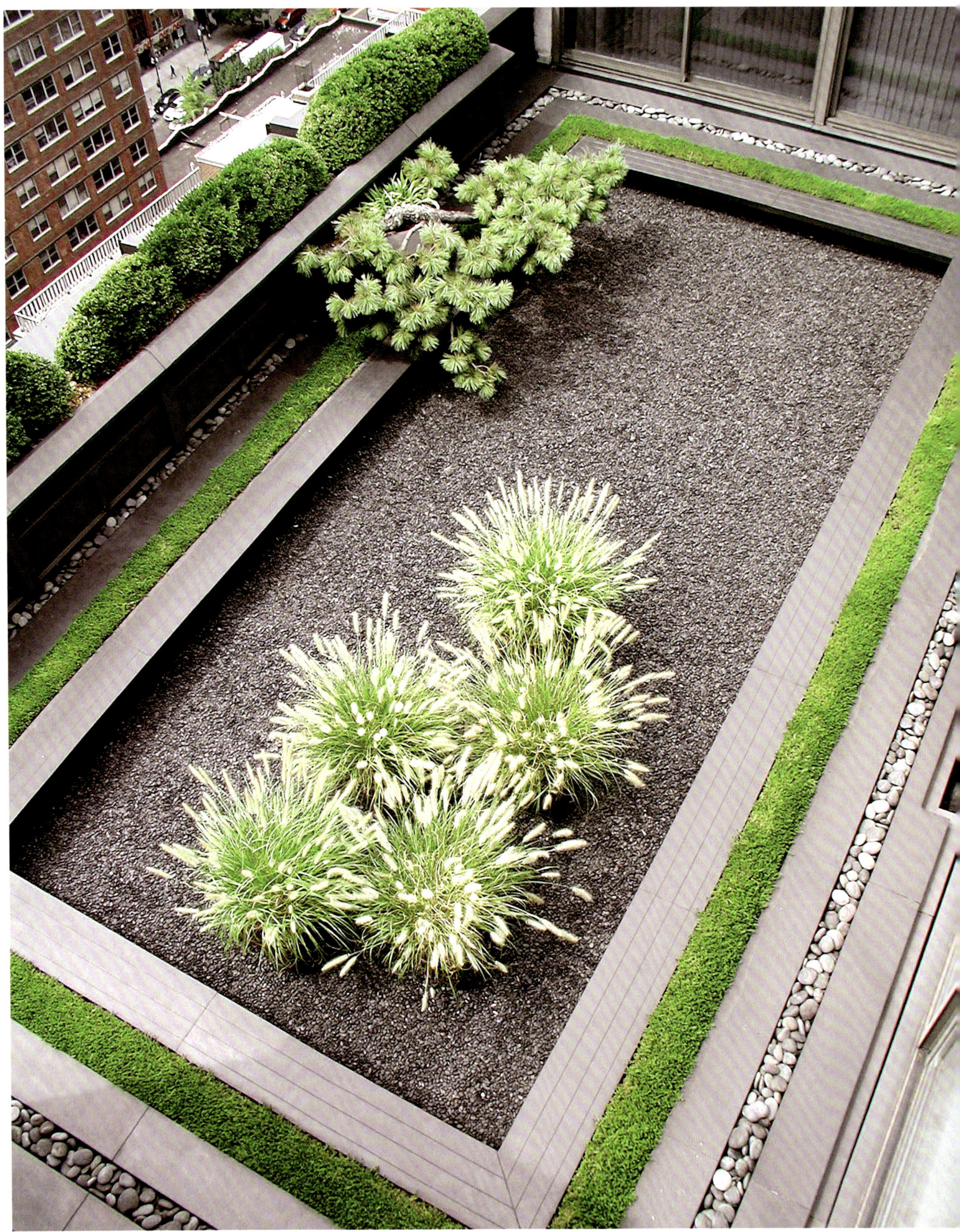

GEOMETRIC

I met with an advertising agency in 1985 that wanted a garden outside of their executive office windows in a 512-square-foot, partially walled space. Manhattan rooftop weight requirements can be stringent, so when I asked what weight was allowed, I was told *no weight*, especially in the center of the space. There was the challenge.

Inspired by the Zen garden Ryōan-ji in Kyoto, Japan, my concept for the space was to fill the bulk of the area with small black Japanese pebbles only two pebbles deep. Around the perimeter—minimal weight was permissible close to the structural walls—I designed a continuous platform of lightweight painted galvanized sheet metal with two four-inch deep channels for sedum *Sedum sexangulare* and river stones. Planter boxes with clipped boxwood were cantilevered off the parapet to keep weight off the roof. I also covered the front of the boxes with a metal skirt to match the platform. A group of 12-inch-deep boxes of fountain grass *Pennisetum alopecuroides* were placed in the field of small black stones for movement in the wind at one end of the still rectilinear viewing garden. A few years later, I was asked to design a conference garden where meetings and lunches could take place in a space adjacent to the viewing garden. However, I was allowed to occupy only 800 square feet of the large roof.

Realizing that I would need a fence and that bolting posts for a fence to the membrane of the roof wasn't possible, I designed a continuous deck with an attached Japanese style fence to sit on the roof and distribute the weight of planter boxes filled with clipped boxwood *Buxus 'Green Mountain.'* To complement the tightly clipped boxwood, bold-foliage perennials like *Hosta plantaginea* and *Iris ensata* created a peaceful, enclosed island on a New York City rooftop.

OPPOSITE Fountain grass *Pennisetum alopecuroides* sits in a field of small Japanese stones that provide softness and movement in this rectilinear garden, along with a pine *Pinus sylvestris 'Hillside Creeper'* and a boxwood hedge. The perimeter platform is at the height of the windowsill, with channels of stonecrop *Sedum sexangulare* and river stone.

OVERLEAF LEFT A corner of the low platform shows small Japanese river stones, channels of stonecrop, and Mexican beach stones.

OVERLEAF RIGHT This section of the conference garden has been planted with iris *Iris ensata*, Russian *arborvitae Microbiota decussata*, sheared boxwood, bamboo *Fargesia nitida*, and large-leaved plantain lily *Hosta plantaginea* for textural contrast.

PAGE 66 A Japanese-style gate was installed at the entrance to the conference garden. The large leaves of *Hosta 'Royal Standard'* contrast with the finer textures of boxwood, moss, pine, and weeping hemlock *Tsuga canadensis 'Pendula.'*

PAGE 67 A pot of fine-leaved Mexican feather grass *Nassella tenuissima* is next to hosta and black cohosh *Cimicifuga racemosa*. A pine *Pinus thunbergii 'Thunderhead'* and large boxwoods were planted in front of the fence in the rear.

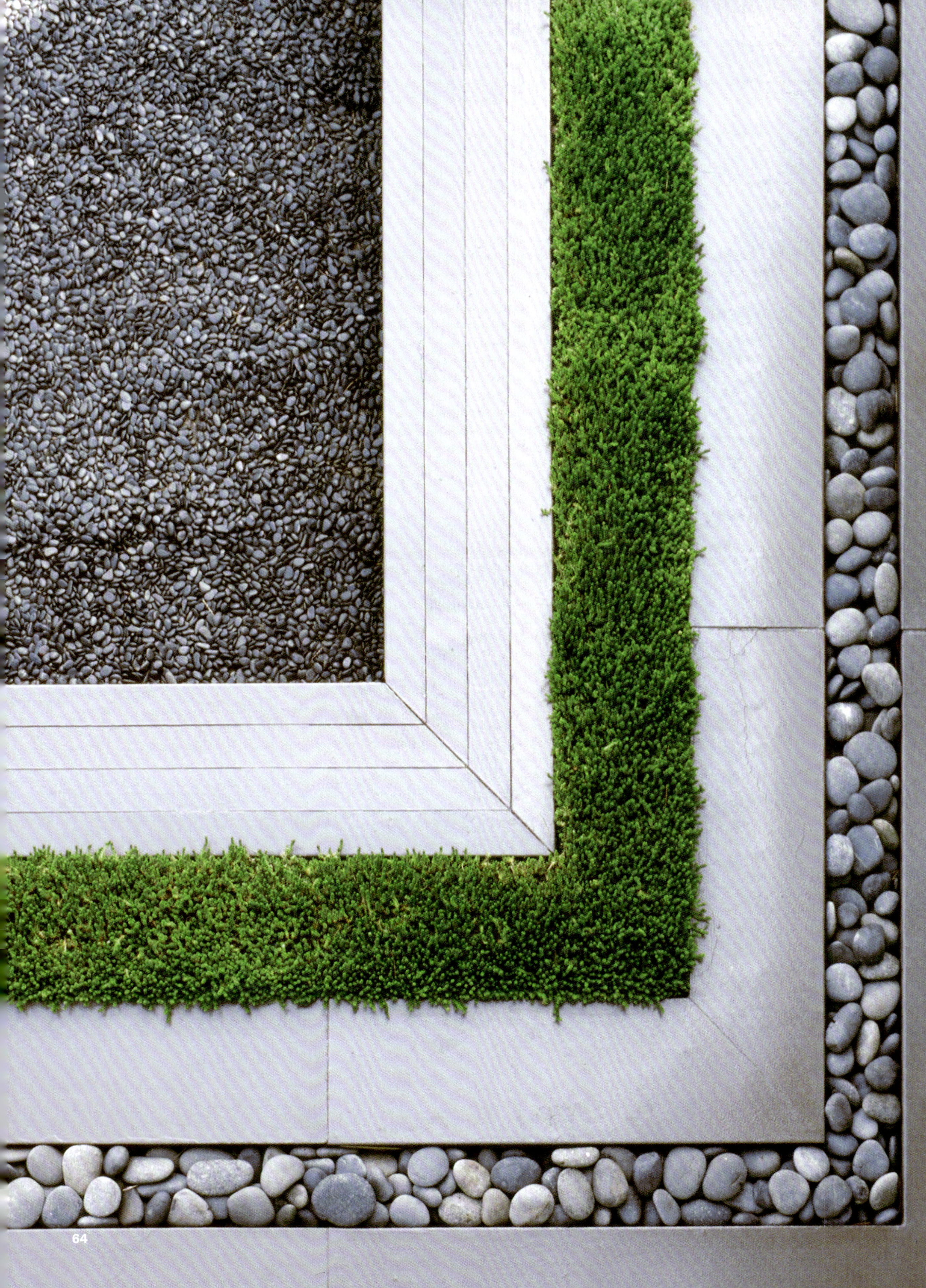

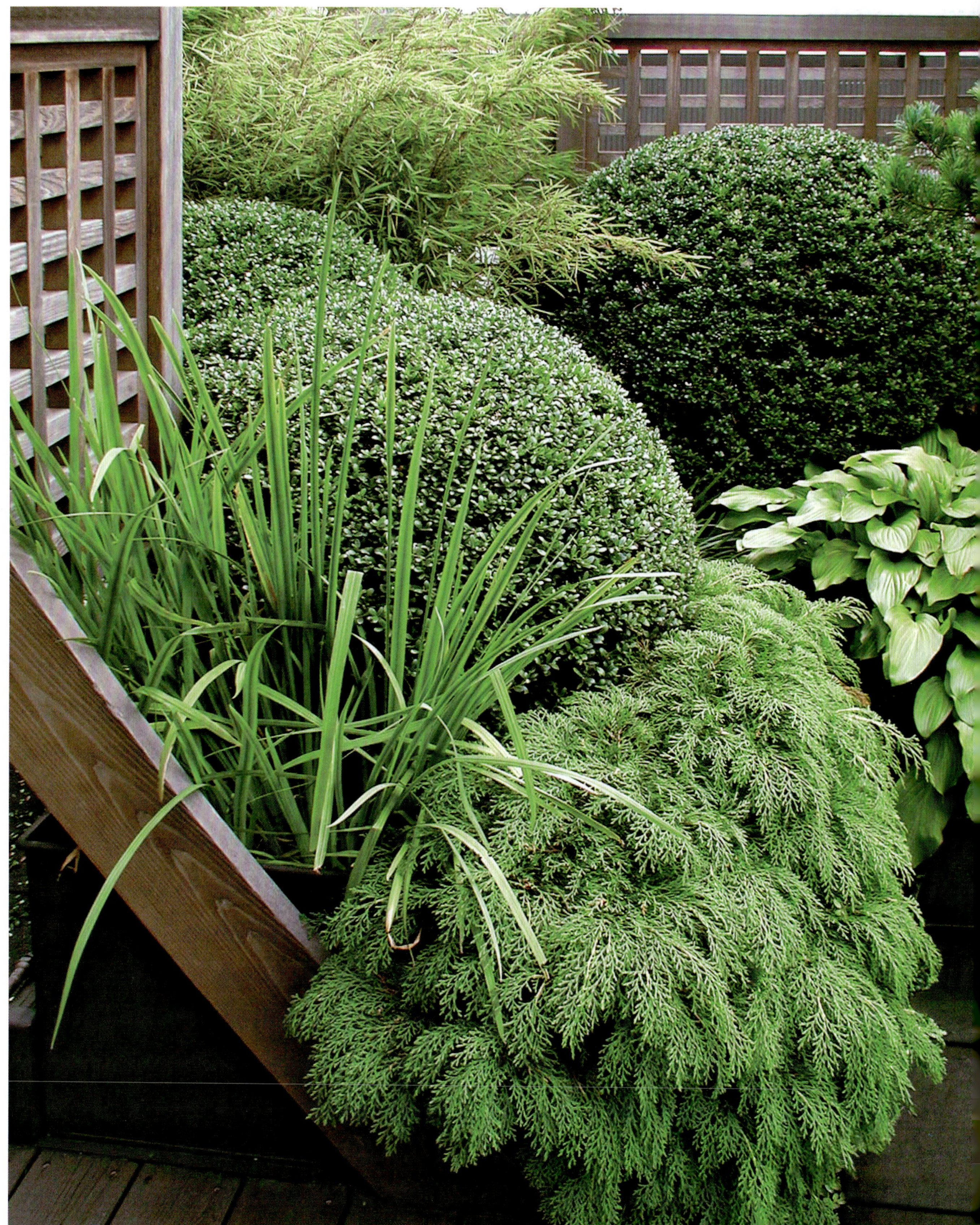

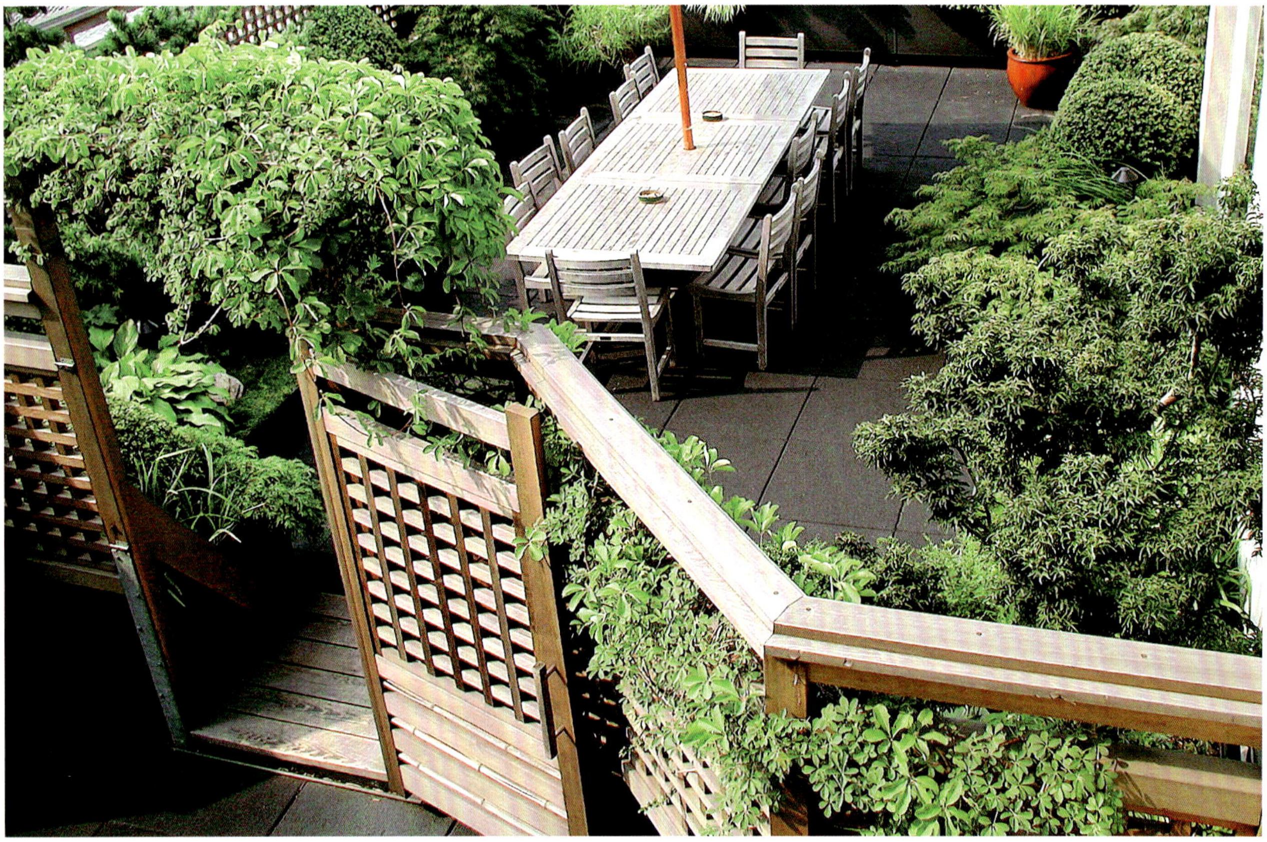

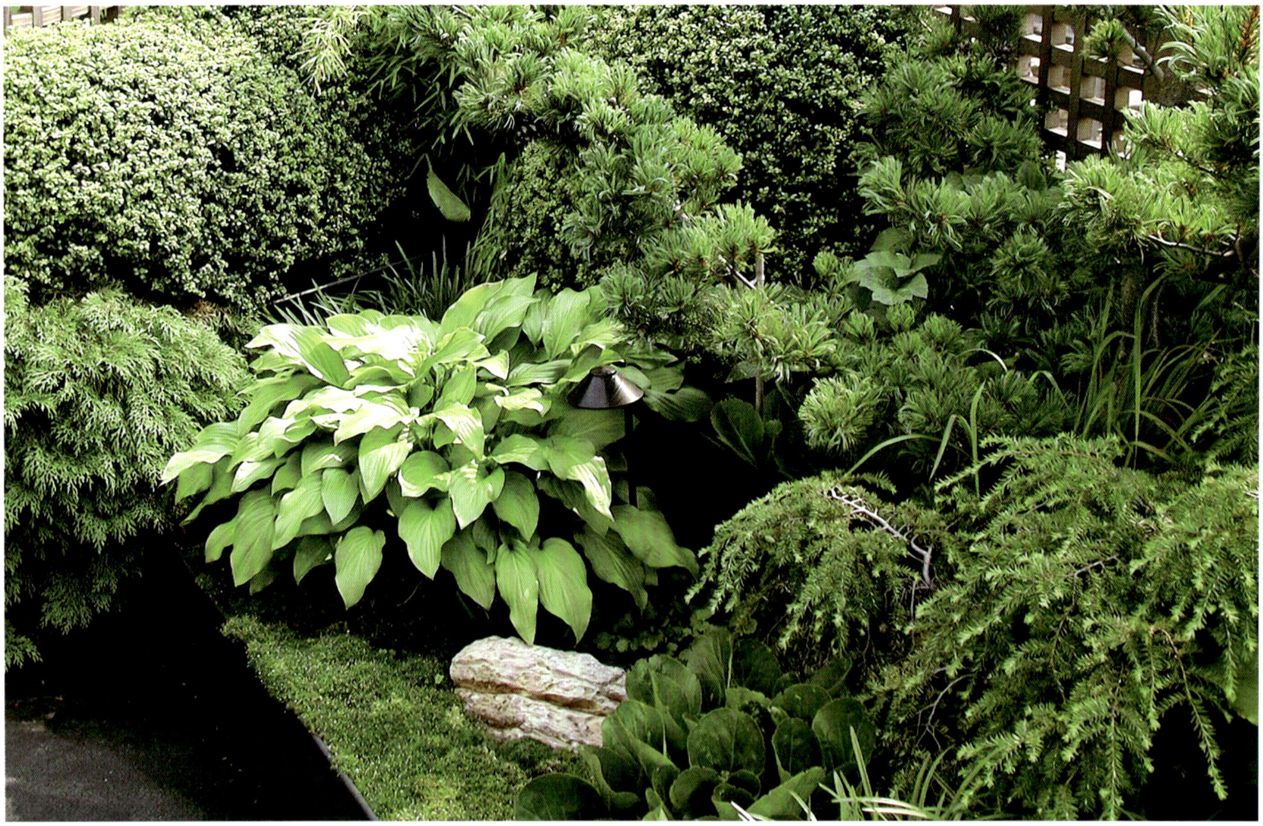

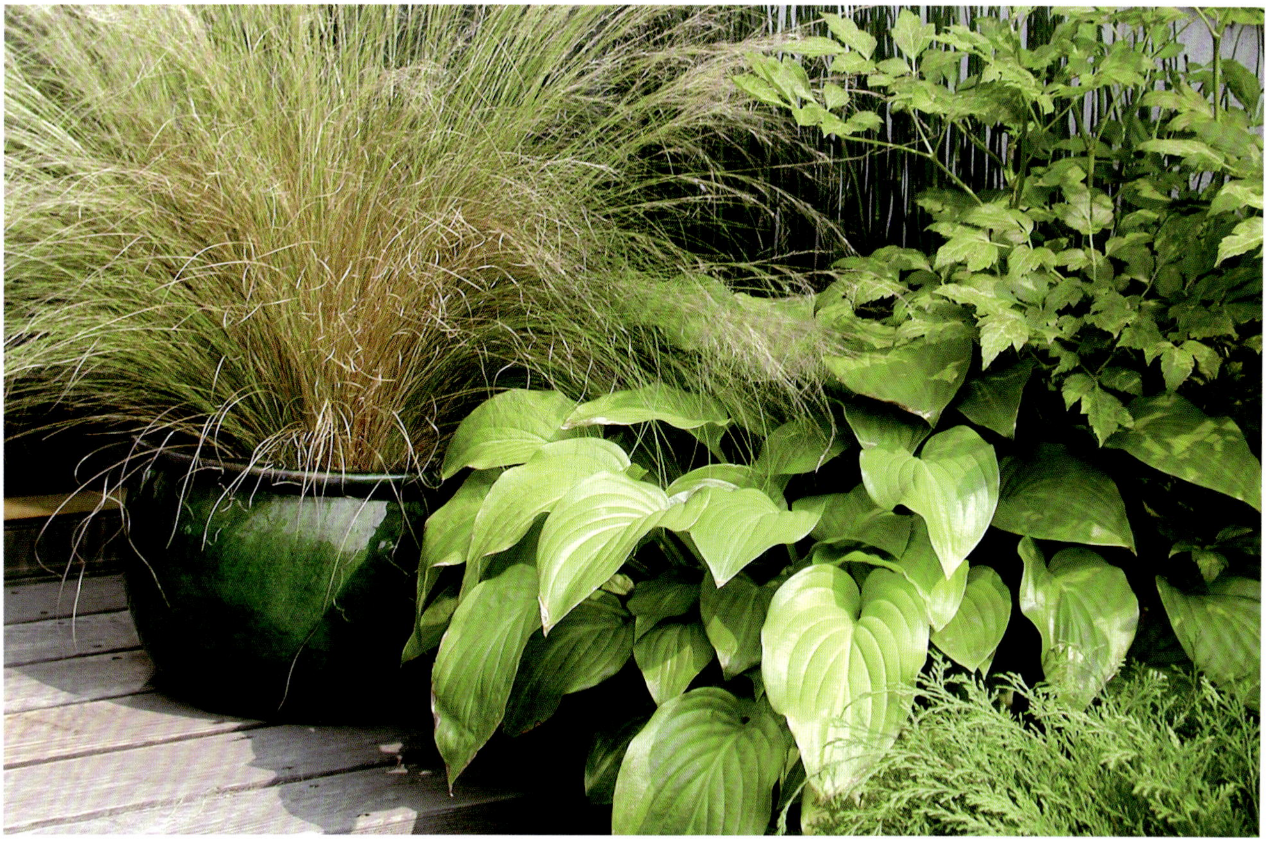

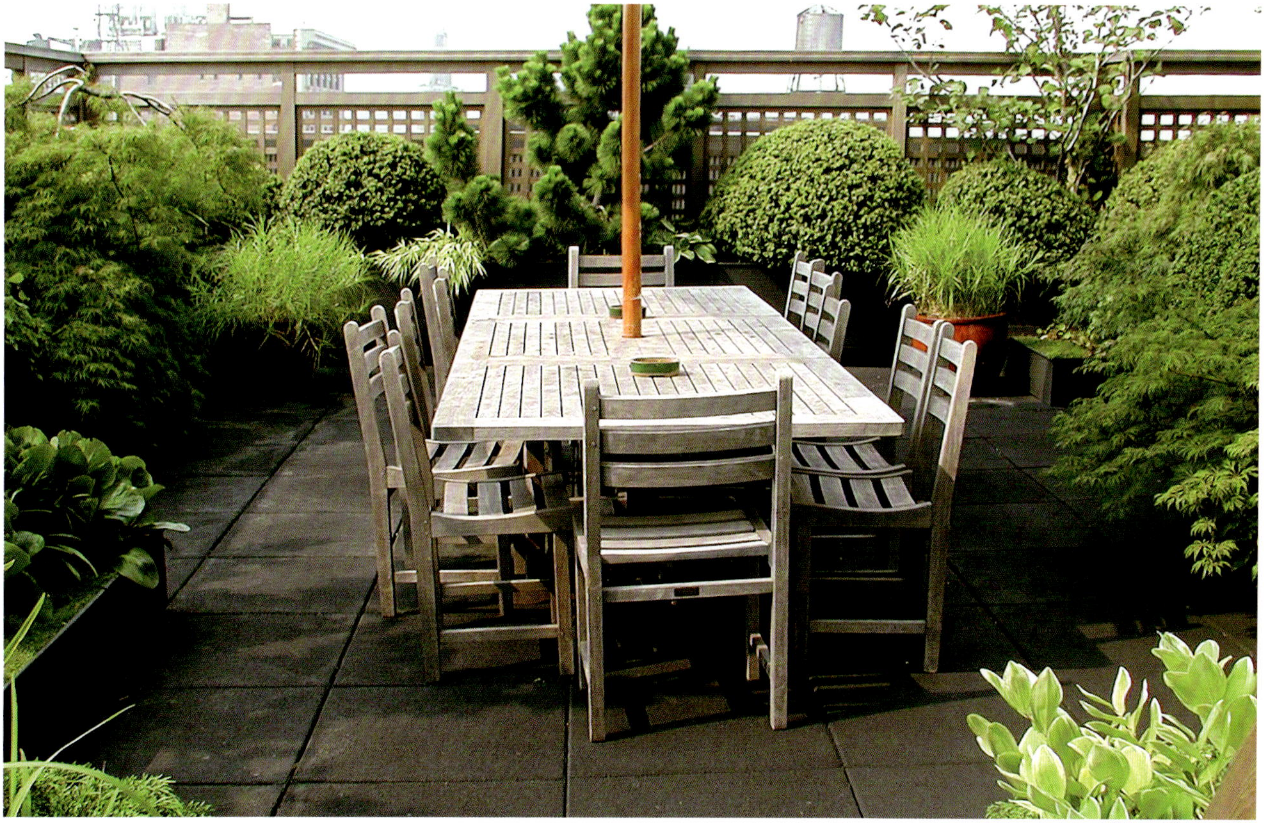

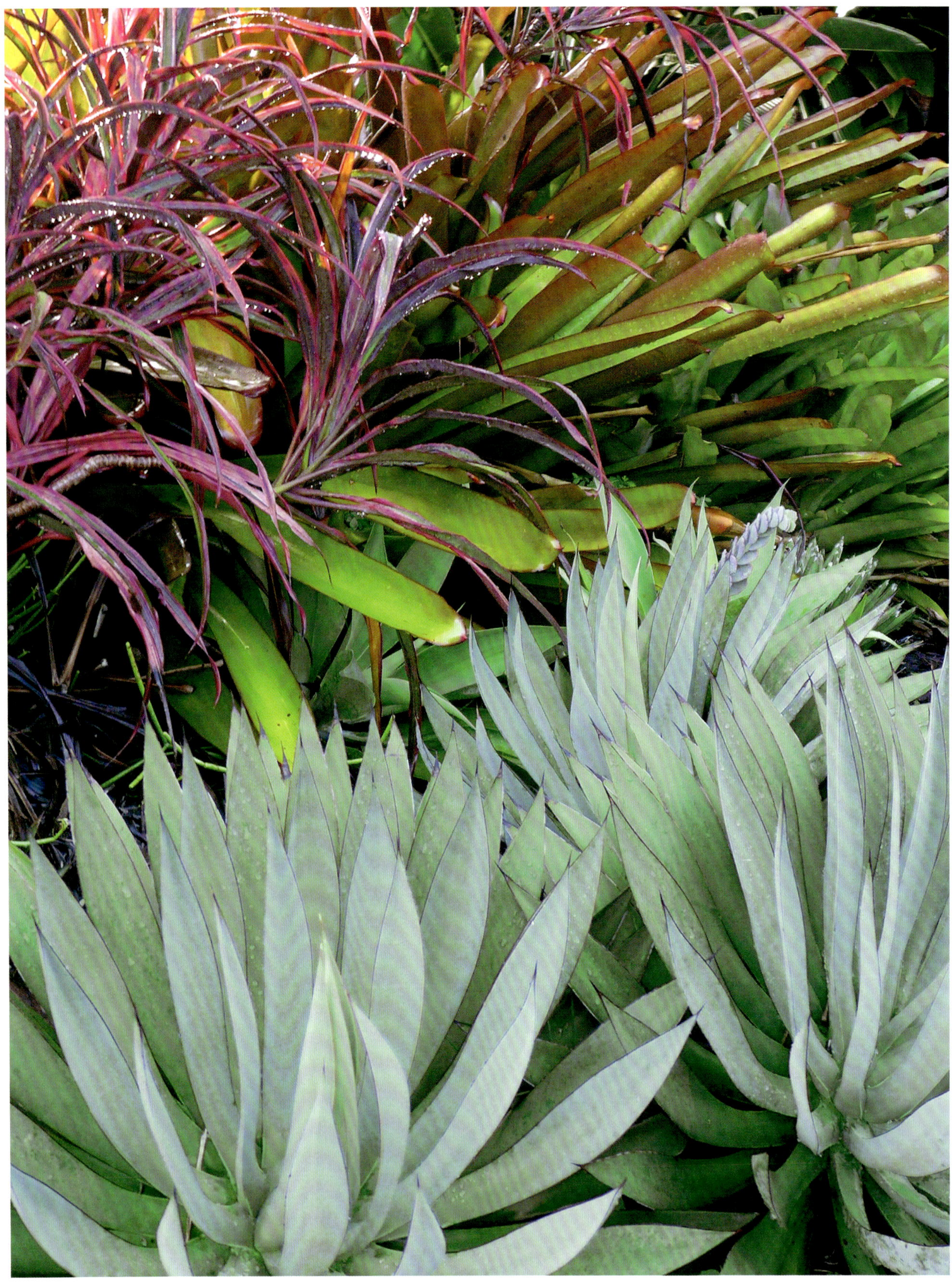

EXOTIC

OPPOSITE In the succulent garden, *Agave attenuata 'Red Margin'* was planted with bromeliad *Aechmea blanchetiana* and Red *Dracaena* creating a vivid color combination.

OVERLEAF One enters the property at the lower garden. The house on the upper level is painted orange, which determined the red, orange, and yellow palette of the gardens.

In 2008, after 35 years of designing gardens without a garden of my own, my husband and I bought a small three-quarter–acre property on the island of Vieques, off the coast of Puerto Rico. The chief selling point for me was that the property did not have a single plant on it.

In thinking about the landscape, there were numerous issues I had to consider. I would not be living on the island full time, so low-maintenance plants were essential. Tropical plants are beautiful and exotic but, like with most plants, you have to know their growing requirements. Vieques is subtropical, with warm and humid summers and dry winters, so I had to choose accordingly. I wasn't interested in flowers, but wanted to concentrate on leaf color and form. Also, I didn't develop a master plan but wanted to test which plants would survive in my absence for months at a time. I faced a large learning curve so my landscape developed slowly by trial and error.

Plants like agaves and bromeliads were reasonably dependable in this climate. Palms were a definite choice. Other interesting shrubs and trees were a gamble, one I often lost. Decisions on plants were complicated by the fact that plant availability on the island was very limited. It was a challenge, but I persevered.

Everyone's idea of paradise is different. For most people, it is being in a trouble-free or blissful situation of one kind or another. Every gardener knows that gardening is hardly described as trouble-free. And yet, in spite of all the hard work involved in developing a garden or landscape, at the end of the day there is a peaceful satisfaction looking at what you have created that, for me, qualifies as paradise.

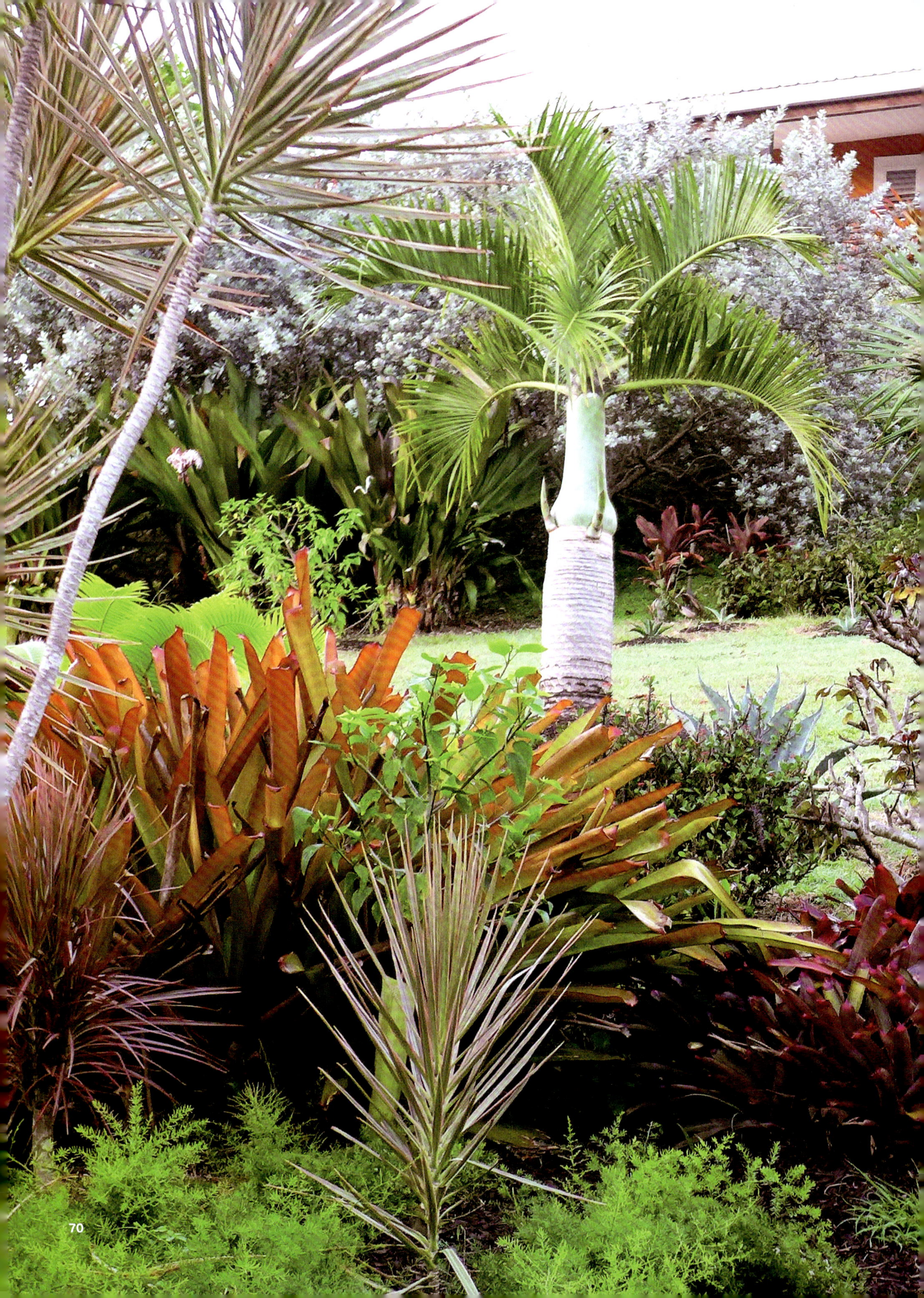

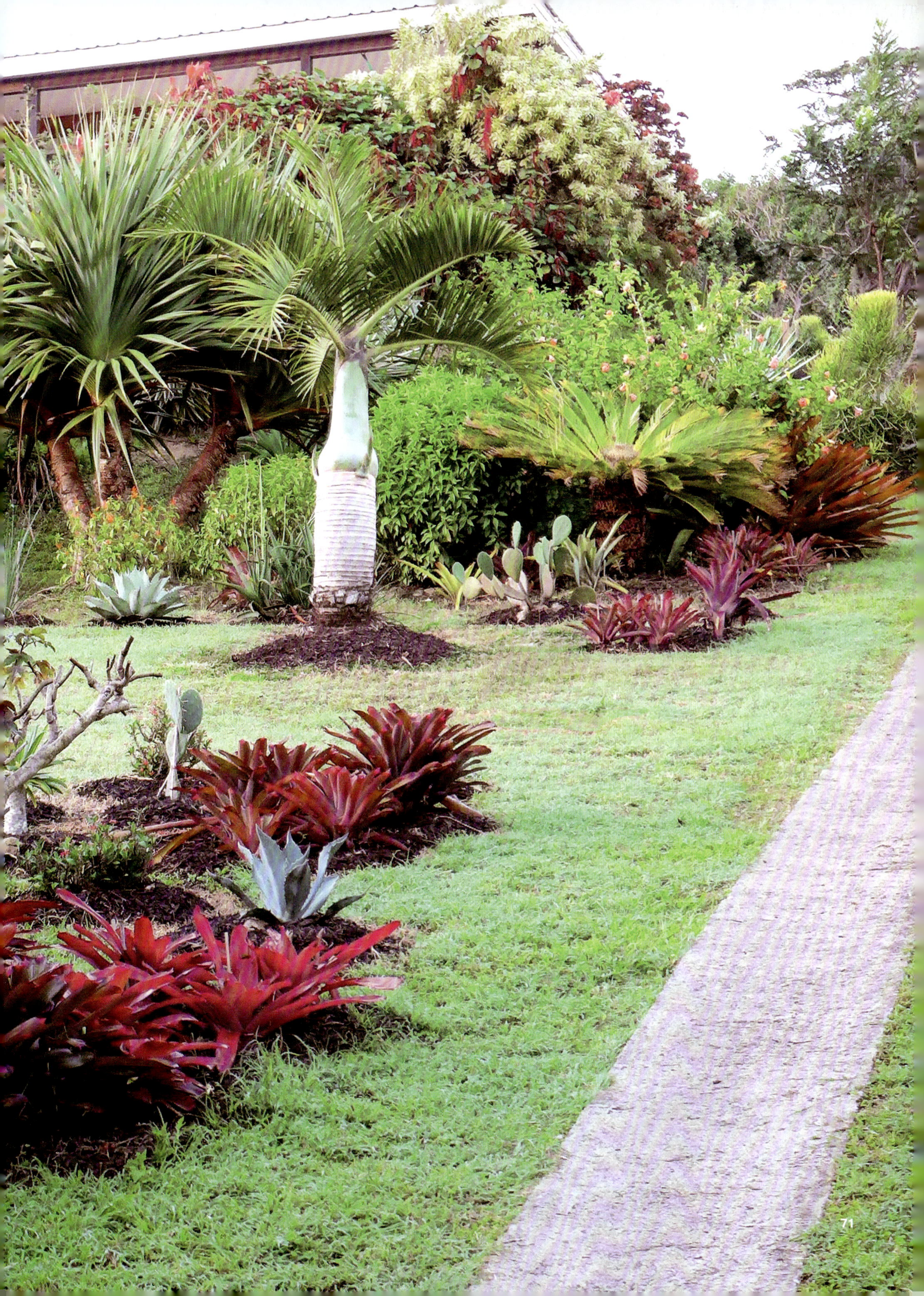

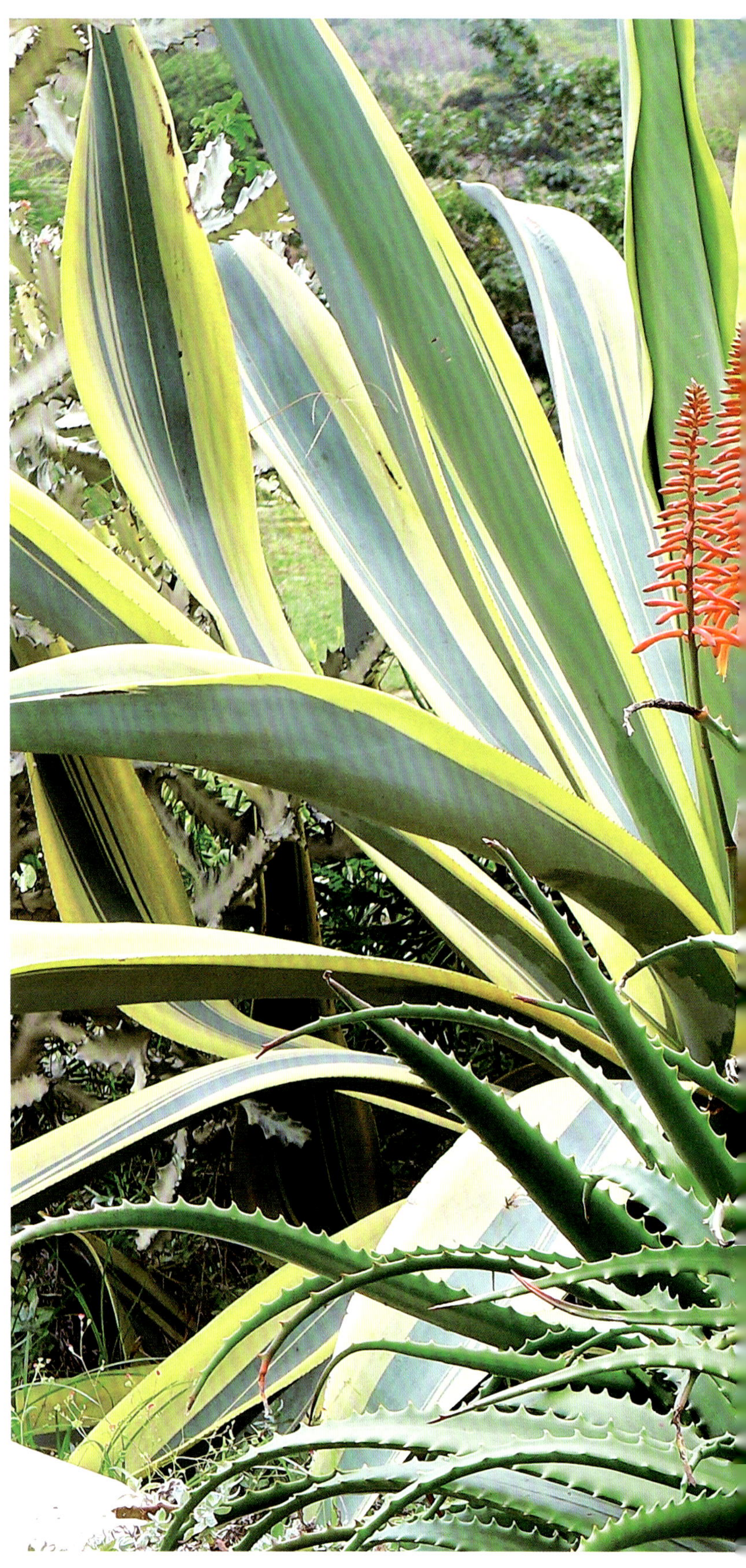

RIGHT Krantz aloe *Aloe arborescens* blooms with Agave *weberii 'Arizona Star'* as its background.

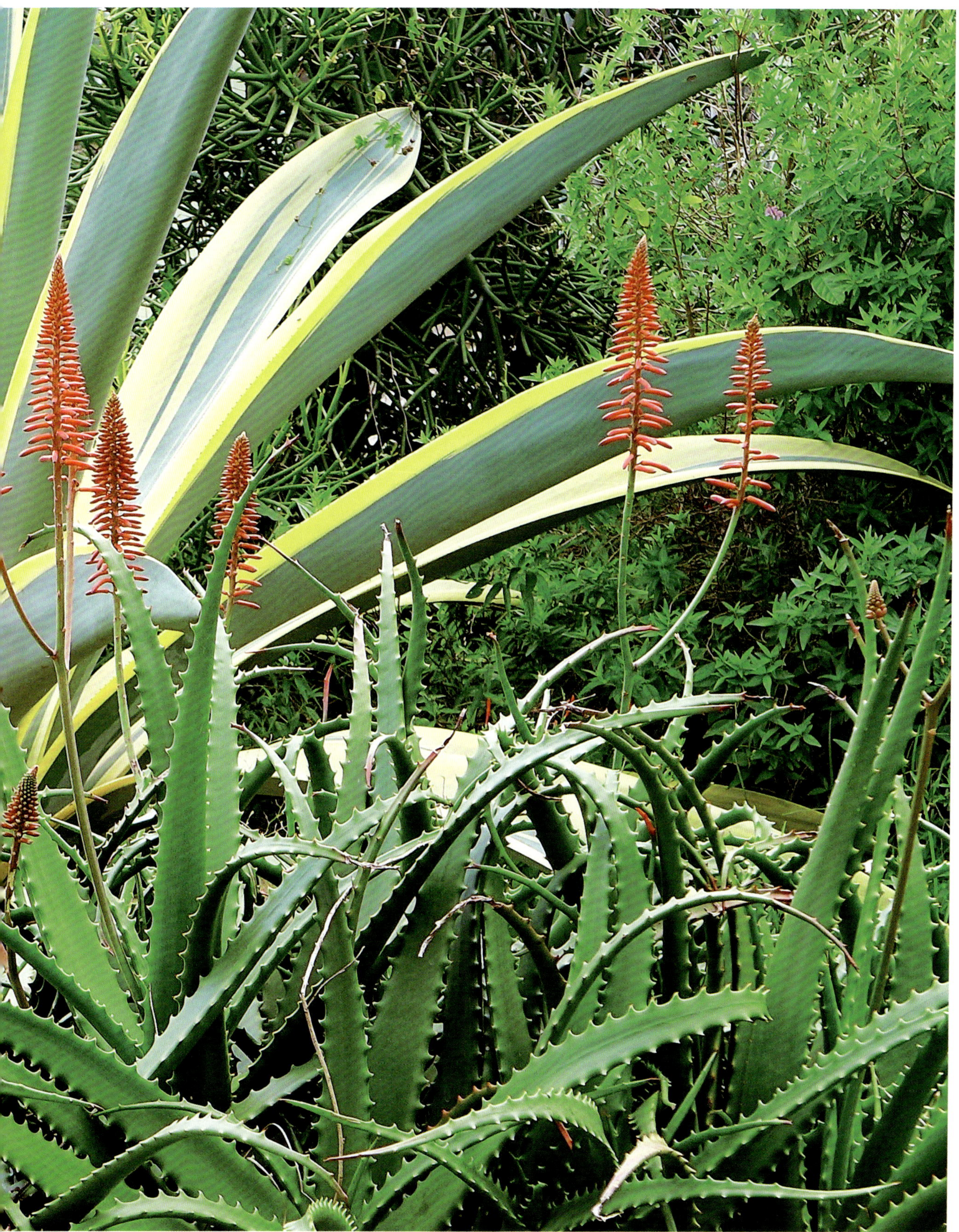

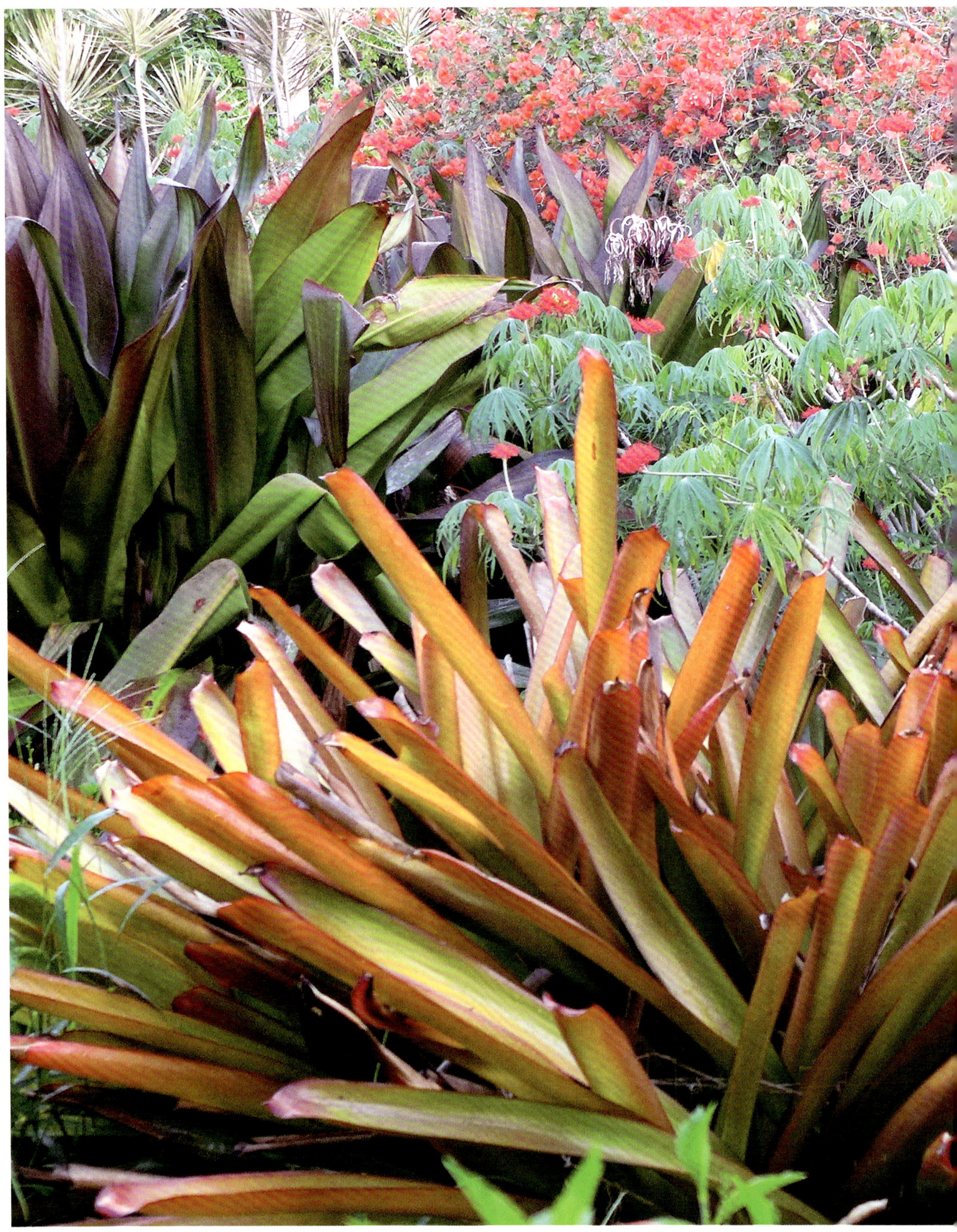

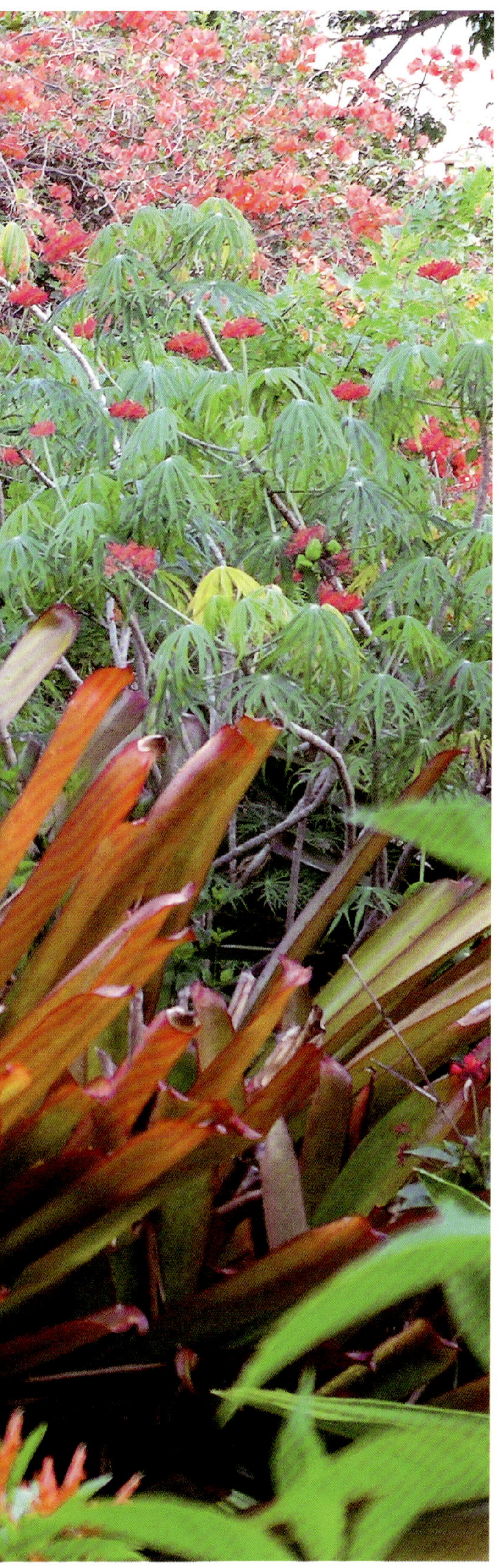

LEFT In the lower garden, orange and red plant combinations set the theme—as with bromeliad *Aechmea blanchetiana* planted with coralbush *Jatropha multifida*, crinum lily *Crinum augustum 'Queen Emma,'* and an orange bougainvillea.

OVERLEAF The upper garden continues the orange and red plant motif. The view from the upper garden shows a Ti plant *Cordyline terminalis 'Peter Buck,'* bromeliad *Aechmea blanchetiana* in bloom in the foreground, and the top of a silver buttonwood tree *Conocarpus erectus var. sericeus* in the lower garden. The silver color complements the intense red and orange hues of the nearby plants.

PAGES 78–79 In the succulent garden, *Agave attenuata 'Kara's Stripes'* was planted with lavender scallops *Kalanchoe fedtschenkoi*, bromeliad *Aechmea mulfordii 'Malva,'* and *Agave victoriae-reginae*. The cool blue color of the scallops works well with the lime-green and pink cast of the agaves.

PAGES 80–81 Leaving the property, one passes through the lower garden with its orange bromeliad *Aechmea blanchetiana*, creating a rhythm in the planting scheme.

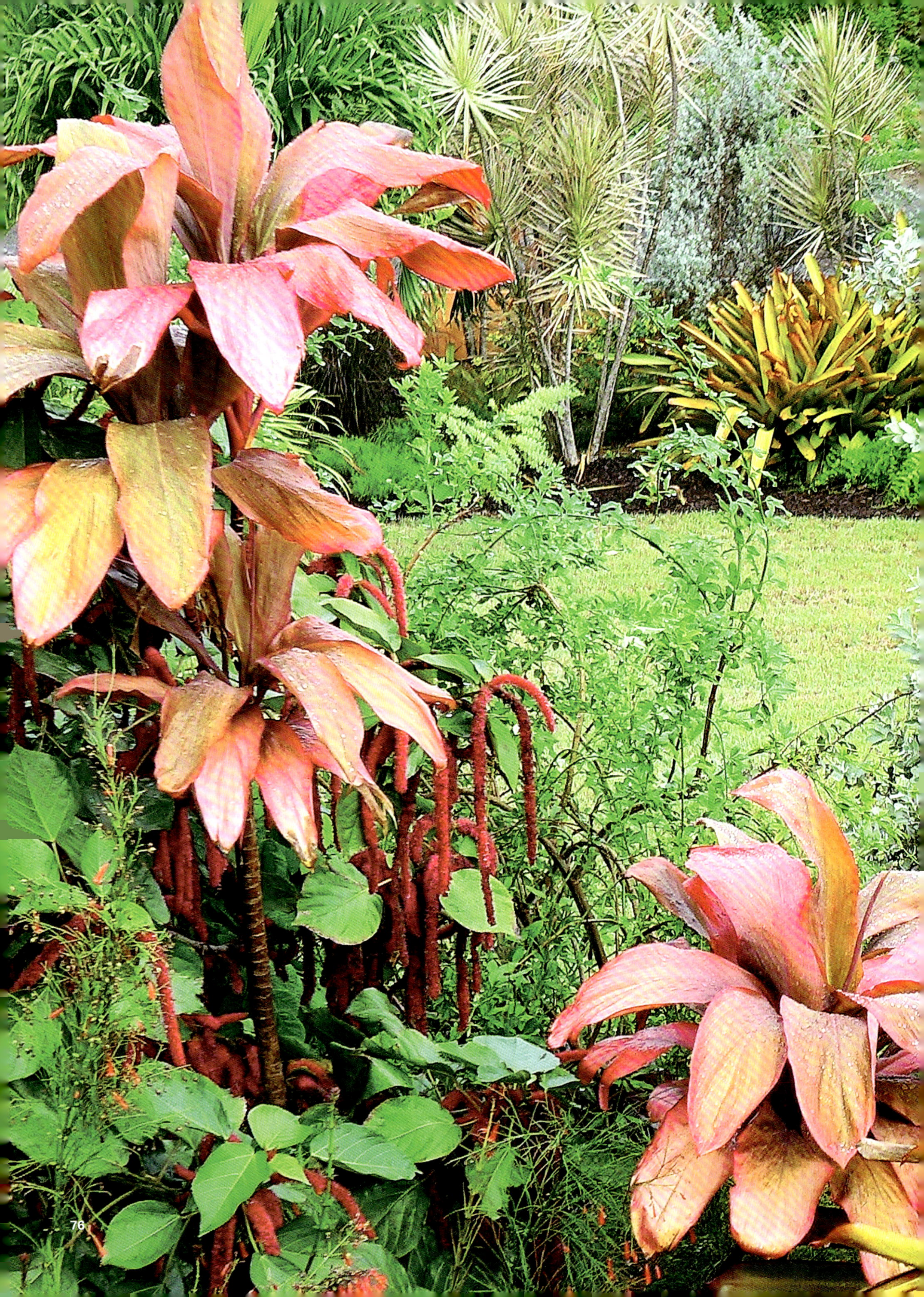

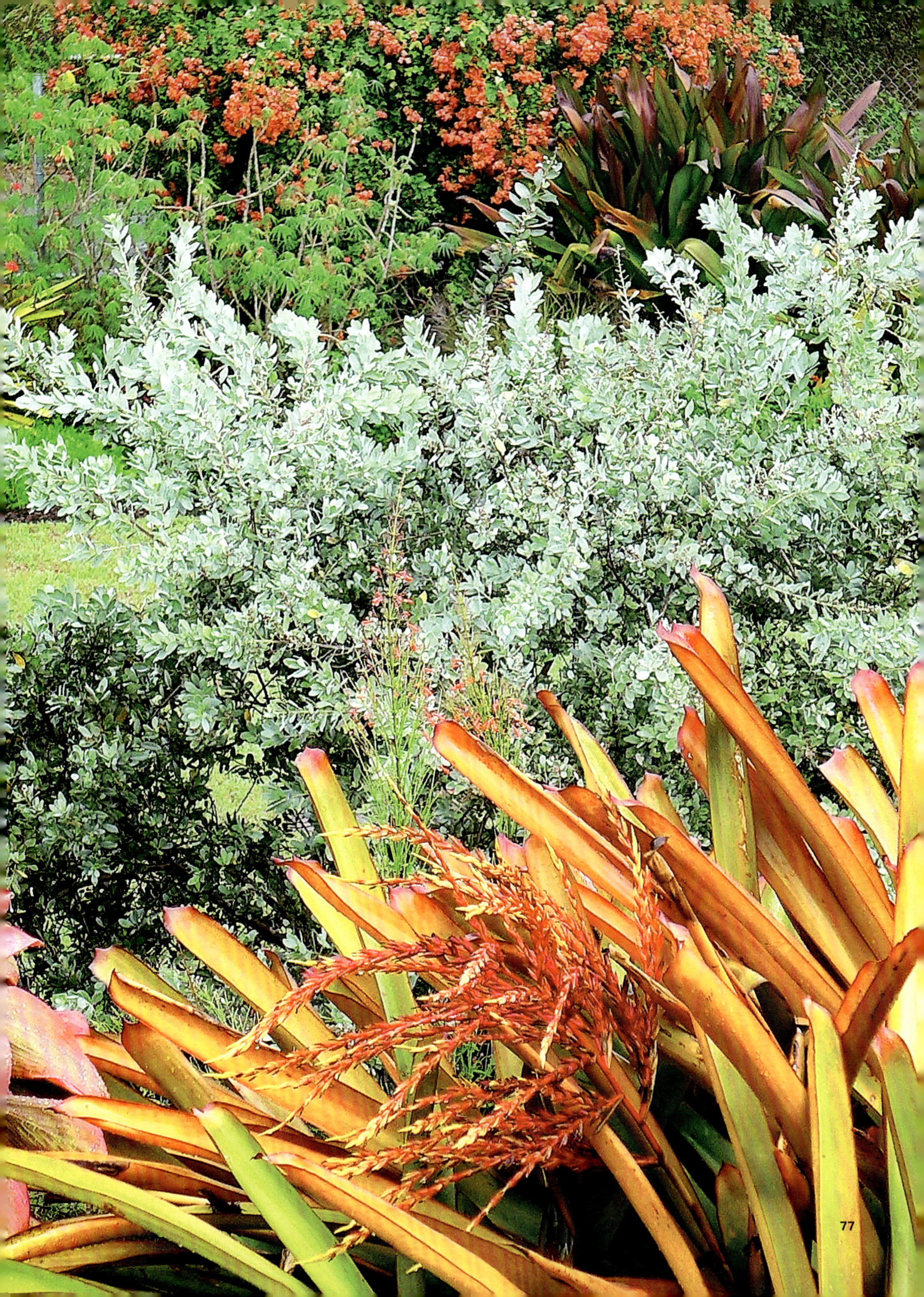

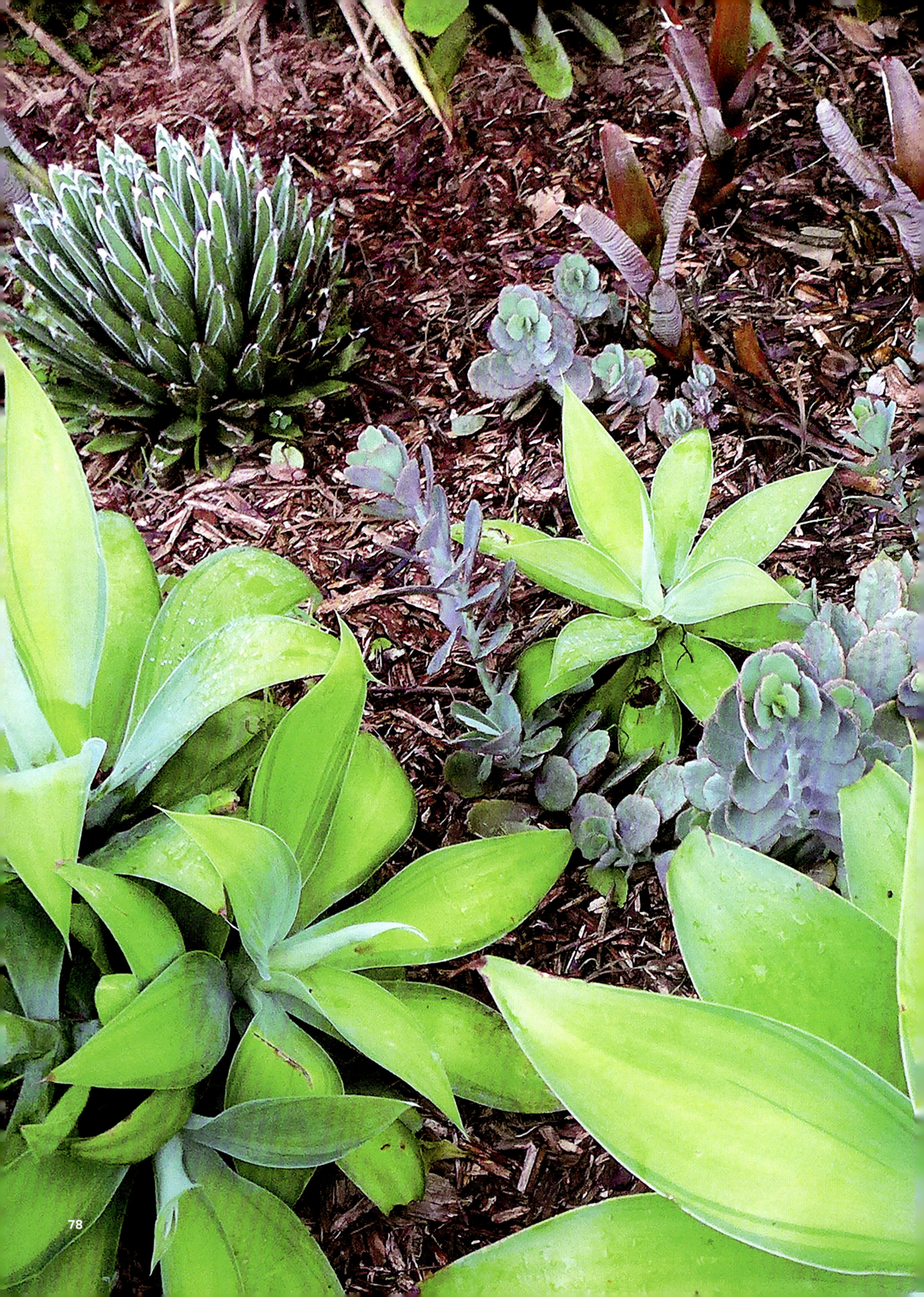

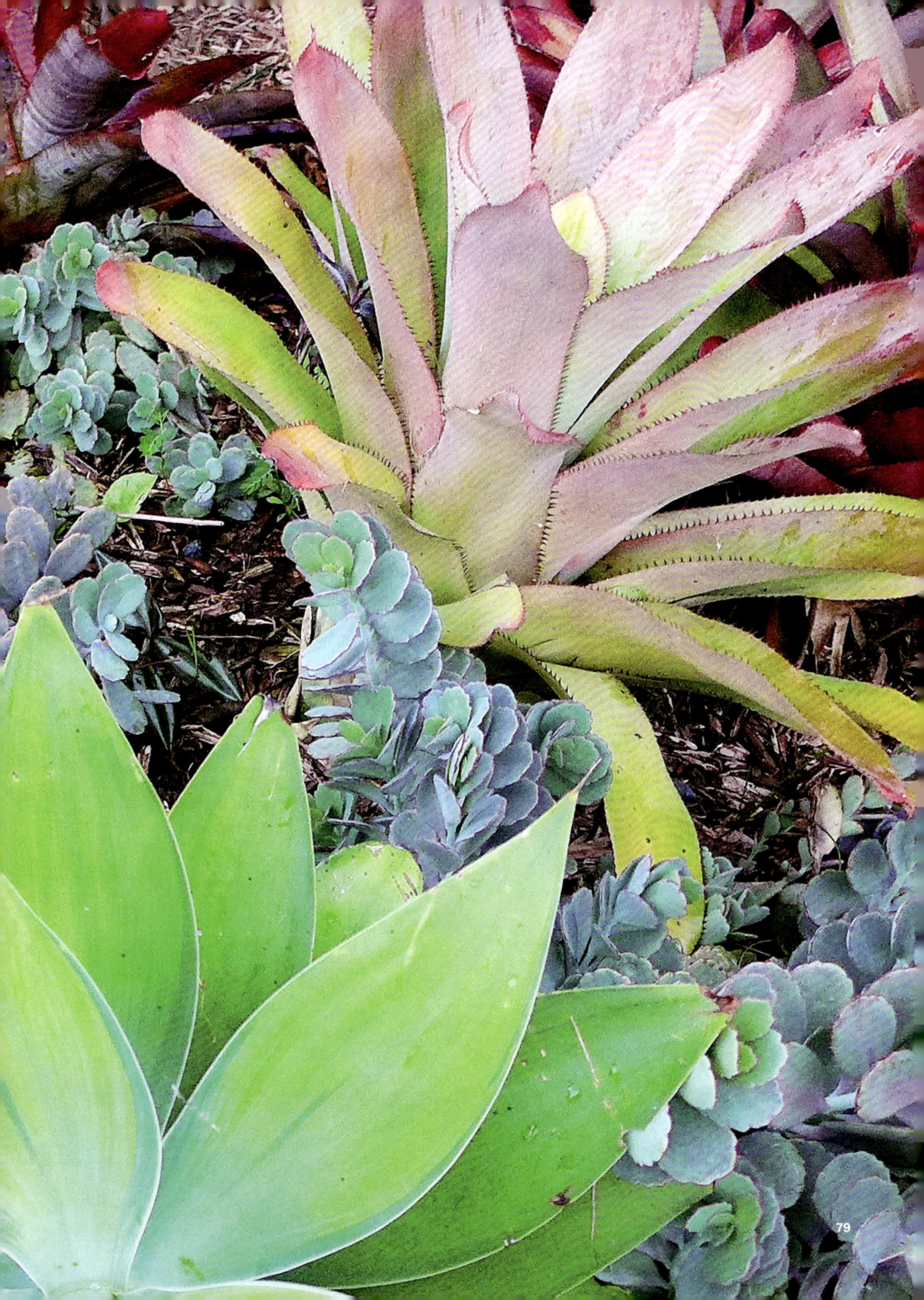

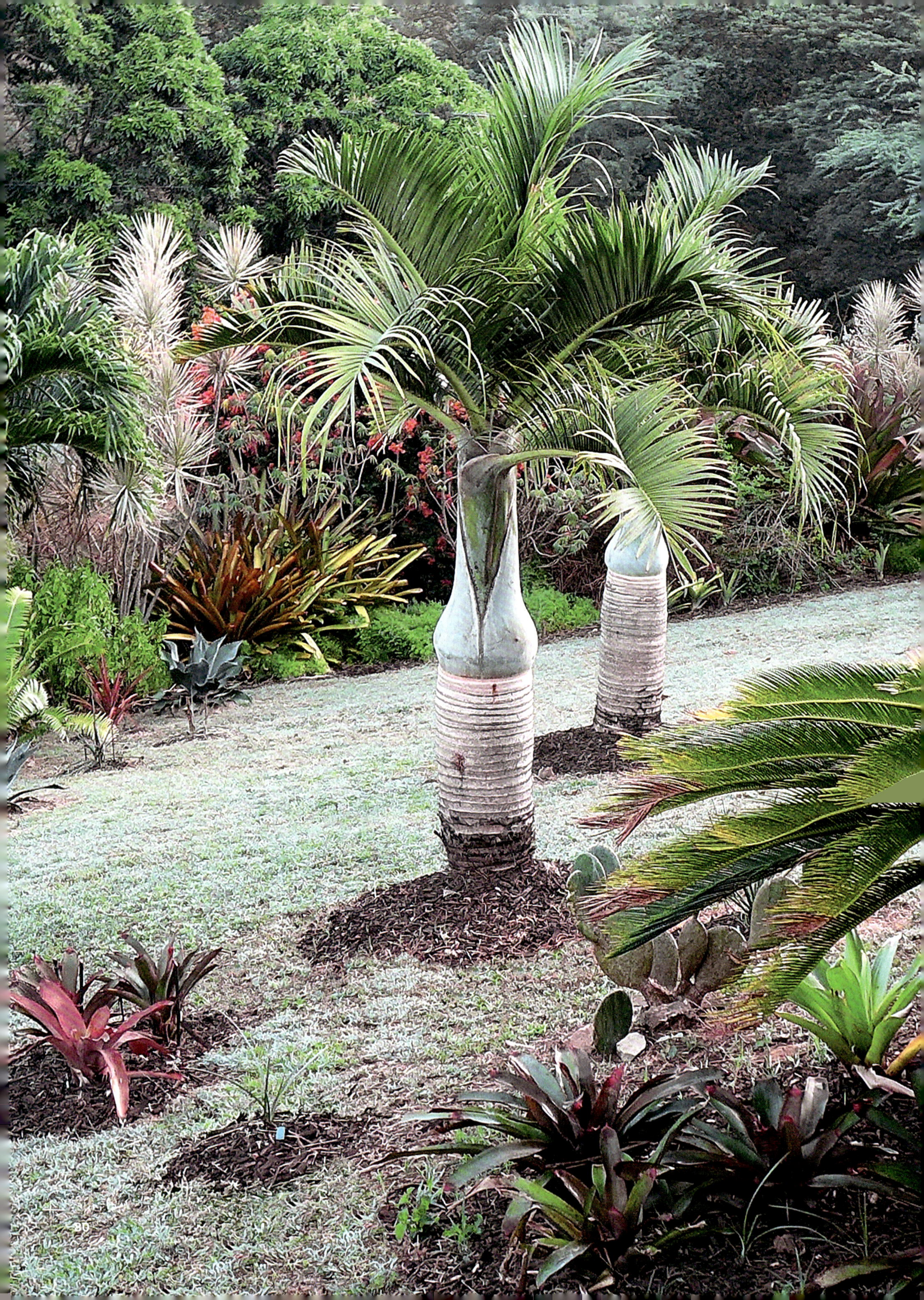

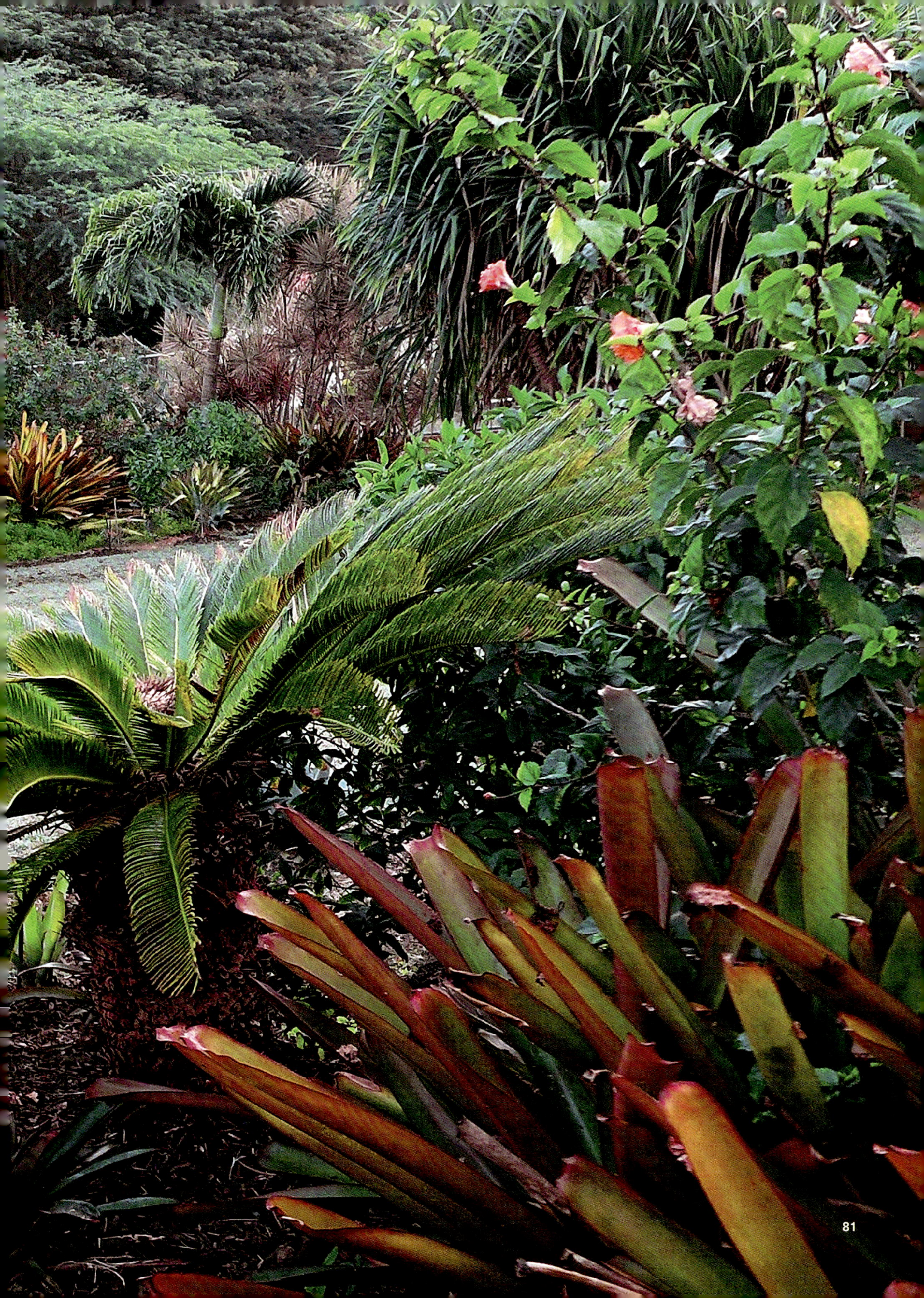

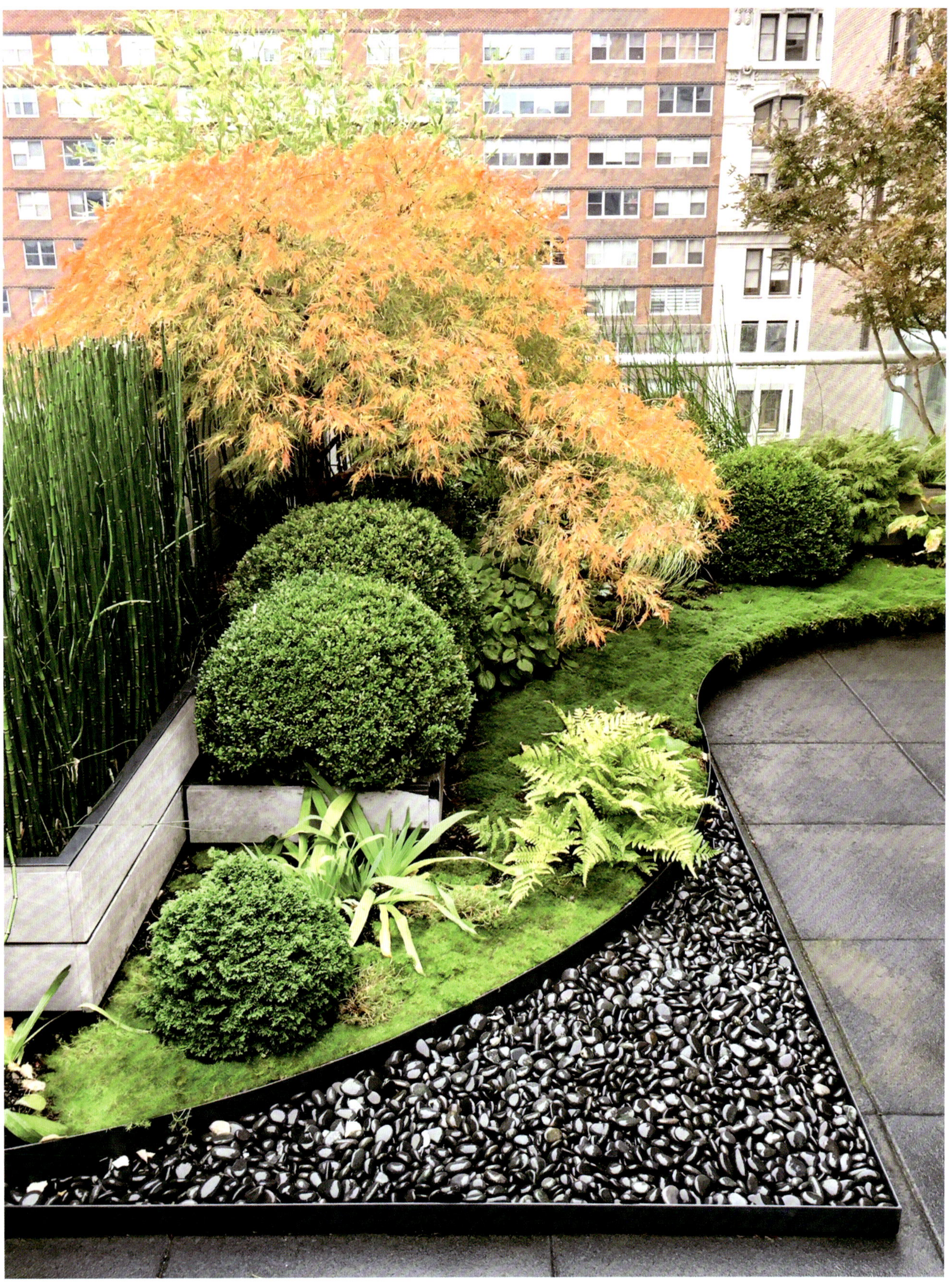

NATURALISTIC

OPPOSITE A detail of a section of the garden, taken in the fall, shows the Japanese maple *Acer palmatum dissectum 'Viridis'* in full color.

OVERLEAF The garden layout includes three separate sections with a deck and an arbor in the upper right-hand corner. The puzzle-like sections suggest an entire woodland.

In addition to planting the floor plane in this 1,000-square-foot New York City rooftop garden created in 2012, planter boxes were made in two or more heights so that when filled, they would create a sense of enclosure, with plants in layers. The three-level composition of boxes gives the illusion of slices of earth sitting on the roof in the form of a natural woodland.

The garden is divided into three separate sections, each fronted with a moss carpet *Minuartia verna* as the unifying element in the total composition. On entering the garden, to the left and the right, one walks through two groups of Japanese maples, *Acer palmatum 'Seiryu,'* surrounded by perennials and moss. The third section continues the woodland theme with the addition of bamboo *Phyllostachys bissetii*, scouring rush *Equisetum hymale*, and sheared boxwood *Buxus 'Green Mountain.'* The garden also has a kitchen and covered arbor for dining.

The clients for this project live in Scotland, with a beautiful garden. They are English and avid plant lovers. This garden, though Japanese in inspiration, is about the subtlety of shades of green and the beauty of plant textures, a subject that transcends cultural boundaries. With botanical Latin used universally as the language of plants, I've been able to travel, discovering new plants and seeing familiar plants in their native habitats. It's an endless education.

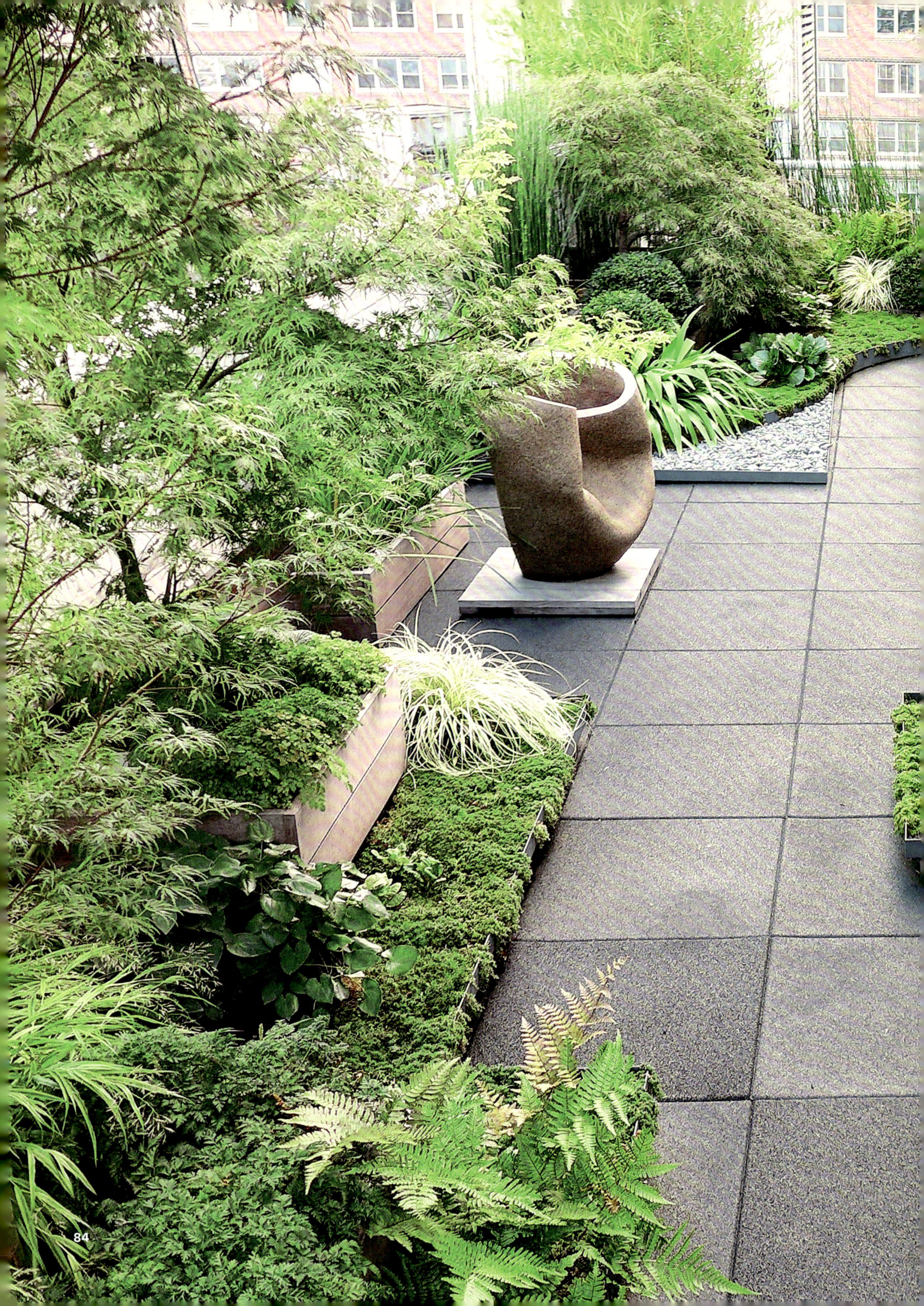

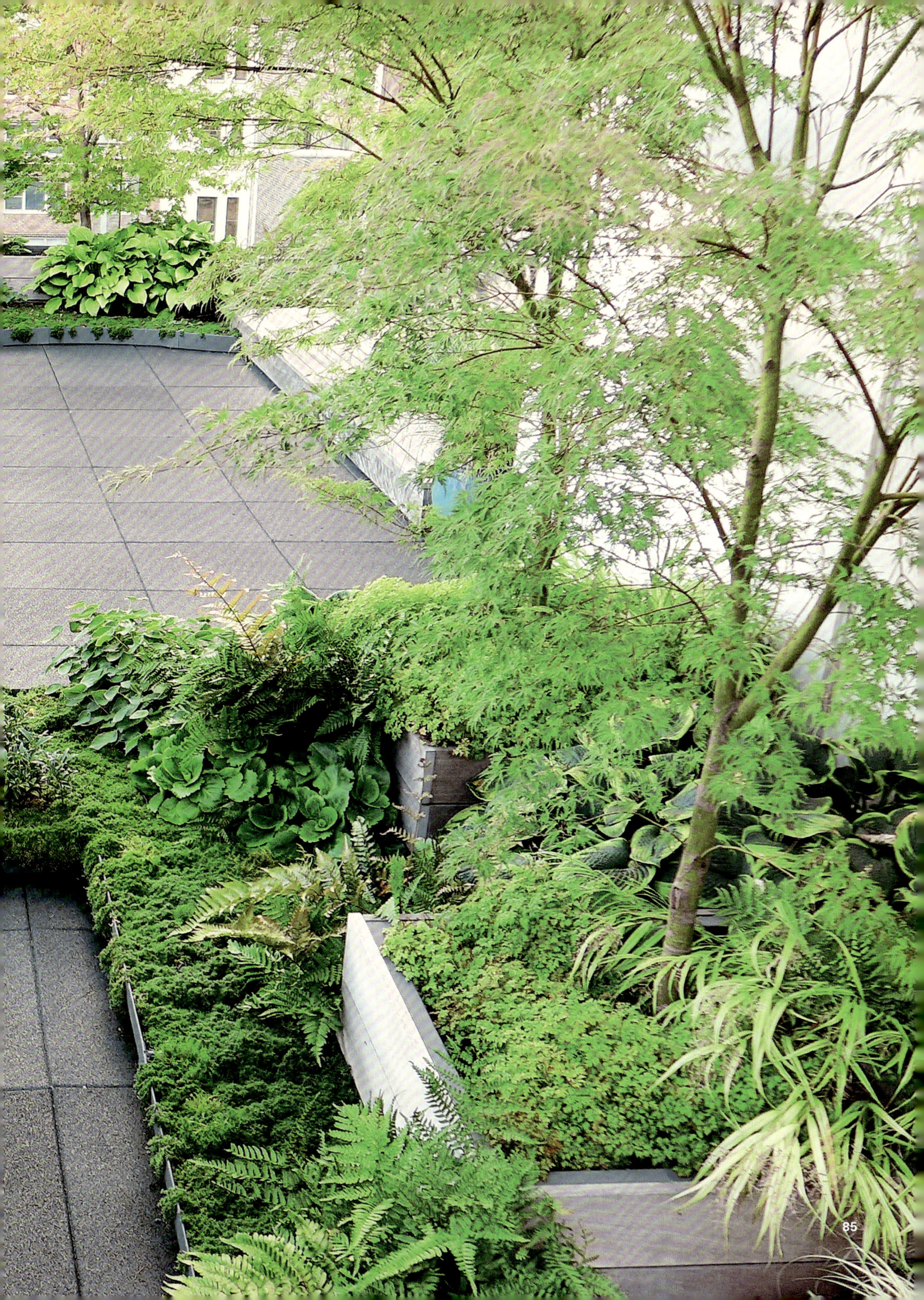

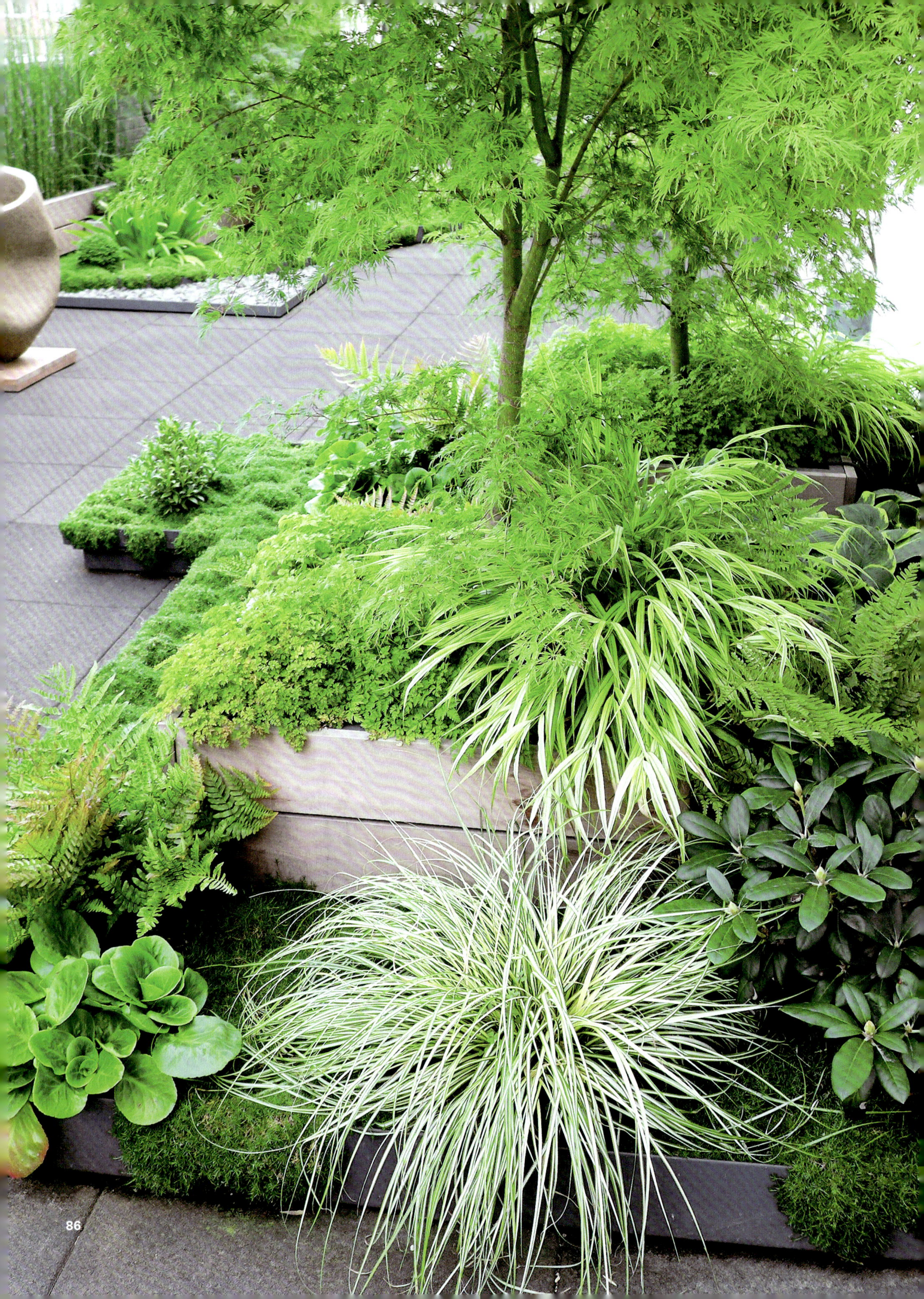

OPPOSITE A sedge *Carex oshimensis 'Evergold'* and *Rhododendron yakushimanum* act as complementing textural accents in an area of the garden under the maples.

RIGHT Maples *Acer palmatum var. dissectum 'Seiryu,'* are repeated on this side of the garden with moss and woodland perennials.

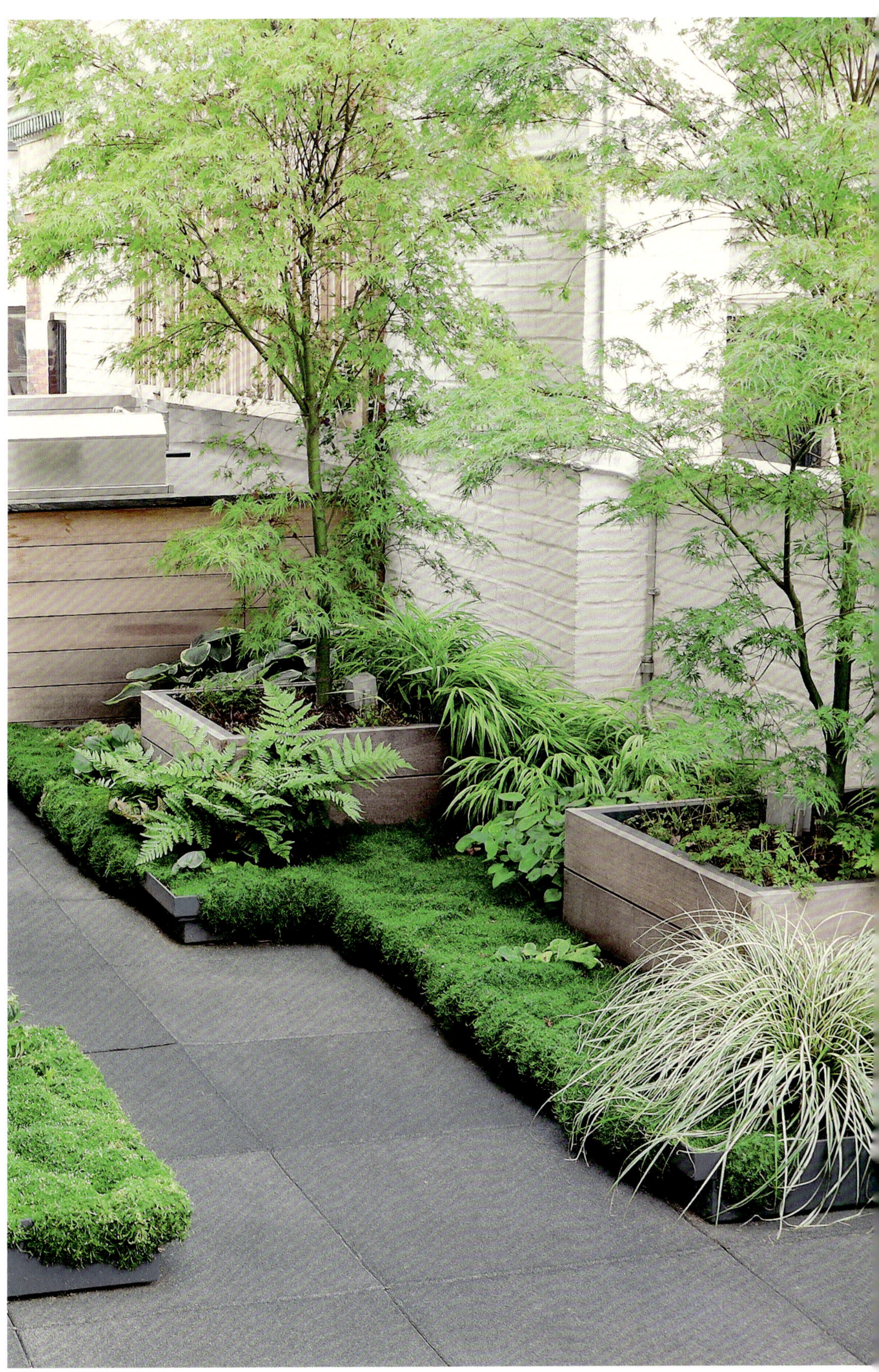

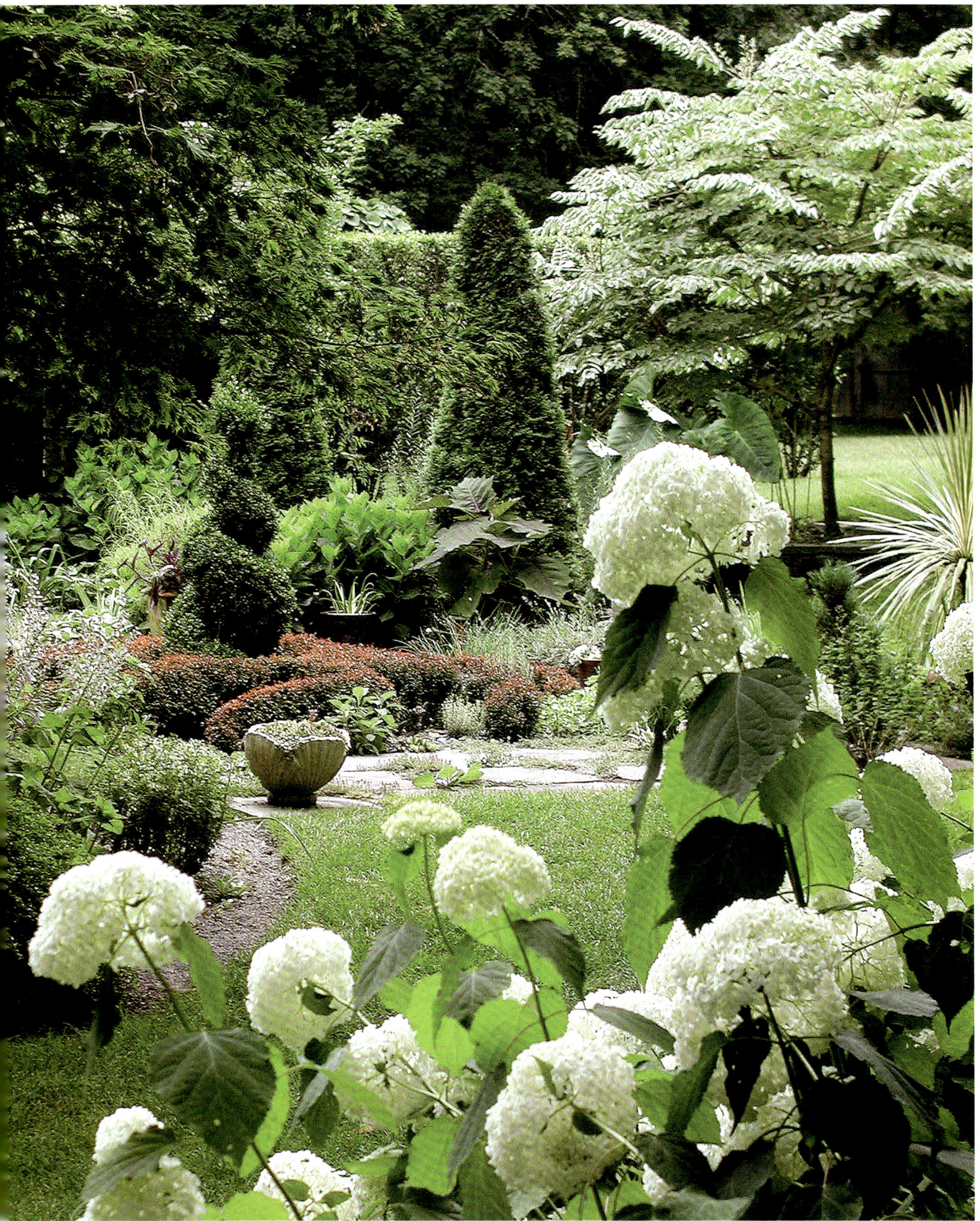

PAINTERLY

OPPOSITE The octopus herb garden, seen from the woodland, is surrounded by plants.

In 1987, when I started J. Mendoza Gardens, I received a call from the owner of this Sag Harbor, New York, property who needed help moving some hydrangeas. Thirty years and several gardens later, with my work done, I said farewell to the property.

In many ways, my career as a garden designer began with this garden. It was on this two-and-a-half–acre property that I tested new shrubs, trees, perennials, and annuals, experimented with plant combinations and color themes, explored plant layering and spatial relationships in the landscape, combined tropical and temperate plants, and created new gardens for this generous client. As the garden grew, so did I as a plantsman and designer.

Perennials are reliable, hard-working plants. They arrive in the spring, grow and amaze through the season, then die to the ground in the winter, returning the following spring. Oddly, the fact that they grow and die in a short period of time is part of their beauty for me. Every year, one anticipates the arrival of certain plants like old friends as they briefly mark each season.

I created six gardens on the property during this period. They included a main perennial garden, an herb garden in the shape of an octopus, a pool garden, a woodland garden, a dry garden, and a grass garden. Each area contained different plant combinations and color themes.

Many of the gardens I designed over the years no longer exist. Some lasted decades but, in the scheme of things, were fleeting like the plants they contained. I am fine with that. Such is the nature of gardens, landscapes, and nature itself.

RIGHT The stepped dry garden is the first area a visitor sees when entering the property.

OVERLEAF LEFT TOP The octopus herb garden was set in a stone patio surrounded by thymes, rosemary, and chives, with a hydrangea walk in the background.

OVERLEAF LEFT BOTTOM A woodland garden detail shows a boxwood "S" hedge and two pots—one ceramic, and the other a pruned boxwood with white flowers and white foliage that brighten a shady area.

OVERLEAF RIGHT TOP The pool garden features bold-leaved Dutchman's pipe *Aristolochia macrophylla* covering the arbor and lime-green elephant ears in pots.

OVERLEAF RIGHT BOTTOM The hydrangea walk with its variegated Japanese aralia *Aralia elata 'Variegata'* has a bench as its focal point.

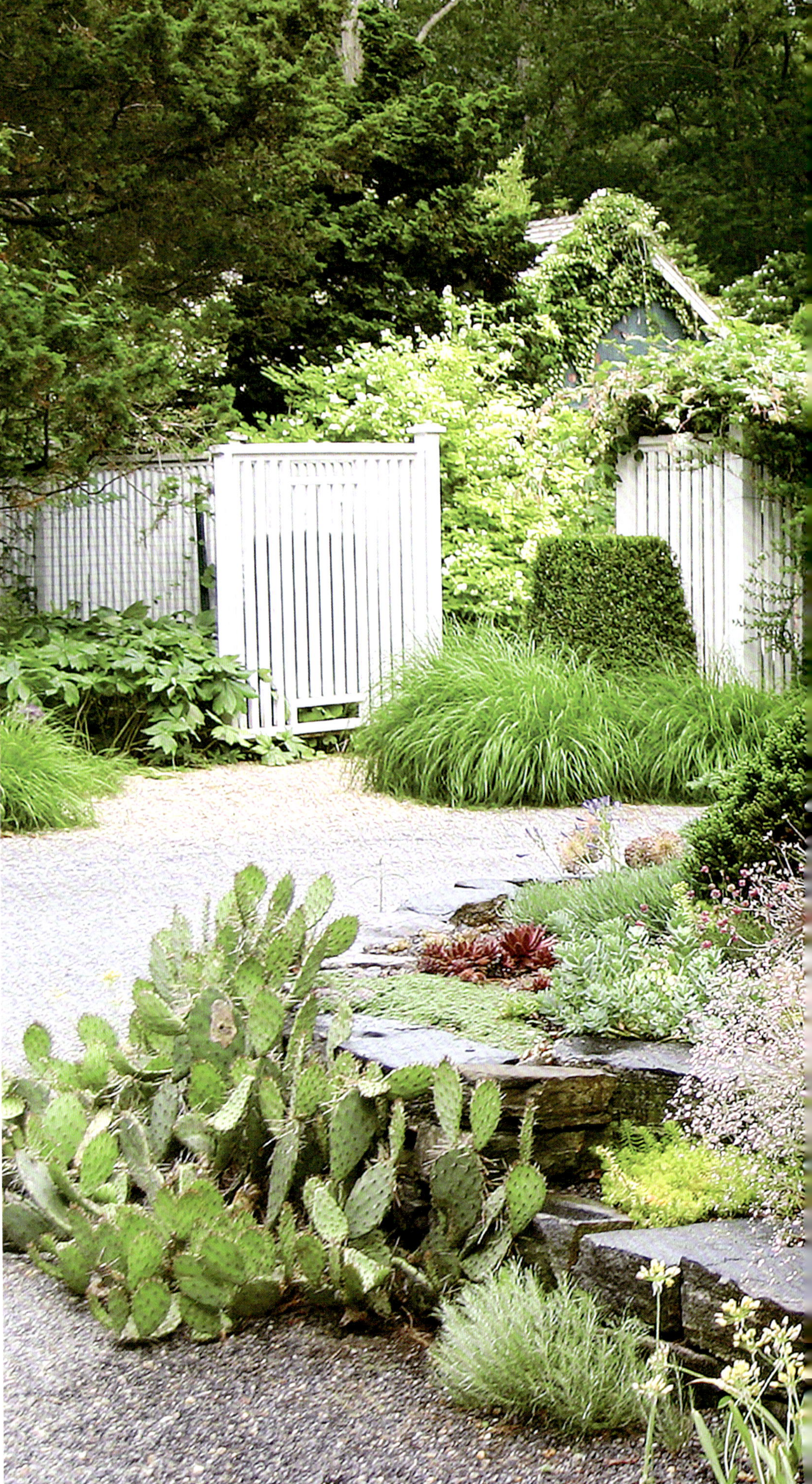

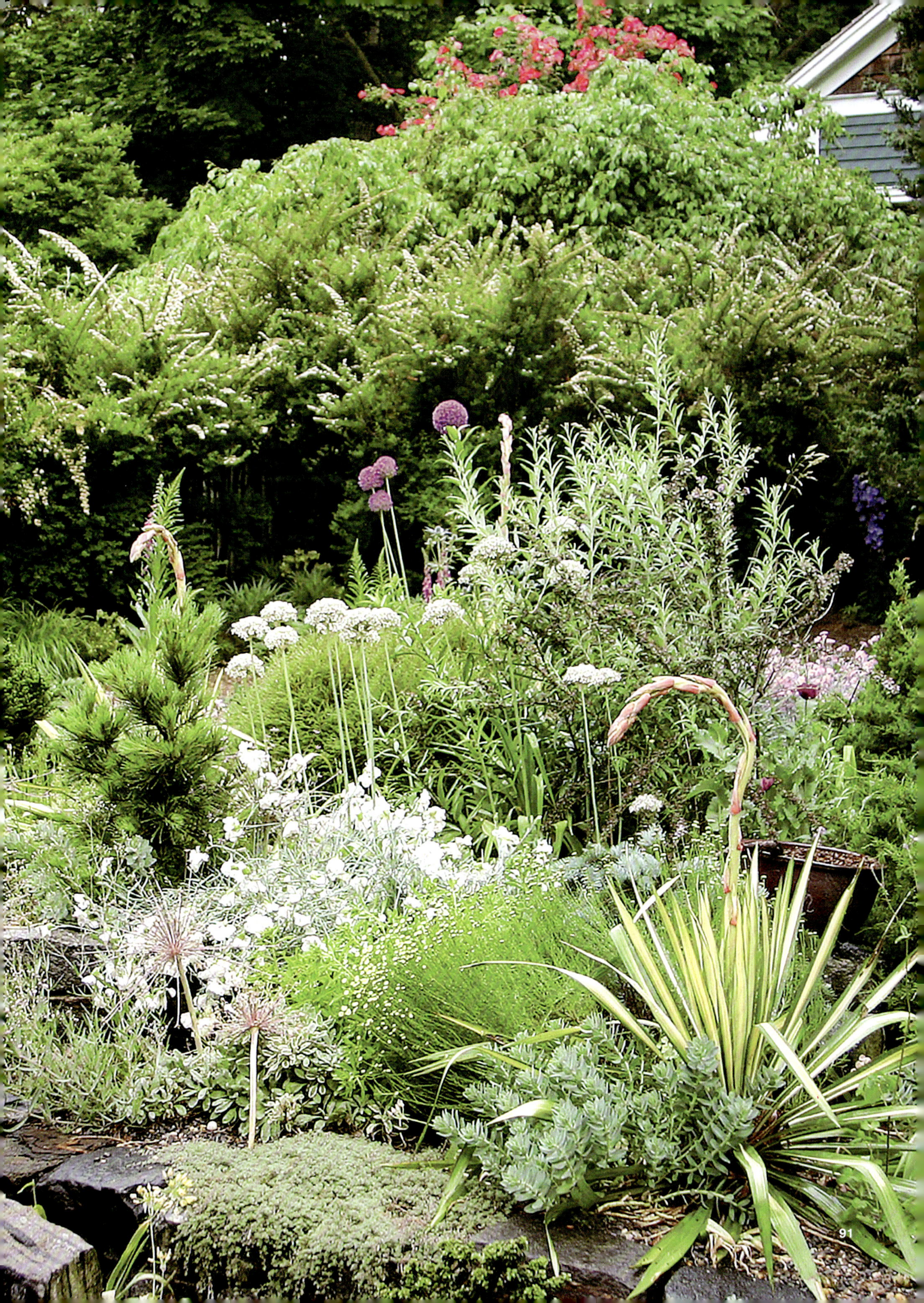

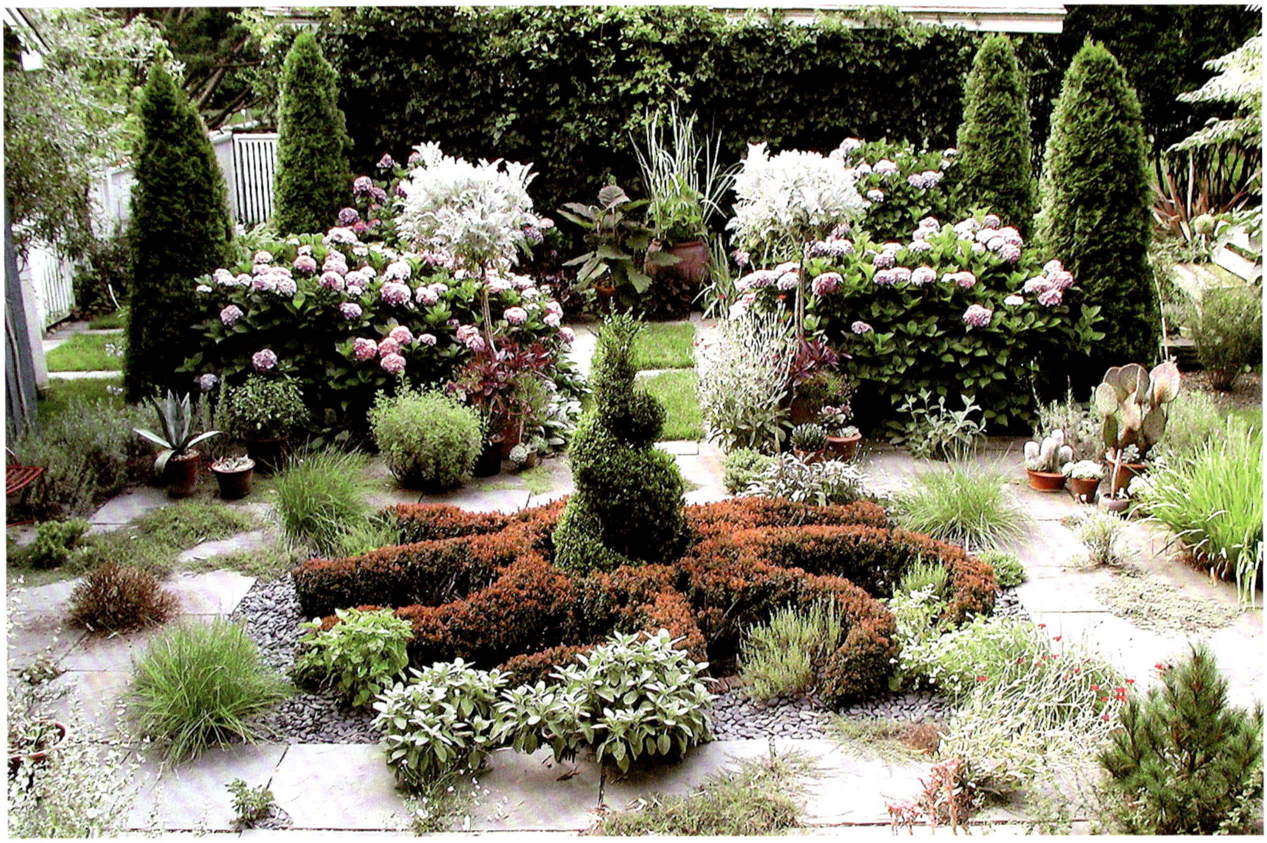

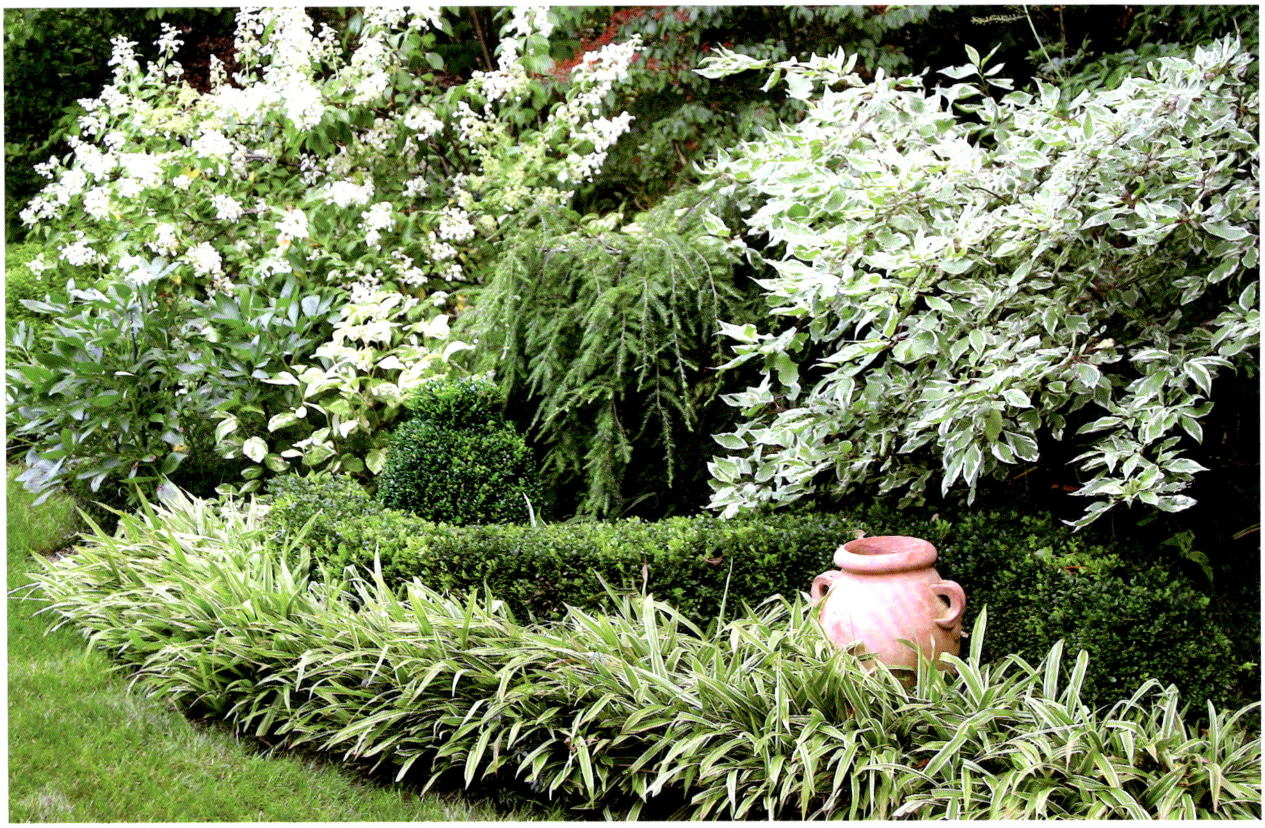

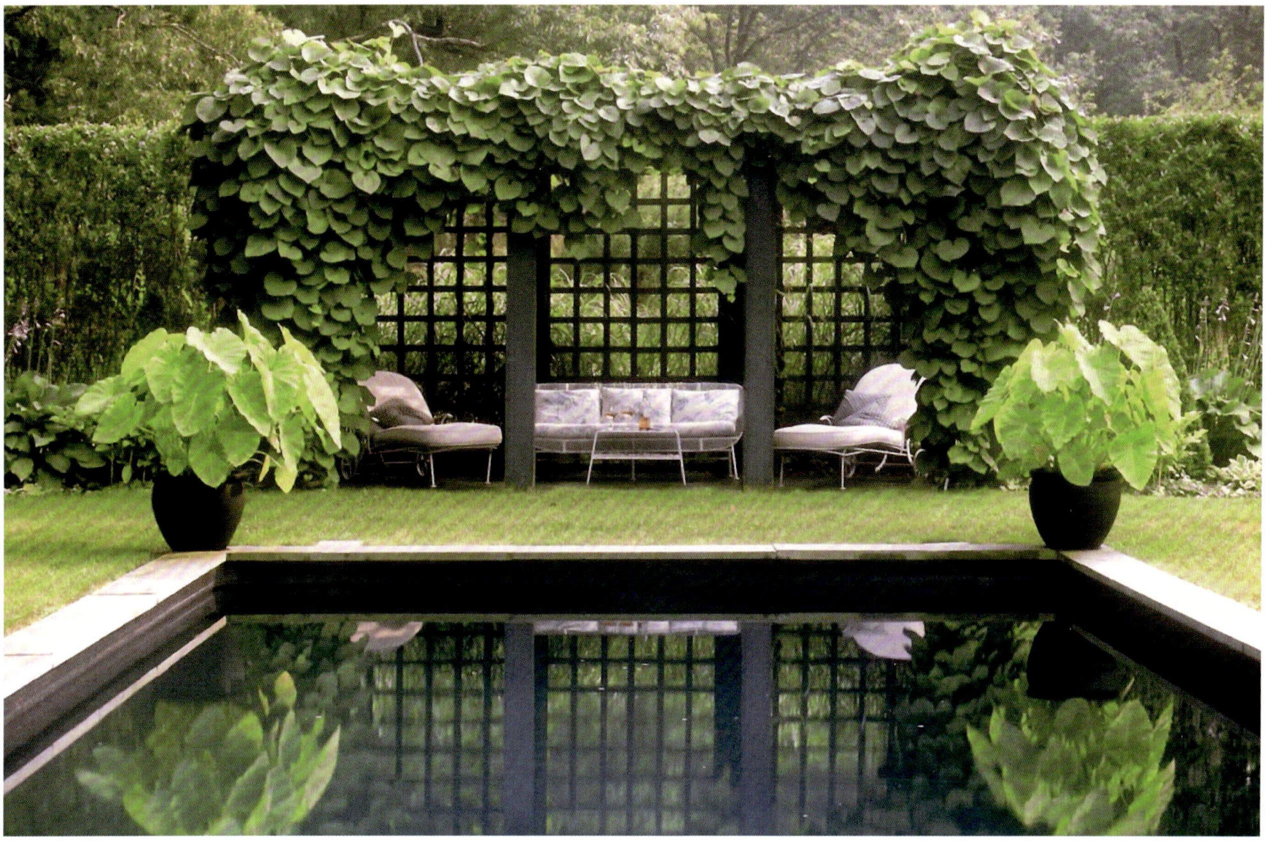

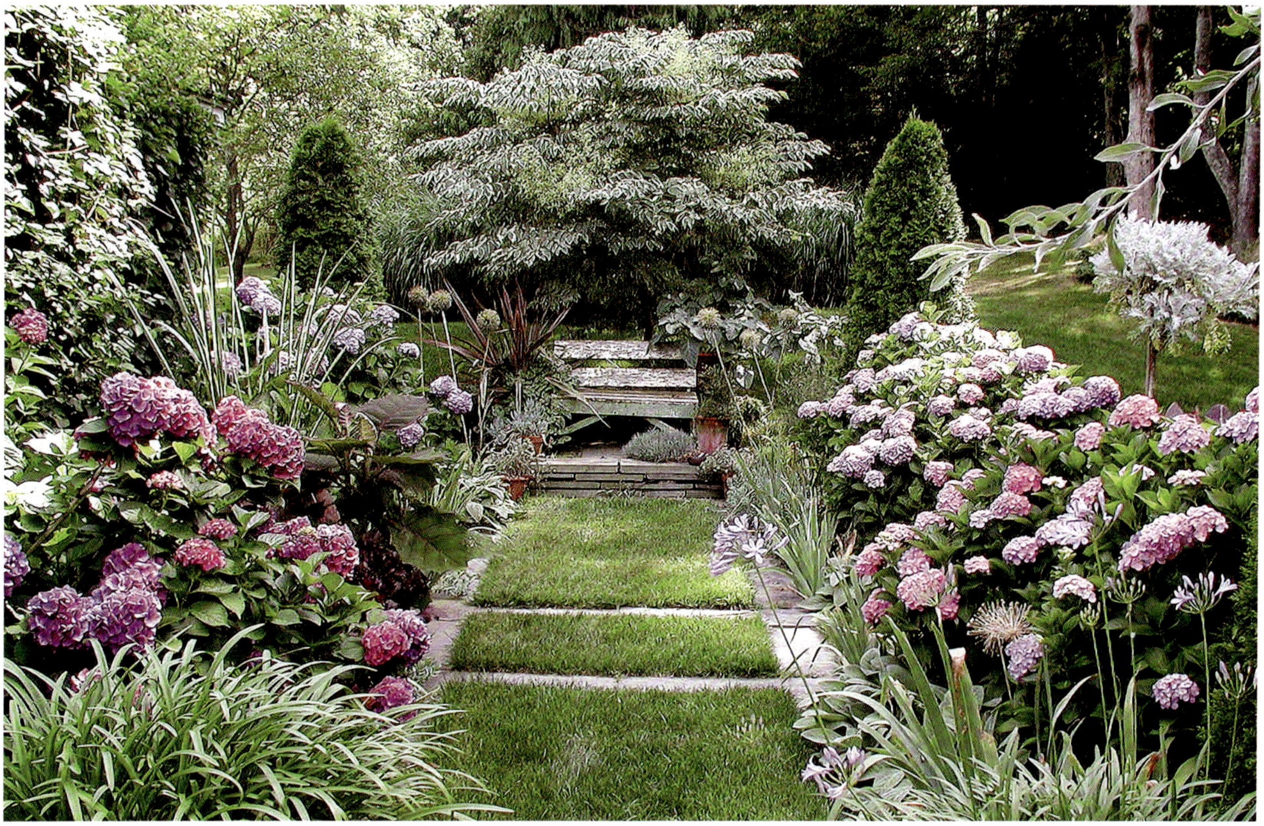

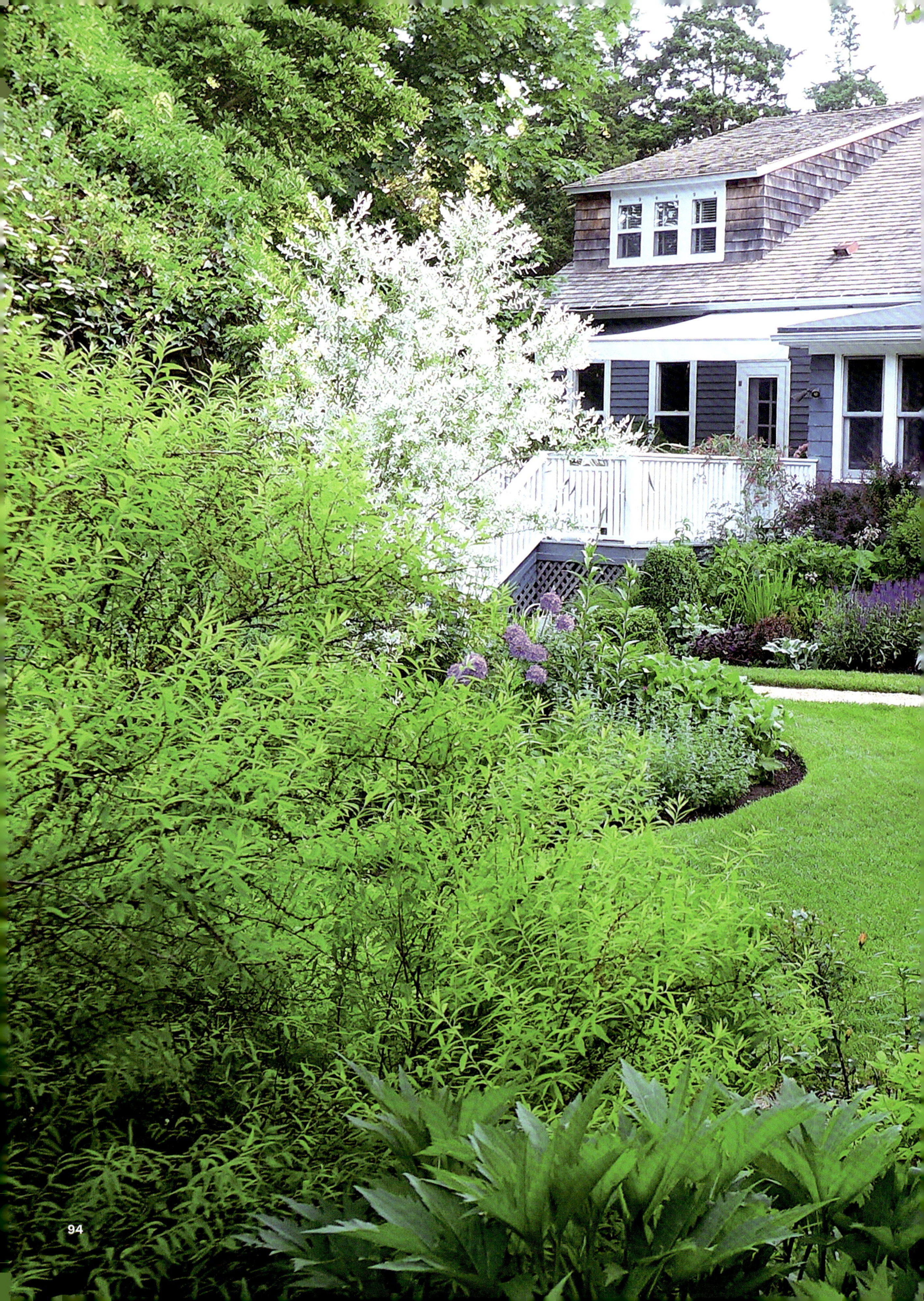

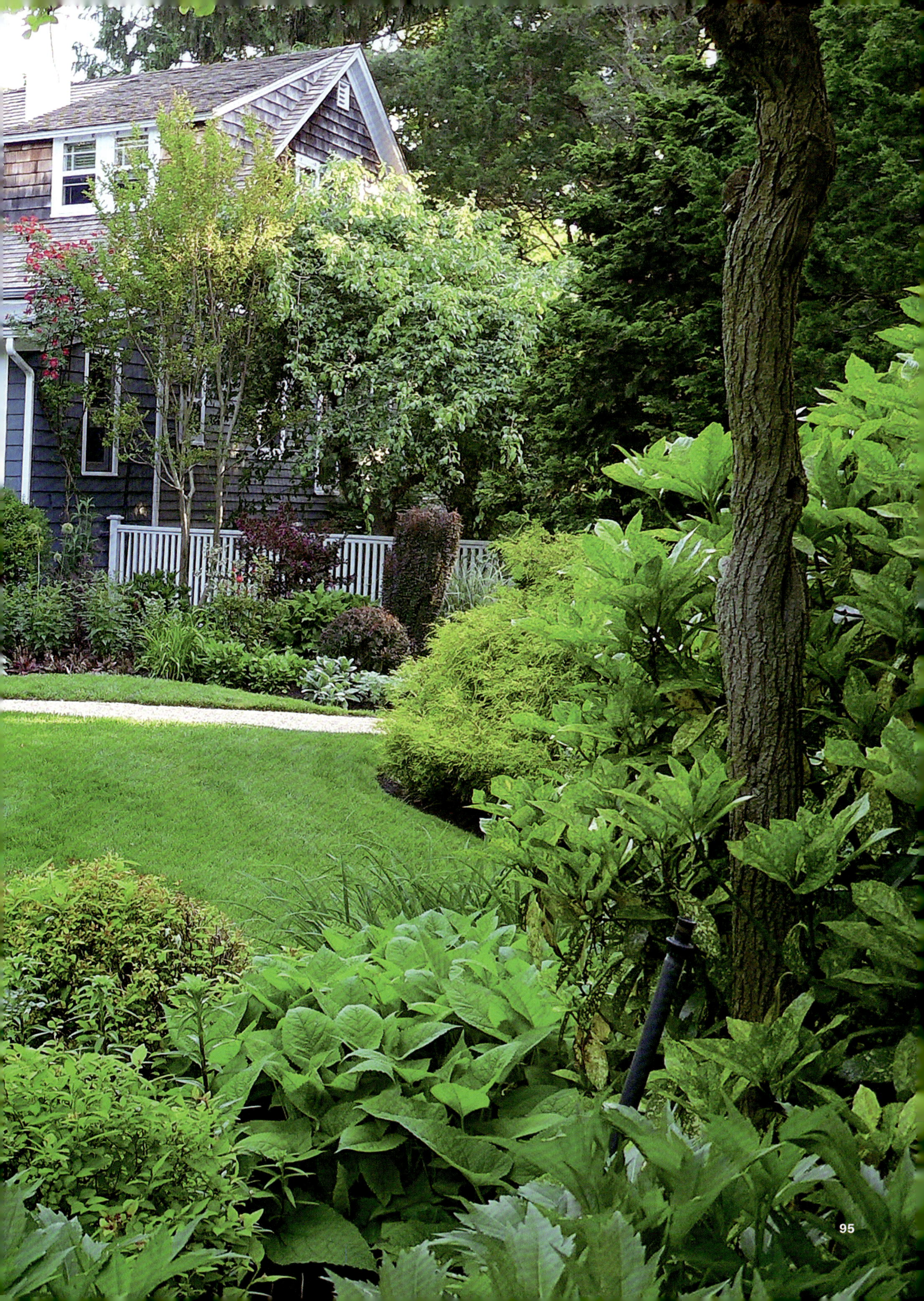

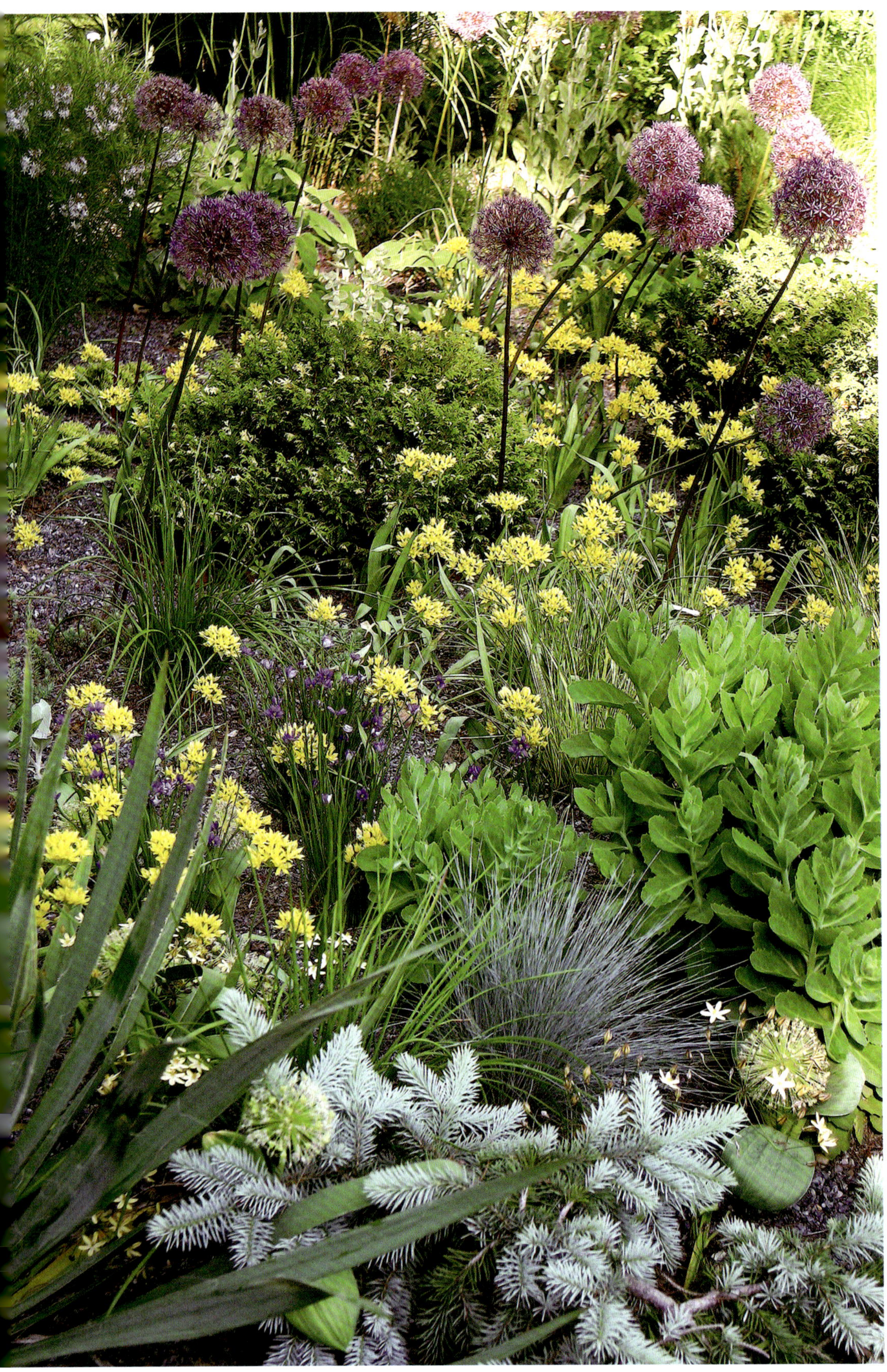

PREVIOUS PAGES The main perennial garden at the back of the house blooms with salvias and alliums in early summer.

LEFT Lily leek *Allium moly* and *Allium 'Purple Sensation'* are in bloom in the dry garden by the parking area. I always looked forward to this moment, when hundreds of delicate yellow alliums were in flower.

OPPOSITE In a perennial garden, annuals are added because they bloom continuously, filling in when perennials are done flowering. Red and orange annuals *Bulbine frutescens*, *alternanthera den. Rosa rubrifolia*, firecracker plant *Cuphea x 'David Verity*,' scarlet sage *Salvia splendens Van Houttei* and orange lily do the trick.

OVERLEAF The perennial garden can be seen from the house. In the foreground, the red-themed bed is planted with mountain fleece *Persicaria amplexicaulis 'Firetail*,' red Japanese barberry *Berberis thunbergii 'Atropurpurea*,' *Rosa glauca*, and *Lilium 'Black Beauty*.'

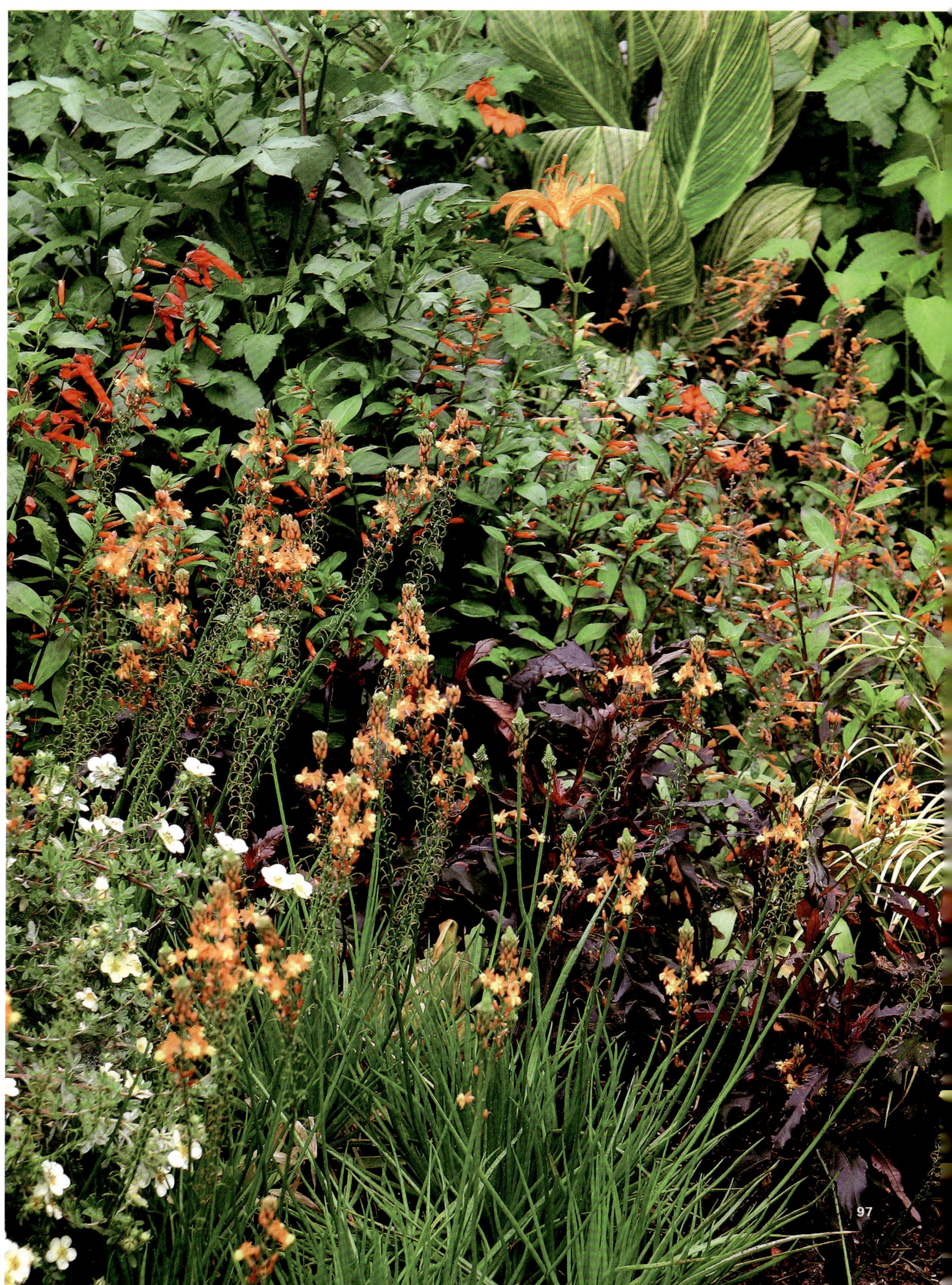

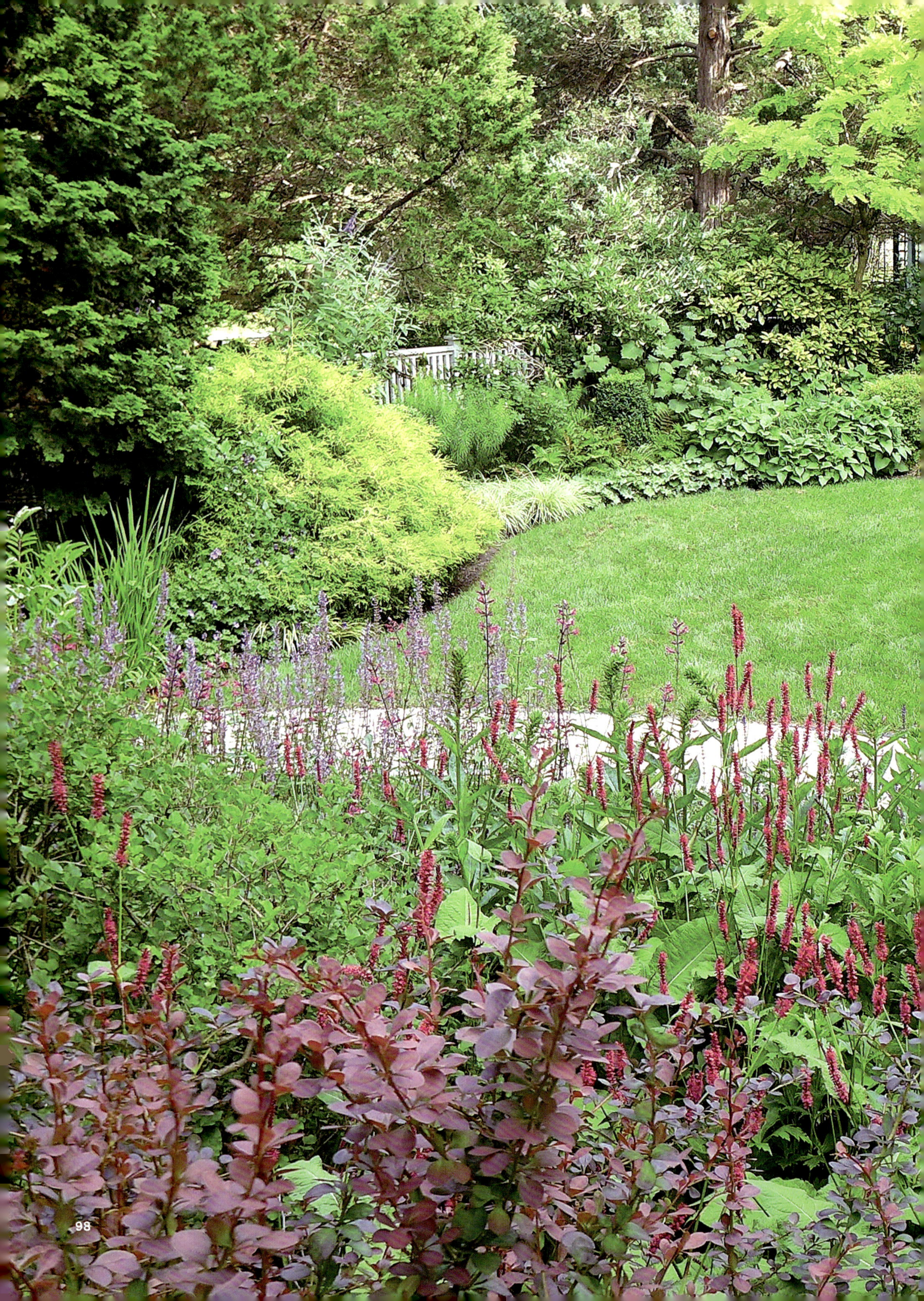

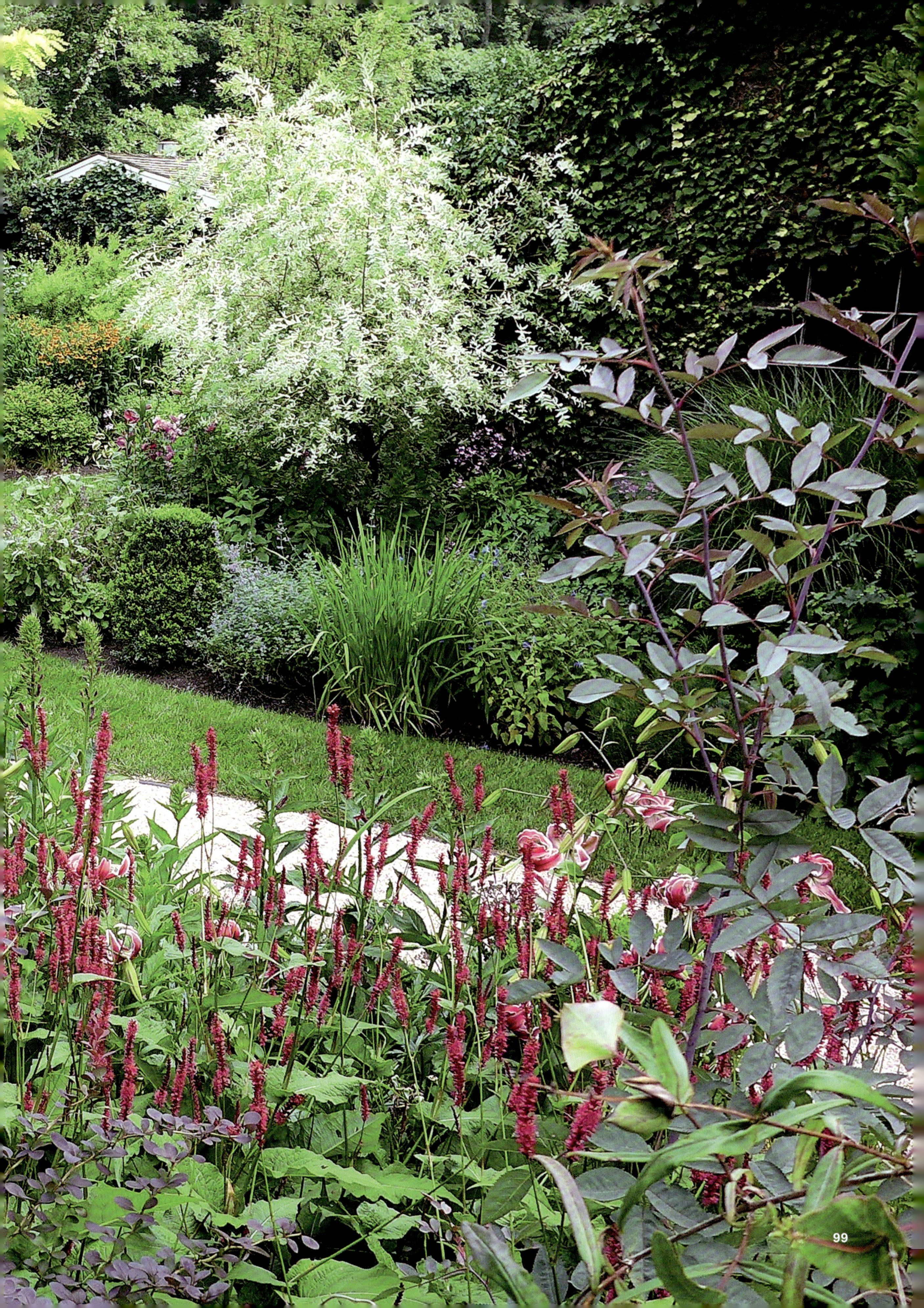

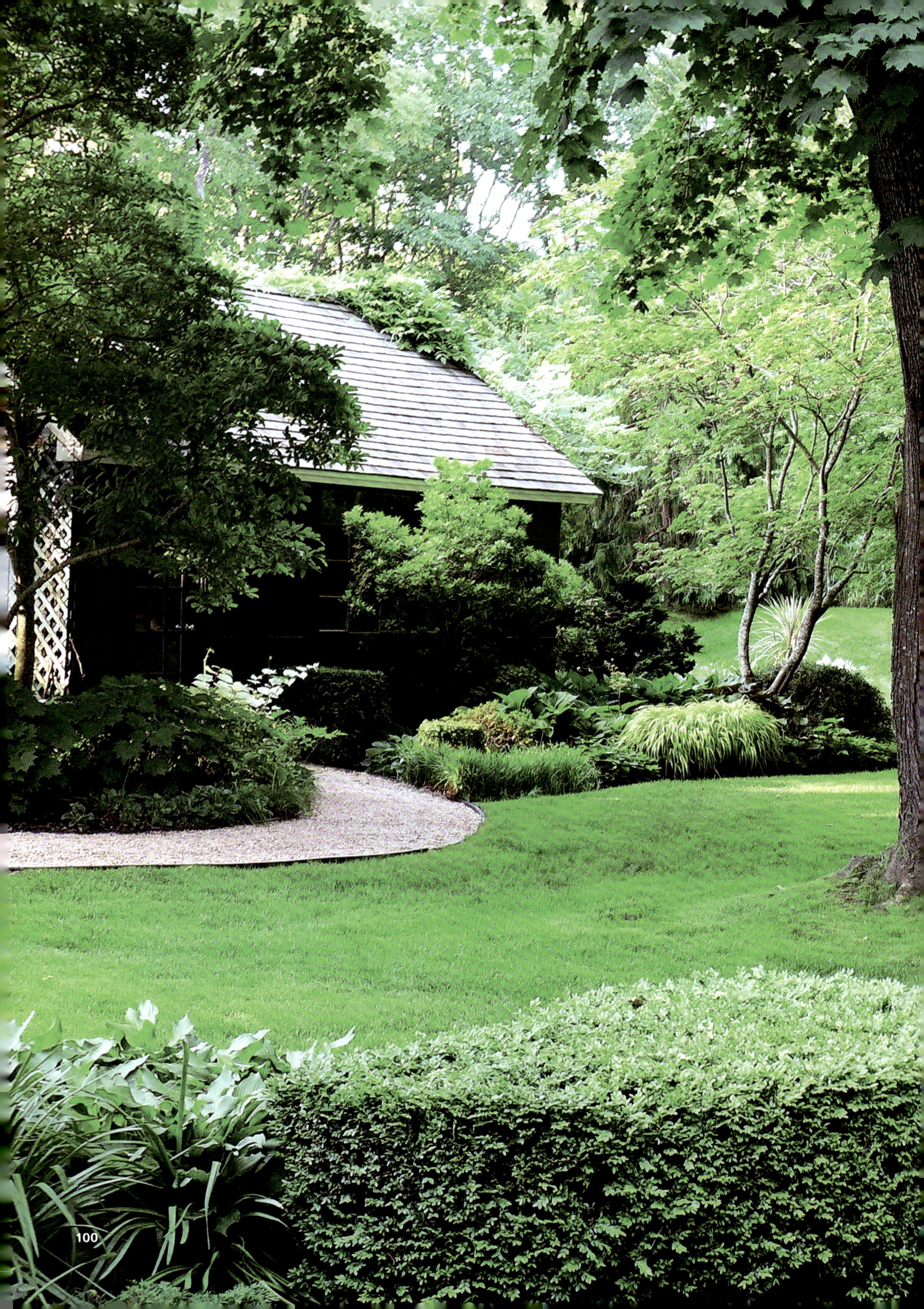

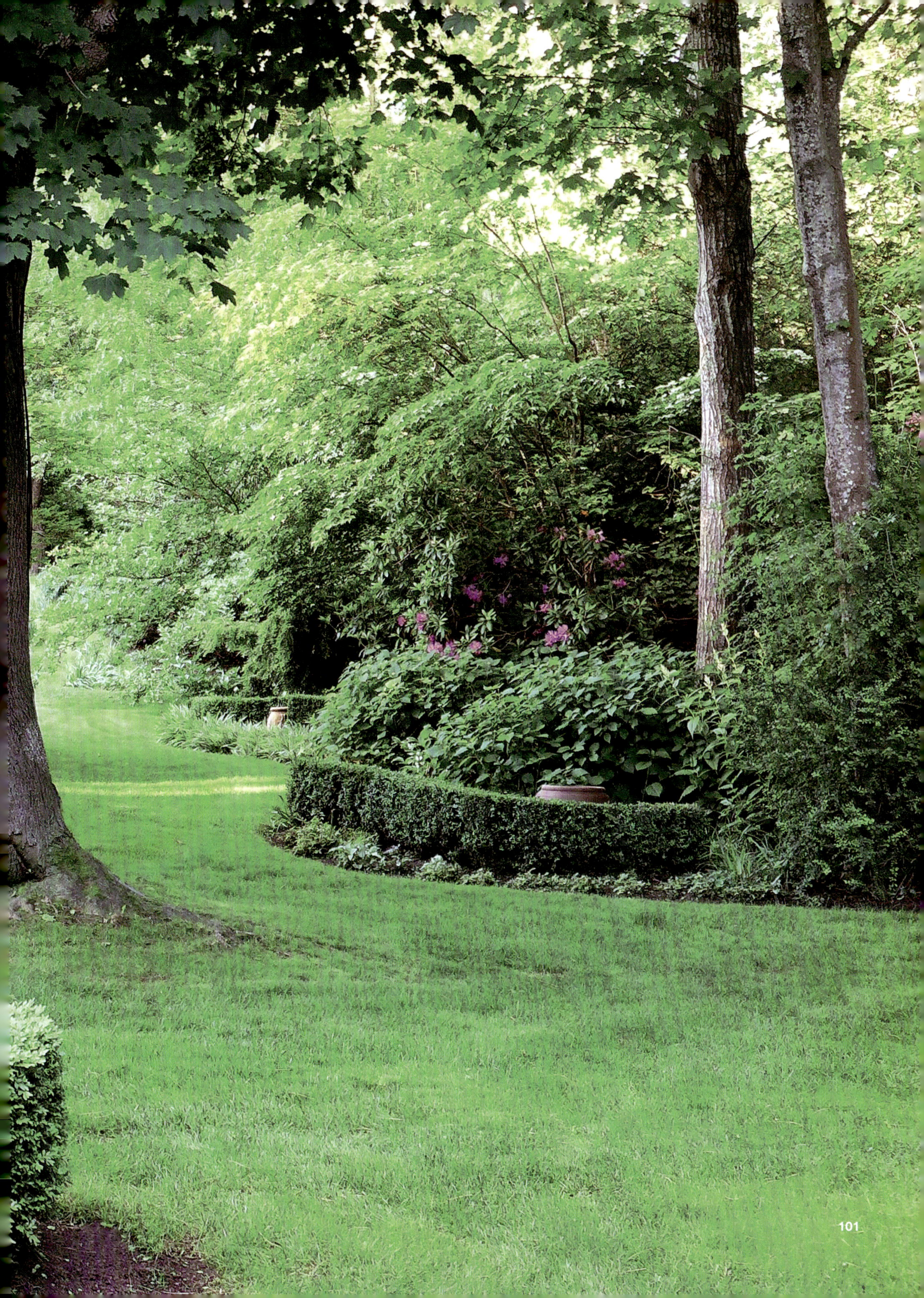

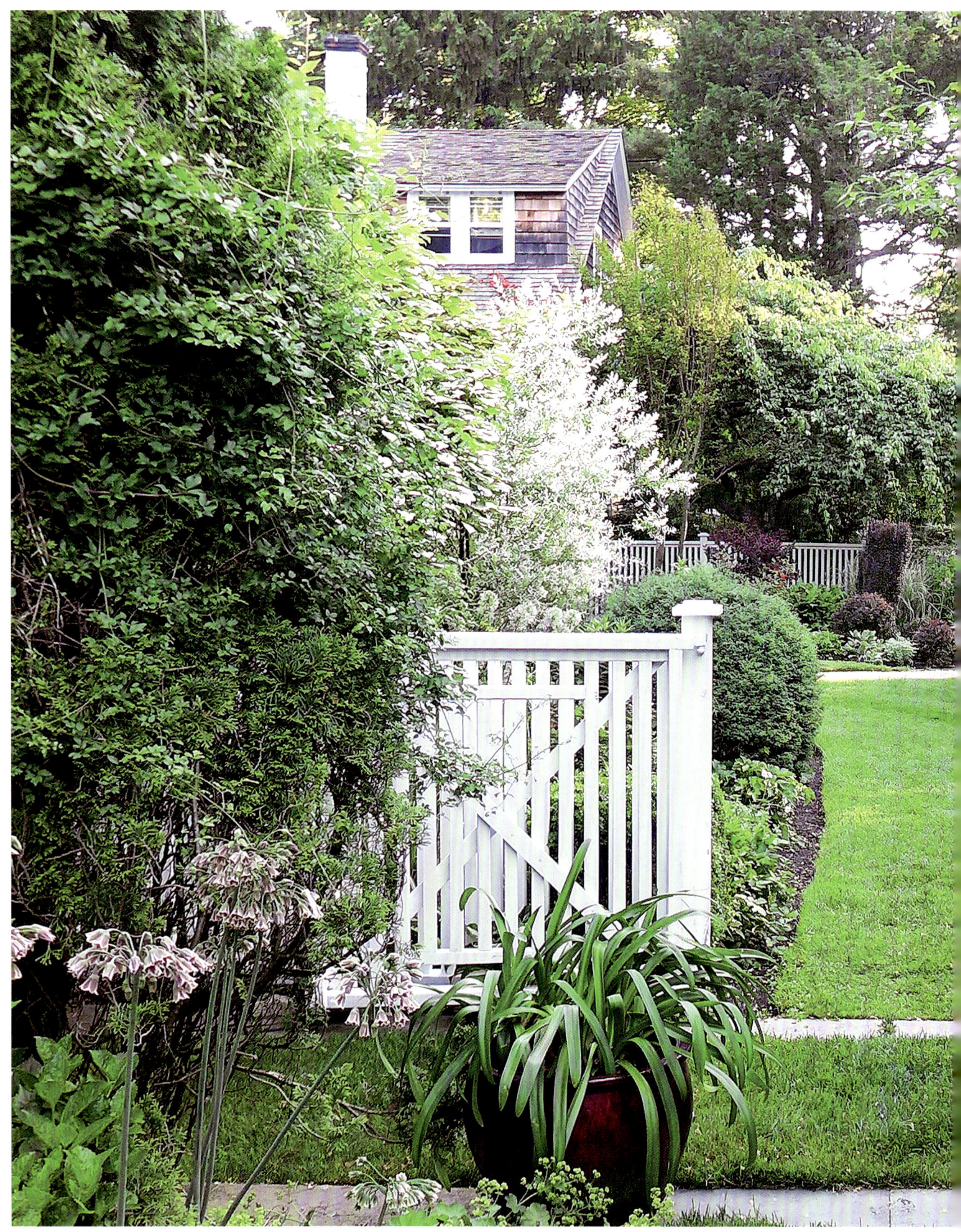

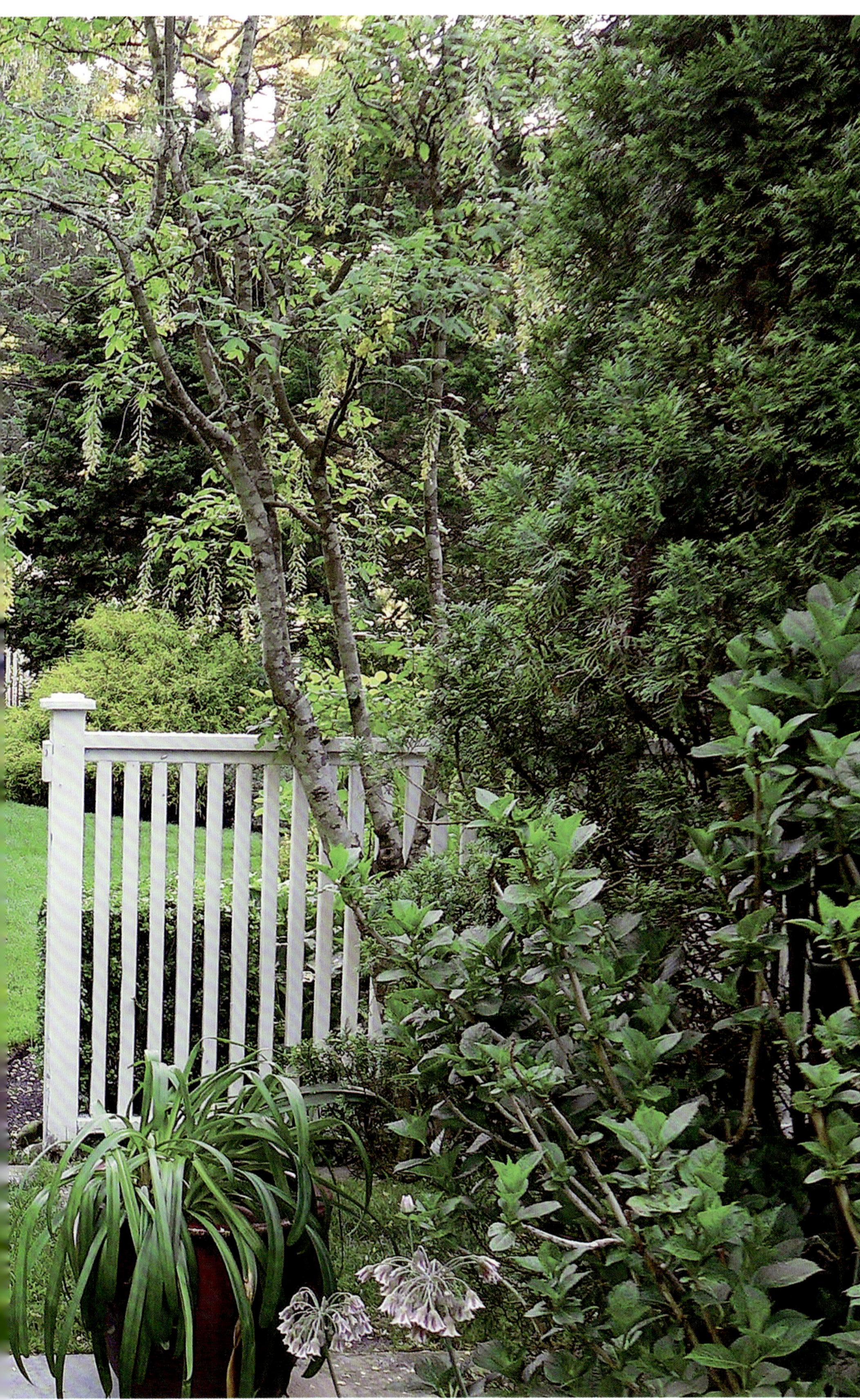

PREVIOUS PAGES
A mature Norway maple *Acer platanoides* reigns over the lawn that separates the woodland garden from the house and the shed gardens. Clipped boxwoods in the shapes of balls, squares, a paisley, and curved hedges unite the three gardens.

LEFT A golden chain tree *Laburnum anagyroides* is in bloom on the right in the perennial garden.

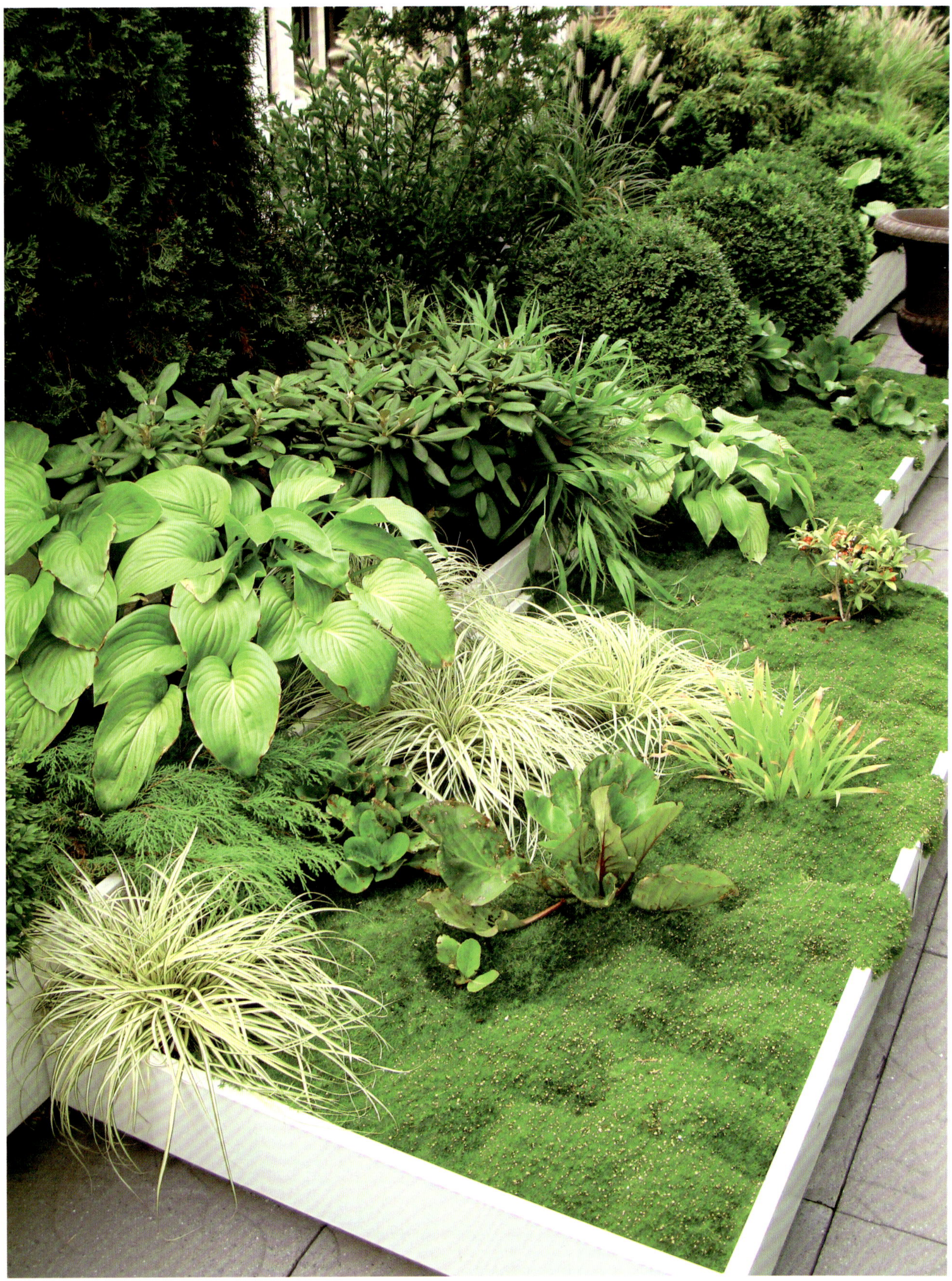

MODERN

Long, narrow terraces create their own set of design problems. In 2007, I designed a garden for this New York City terrace. The building had a tinted glass facade and the client wanted privacy from neighbors looking in.

In Chinese scroll paintings, the viewer follows a figure walking on a winding path through a long mysterious landscape with lookouts and waterfalls as visual pauses and points of interest. In a long garden, a visitor's eye should have a similar experience. In this three-level terrace garden, a long arborvitae hedge, *Thuja occidentalis 'Emerald,'* was planted for privacy. Groups of boxwood and complementary foliage were placed in front of the hedge at intervals to provide a rhythm along the garden's length. In four areas, low six-inch-deep planter boxes project from the boxwood groups with panels of moss and perennials for a restful view. To break up the long hedge, two openings contain trees and shrubs for a textural contrast. Combined, these elements create a sense of complexity and natural interest.

South-facing gardens in front of tinted glass facades sometimes have unexpected issues. With reflected sun, they can be considerably warmer in winter than other gardens, and often create microclimates that prevent some plants from going completely dormant. In other cases plants that are not normally hardy can make it through the winter. There is also the fact that the constant reflected sunlight can badly dry and burn leaves. Sadly, I am afraid global warming will complicate these and related matters even more in the coming years for urban gardens.

OPPOSITE Moss, sedge, iris, and bergenia were planted on the lower level, with hosta *Hosta plantaginea* on both levels. Layering plants adds a complexity to the garden that is closer to the natural world.

BELOW A three-level planter composition shows an opening in the arborvitae hedge that has been planted with a maple and shrubs. Barrenwort and lily turf spill from the upper to the lower levels, merging them.

OPPOSITE Looking east on the terrace, bamboo *Phyllostachys bissetii* continues the effect of a green wall around the garden.

OVERLEAF The western end of the terrace has been planted in front of the hedge with repeating boxwoods, combined with grass, shrubs, and perennials.

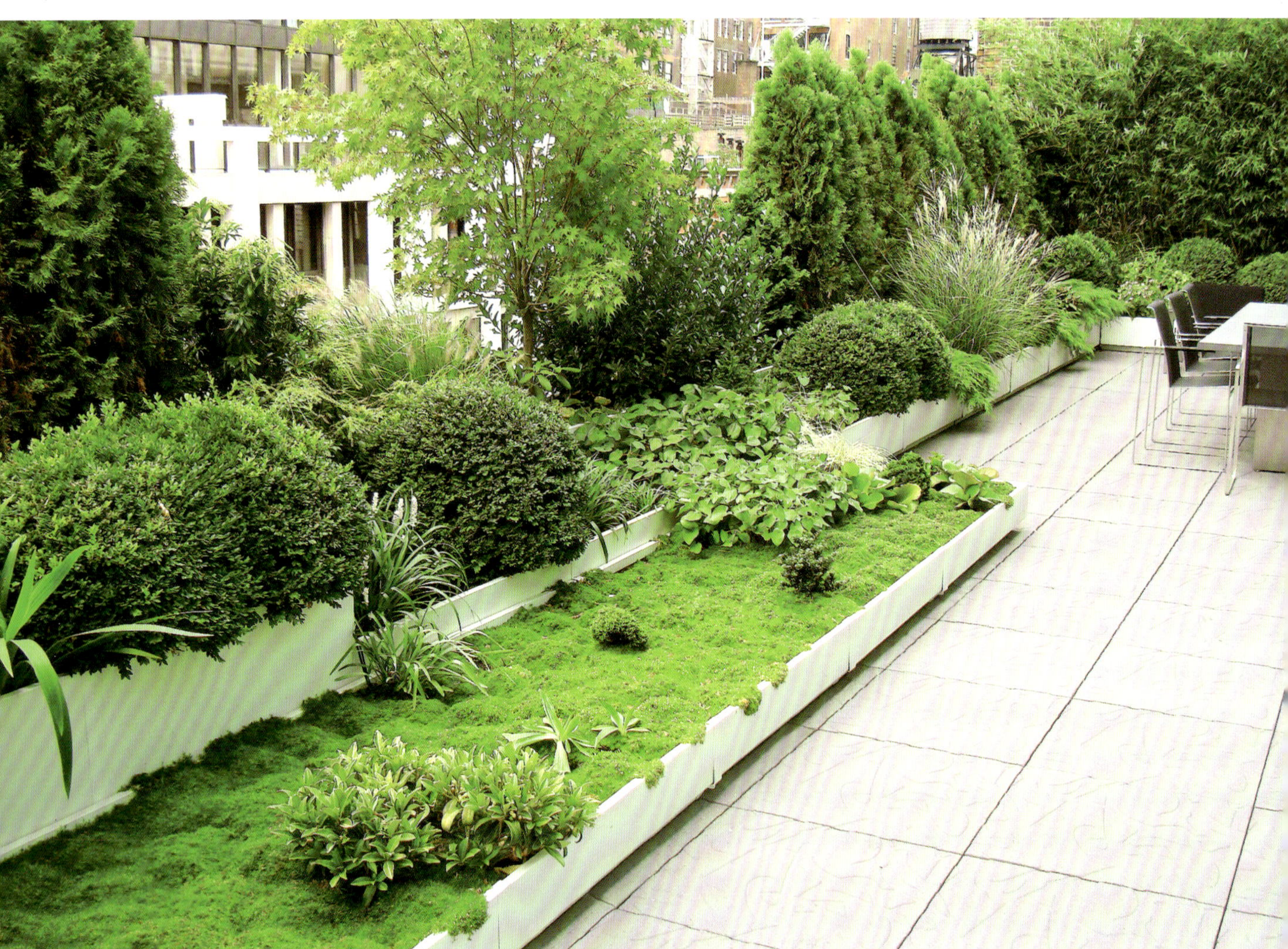

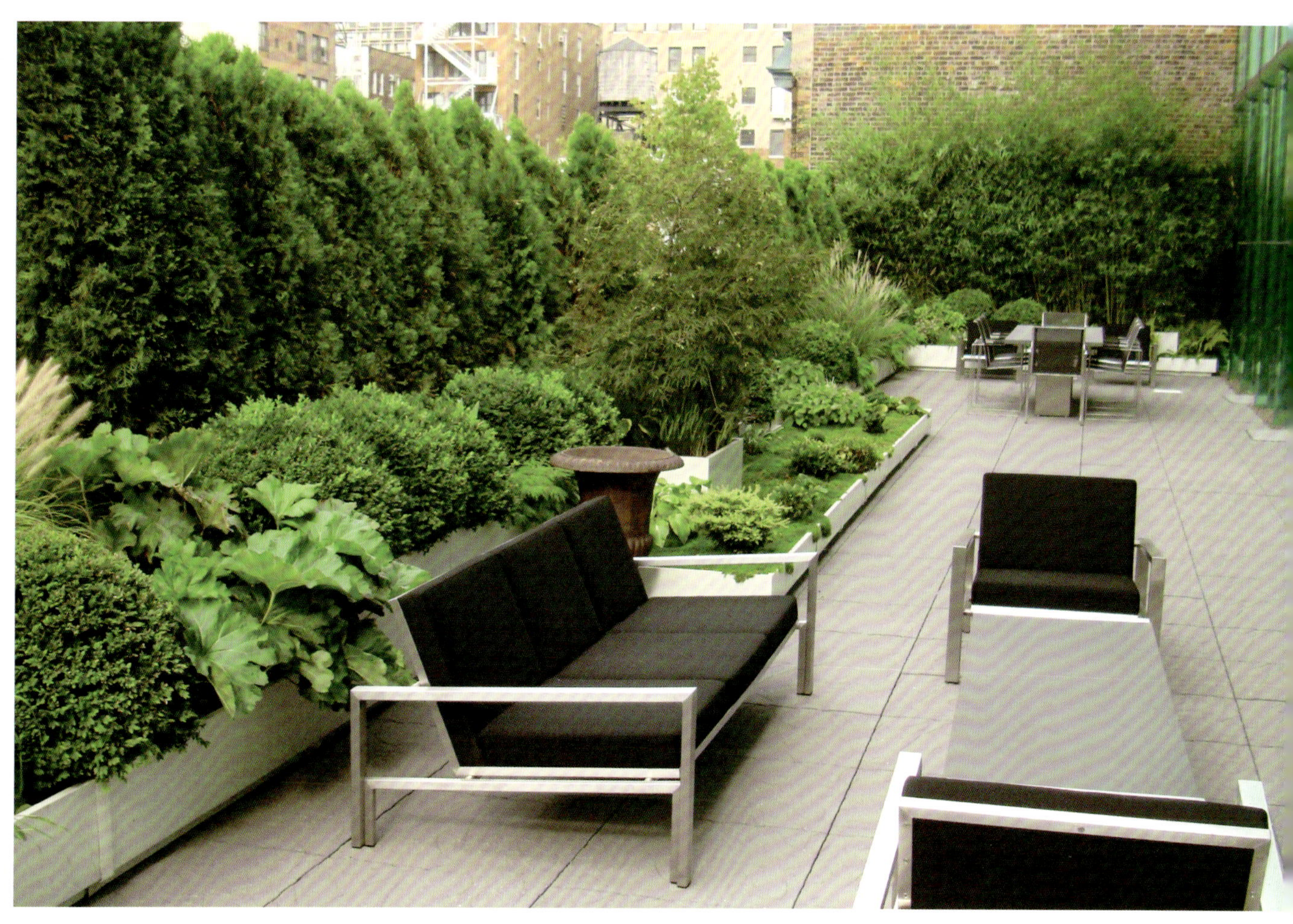

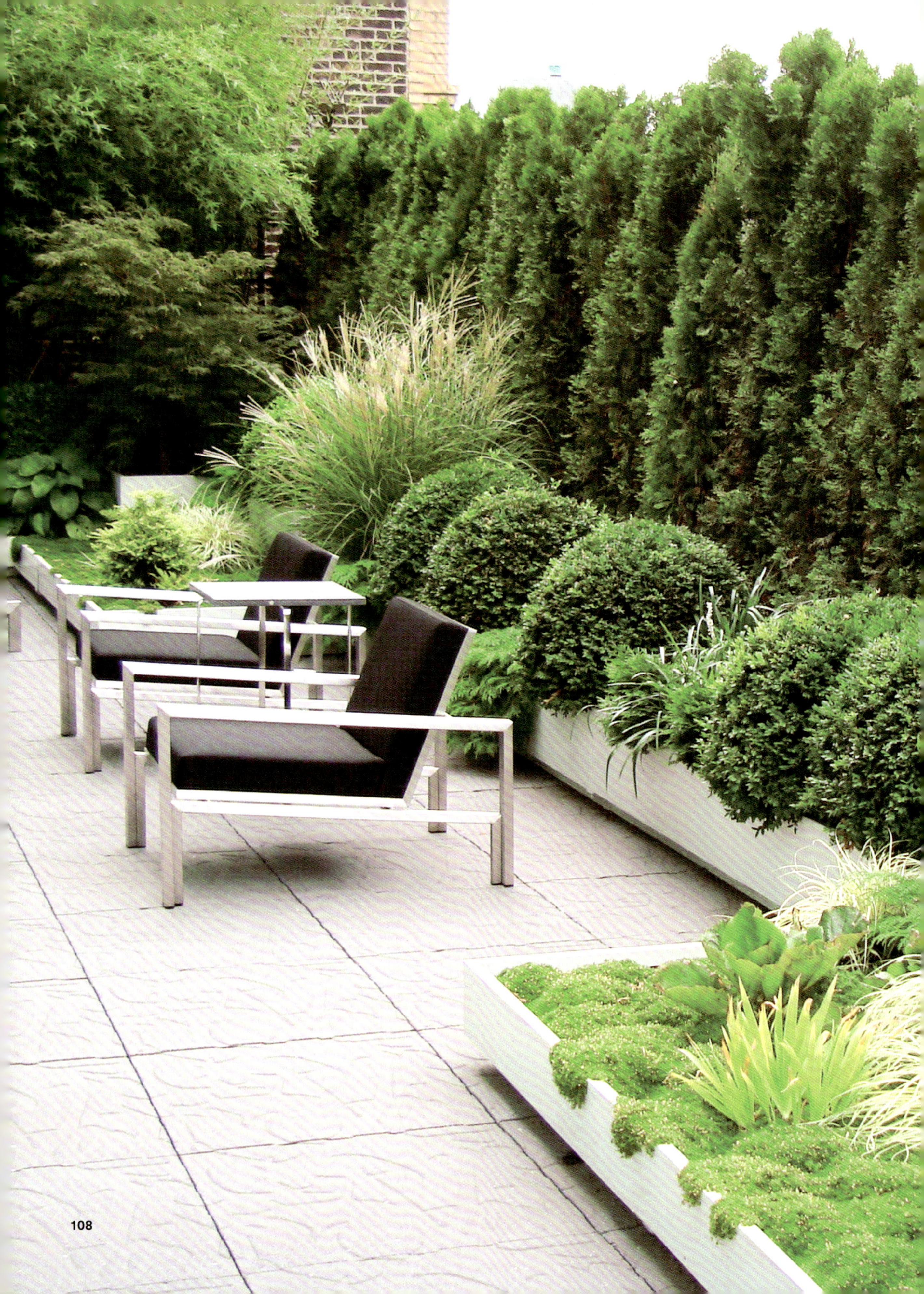

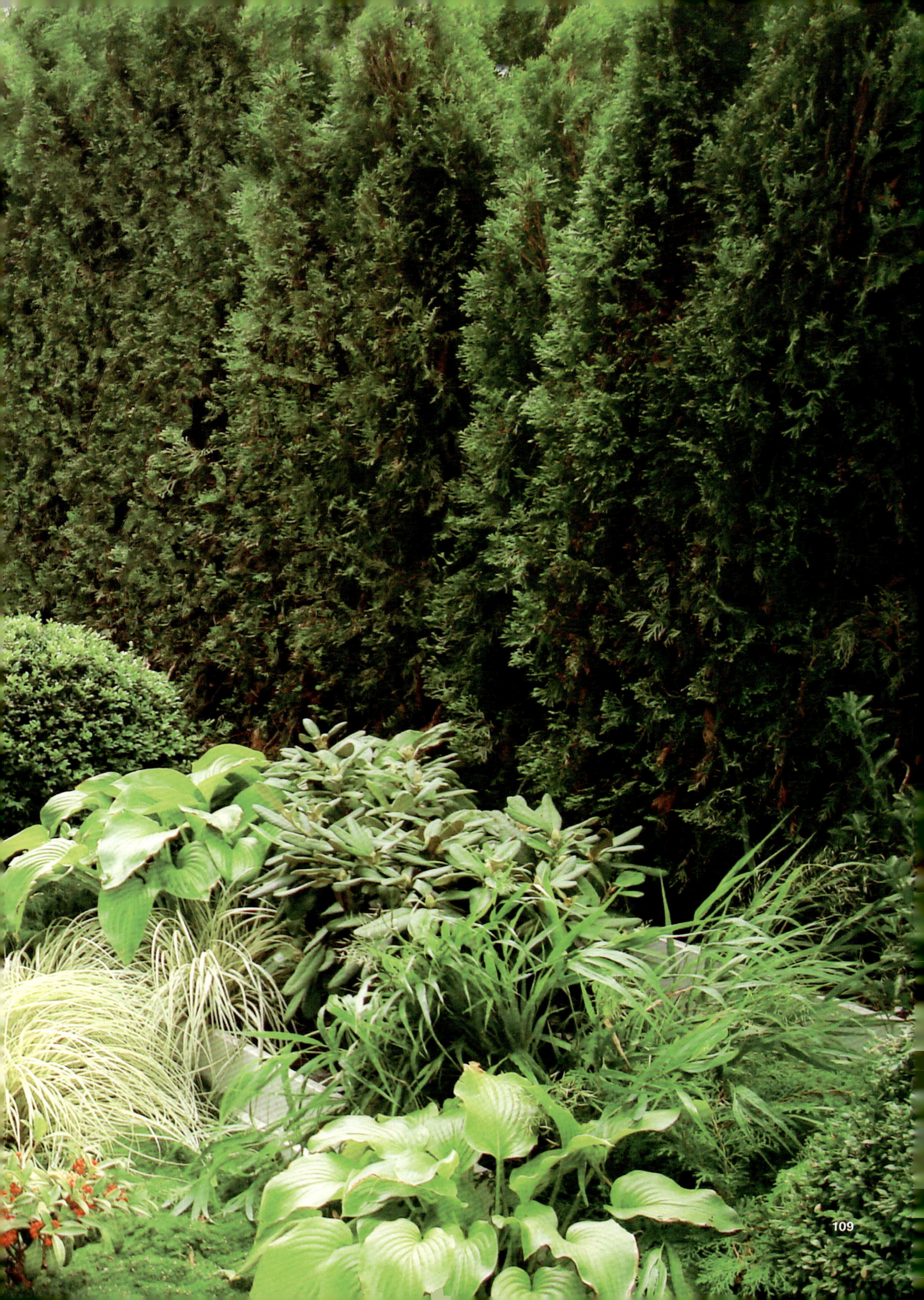

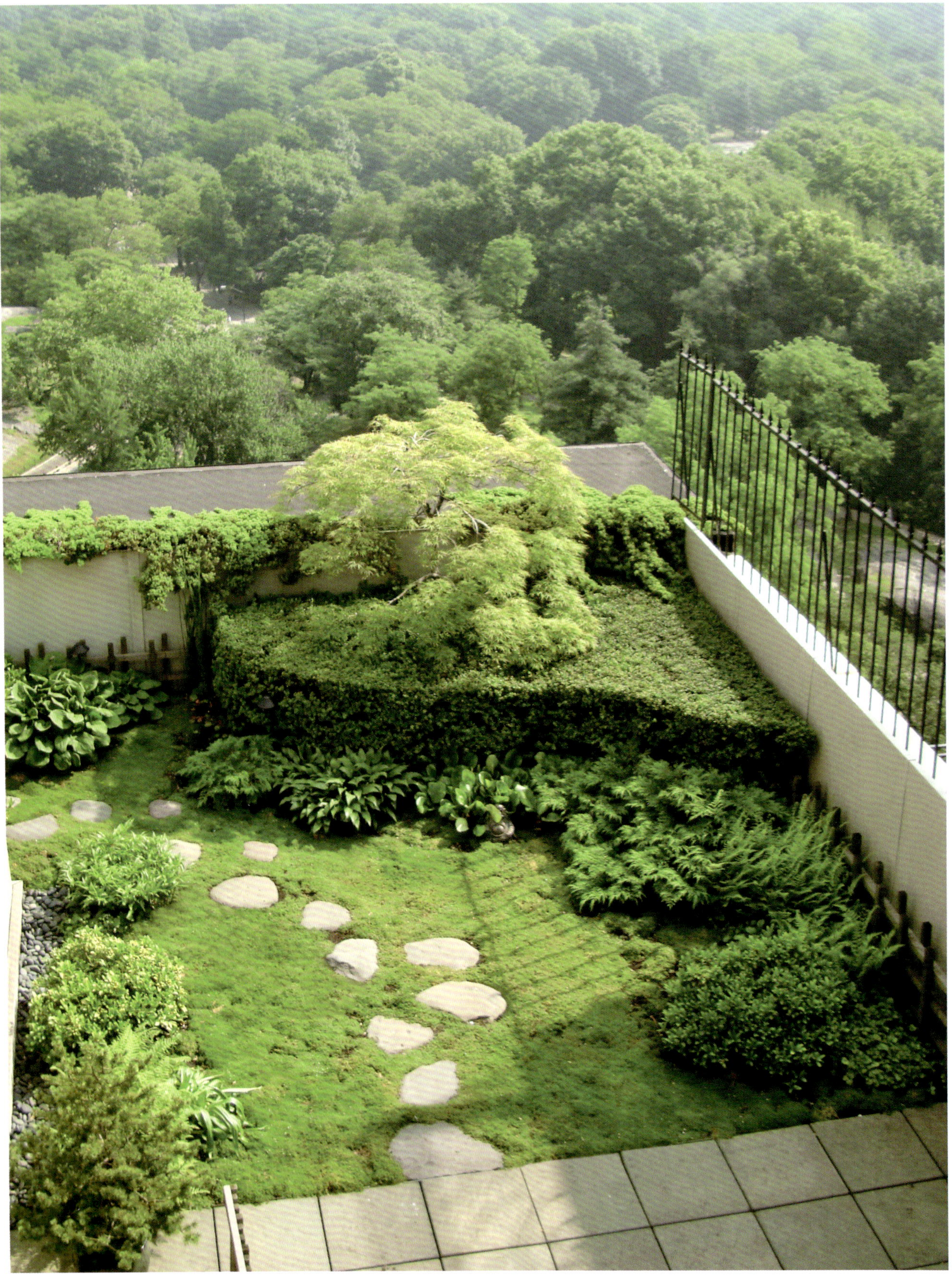

TOPOGRAPHICAL

The Japanese have a term, *Shakkei*, which translates as "borrowed view or scenery." It refers to incorporating a view outside the garden into a garden design. In this New York City garden, designed in 2000, overlooking Central Park, using the dramatic view of the park was unavoidable. As the interior of the residence was designed in a Japanese style, the garden was designed to continue that aesthetic. The issue became one of creating a dialogue between the terrace garden and the trees of Central Park. The parapet of the building was unusually high, and partially blocked the view of the park when one was standing on the terrace. The focus of the garden is a Japanese maple, *Acer palmatum var. dissectum 'Viridis,'* surrounded by a boxwood hedge and a moss garden with perennials, shrubs, and stepping stones. Along the top of the parapet, I planted a low-mounding evergreen, *Juniperus procumbens 'Nana,'* that mimicked the canopy of trees in the distance, melding the park and the garden together.

A second rooftop also belonged to the client. There, I created a deck with an open view of the park, and a border of grass *Pennisetum alopecuroides* in the foreground, with trees to frame the view. From two vantage spots, the gardens take full advantage of Central Park, one of Frederick Law Olmstead and Calvert Vaux's masterpieces.

OPPOSITE The tree canopy of Central Park is the backdrop for this garden.

OVERLEAF The upper terrace garden has a deck and a park view that has been framed by trees.

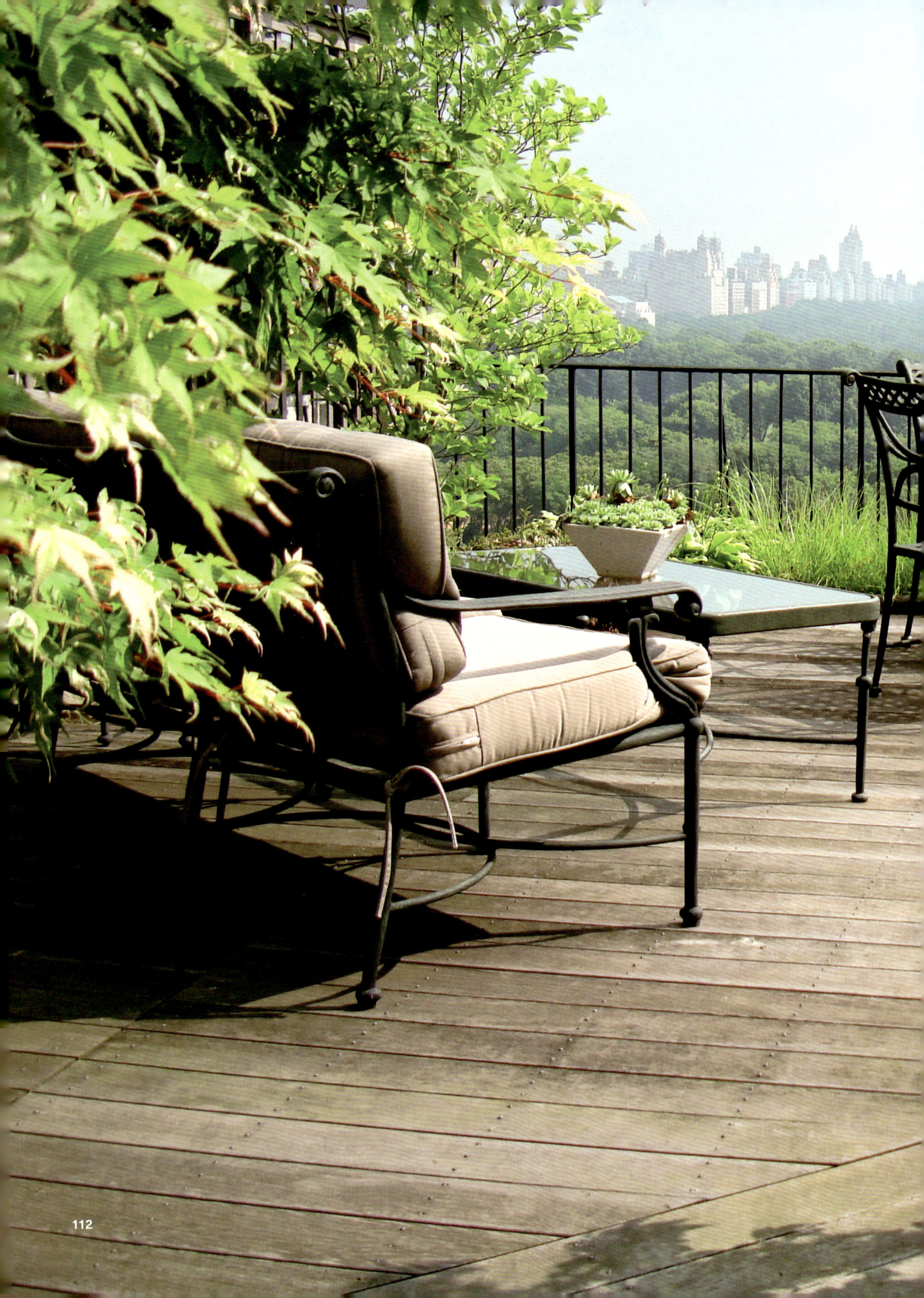

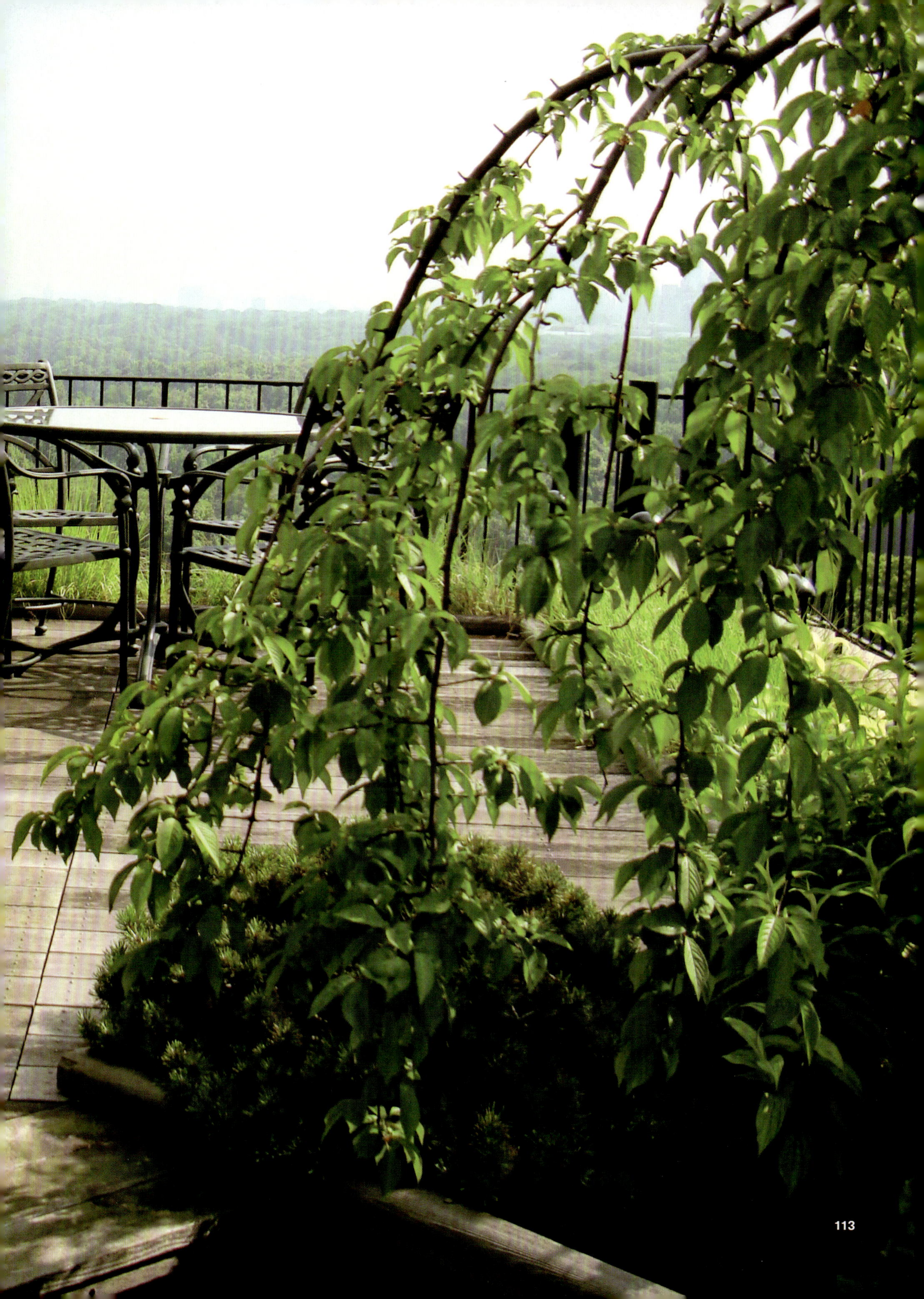

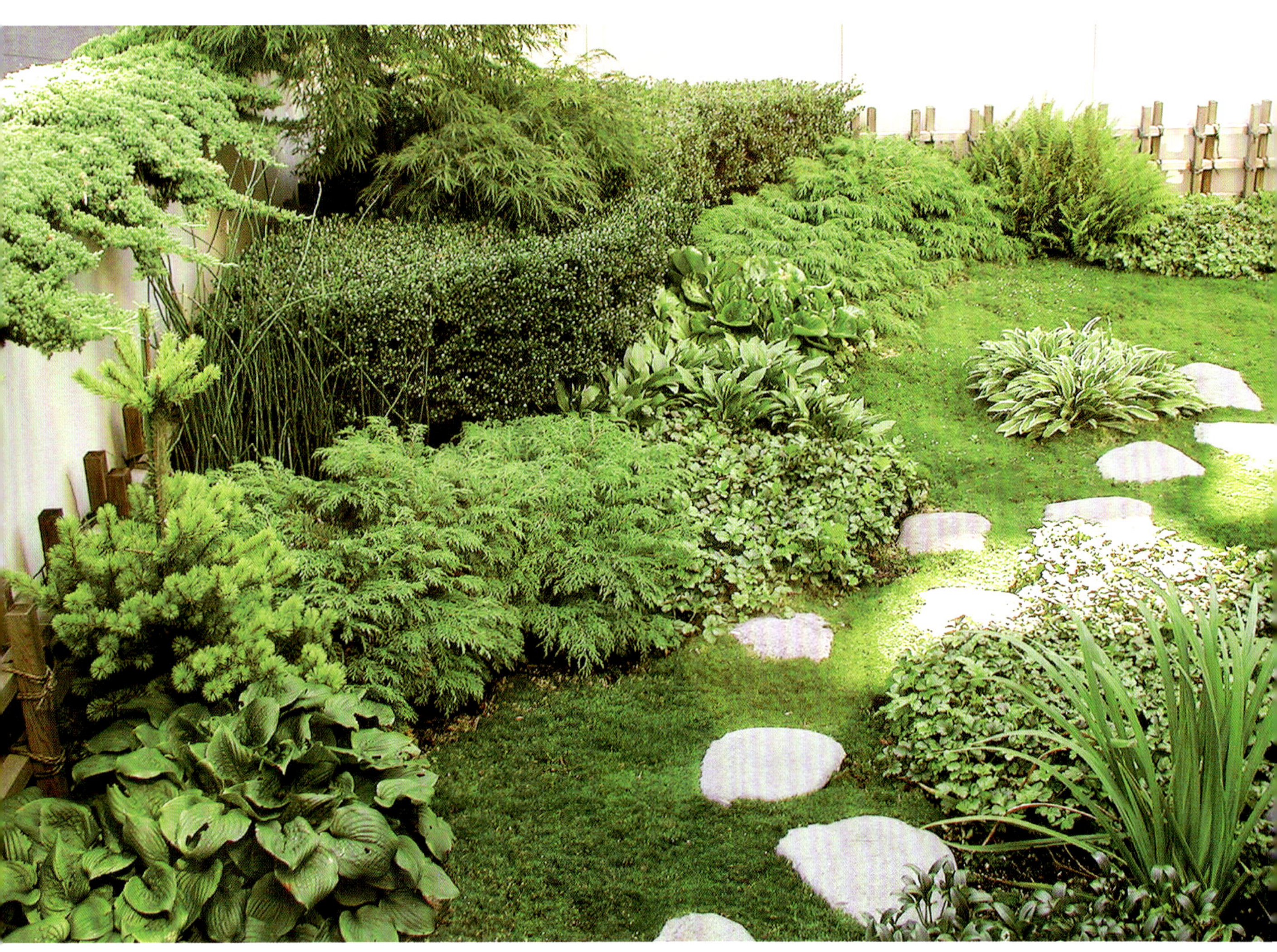

ABOVE The moss garden was planted on the roof in shallow, four-inch-deep containers. Stepping stones and assorted shrubs and perennials were added to the design.

OPPOSITE A maple *Acer palmatum dissectum 'Viridis'* in a curved boxwood hedge can be seen in the south view of the garden. Behind the maple, on the top of the parapet, low-mounding *Juniperus procumbens 'Nana'* mimic the tree canopy of Central Park, bringing the park into the garden.

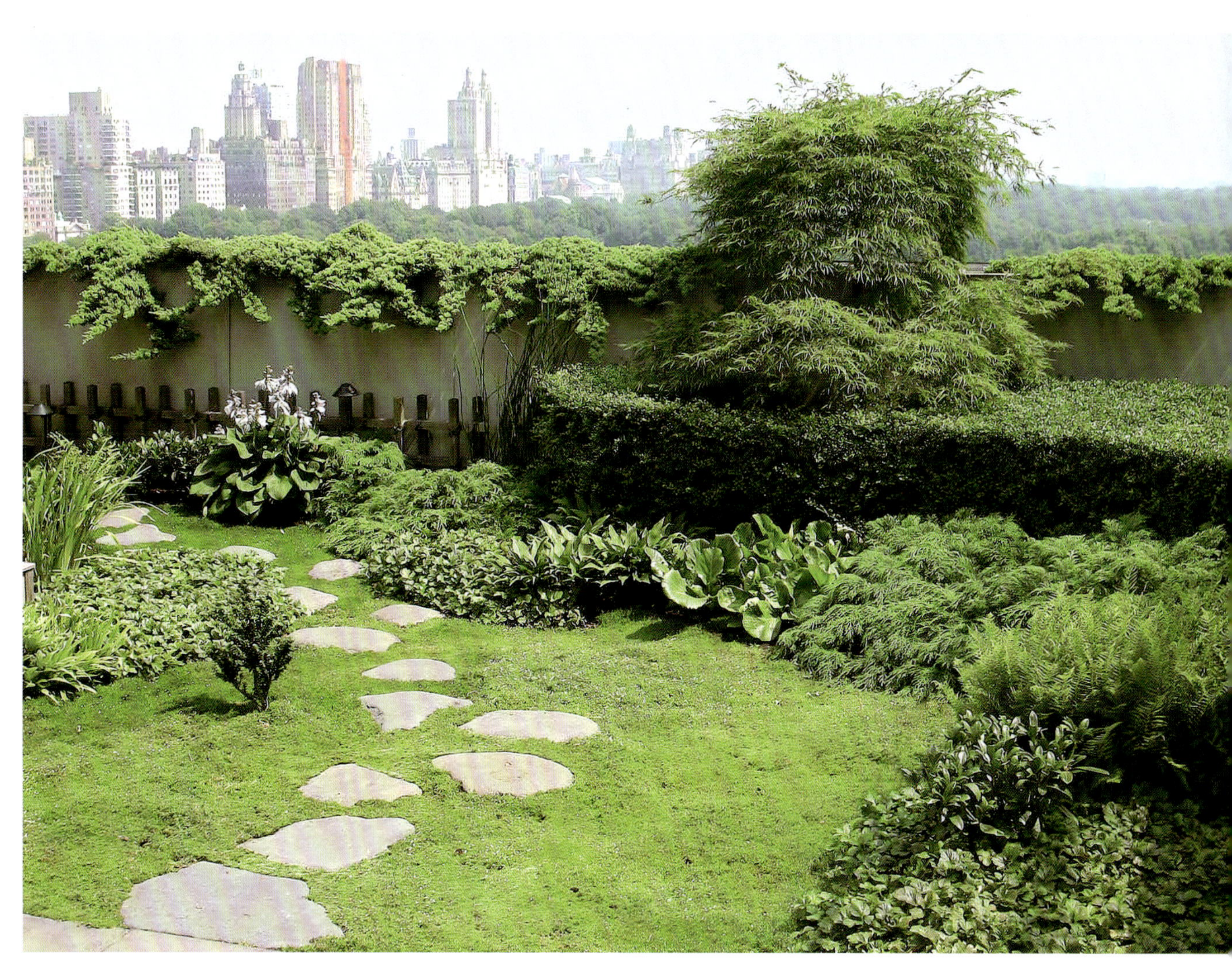

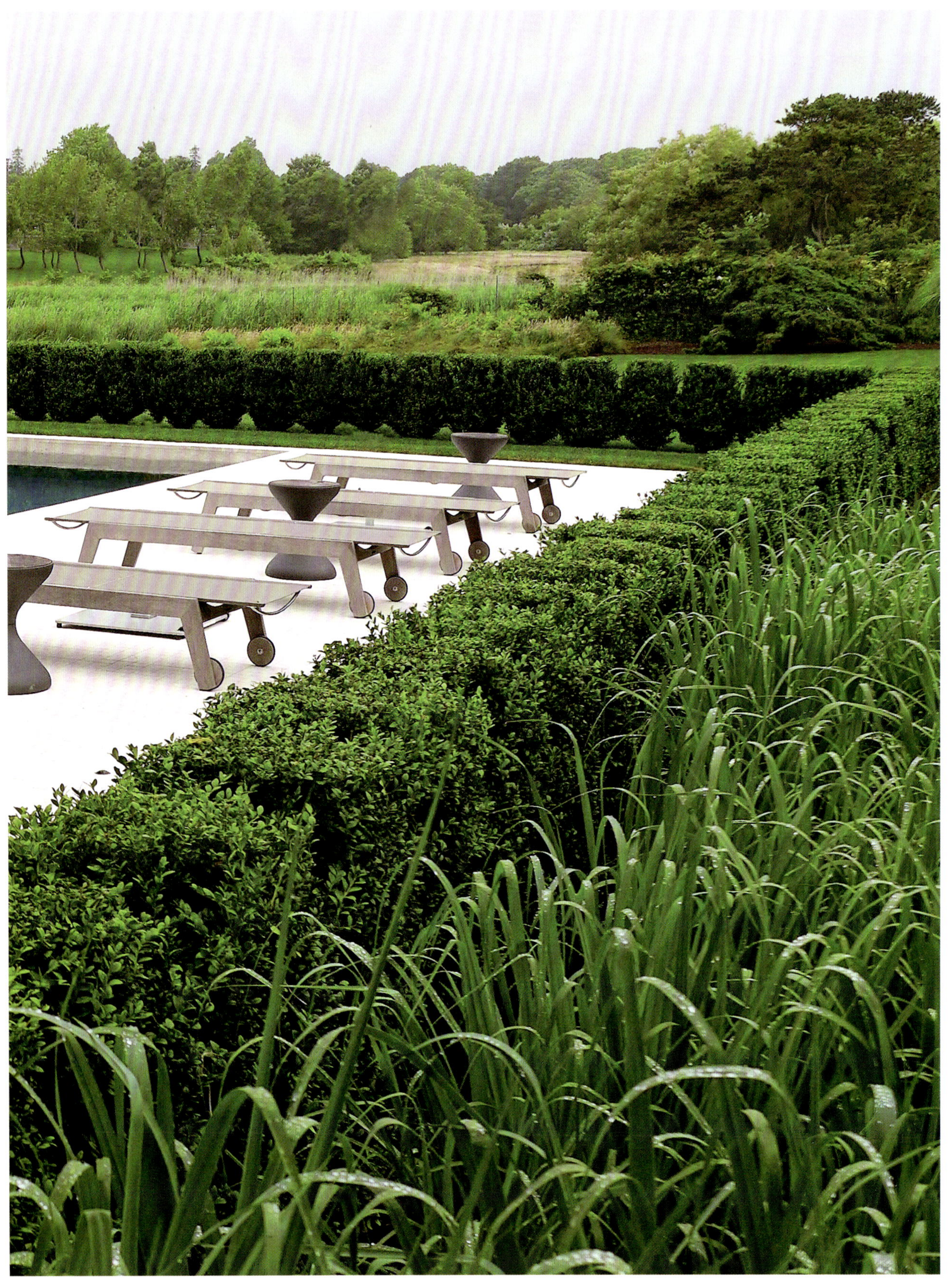

MINIMAL

When clients bought this two-and-a-half-acre property in East Hampton, New York, it had an existing house with a pool on it and was overgrown with trees and shrubs. They bought the property because of its water views, even though the views were partially blocked by a mass of invasive reed *Phragmites australis* that stood 10 feet tall and 60 feet deep in the wetlands portion of the property.

Bates Masi Architects, a firm based in East Hampton, New York, was hired to design a new house. In 2015, my office was asked to join the project team. All wetland removals and re-vegetation plans had to be submitted and approved by the local, state, and federal agencies. After receiving the necessary approvals, we removed the reeds and the wetlands were re-vegetated, revealing the beautiful water views. The landscape was designed to complement the minimal geometric architecture of the new house, with its strong lines and clean surfaces.

The house has four structures, with a central courtyard that is open to the elements. One circulates around the courtyard from one living area to another. The courtyard garden is designed as a simple space with a single tree *Acer palmatum dissectum 'Seiryu'* standing in a mass of dwarf mondo grass *Ophiopogon japonicus 'Nanus'* and a rupturewort area, separated by a gentle "S" curve. Stepping stones lay across the mondo grass, and five sheared boxwood shapes add accents to the composition.

OPPOSITE This landscape is composed of varying shades of green, with plants chosen for their scale and texture. Looking across the property, one can see a corner of the swimming pool and the open blades of the grass *Panicum virgatum* that contrast with the tight architecture of the new, sheared boxwood hedge.

OVERLEAF Approaching the striking, minimal shapes of the house—designed by the East Hampton, New York-based firm Bates Masi Architects, one drives along a quiet allée of Japanese Stewartia *Stewartia pseudocamelia*.

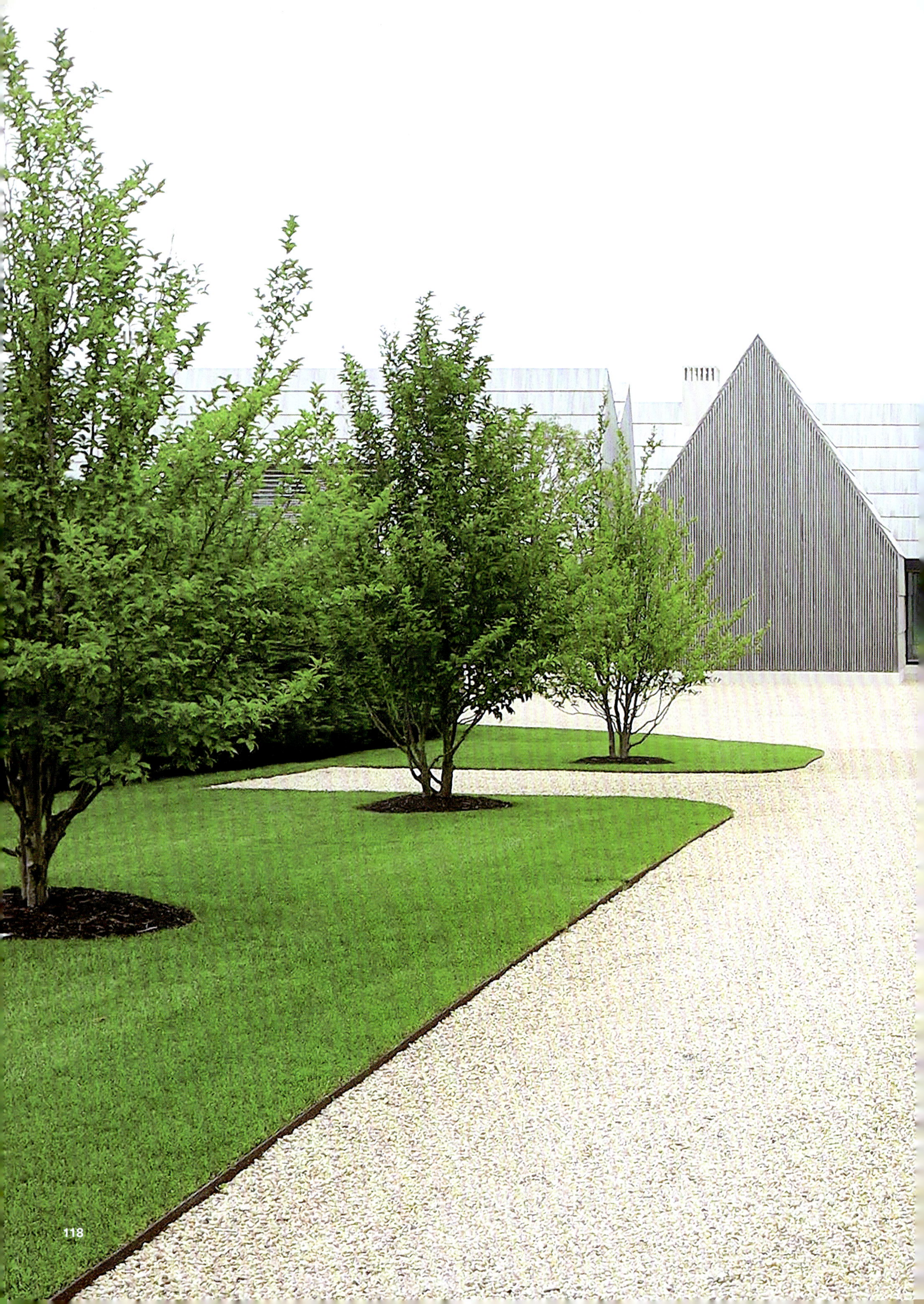

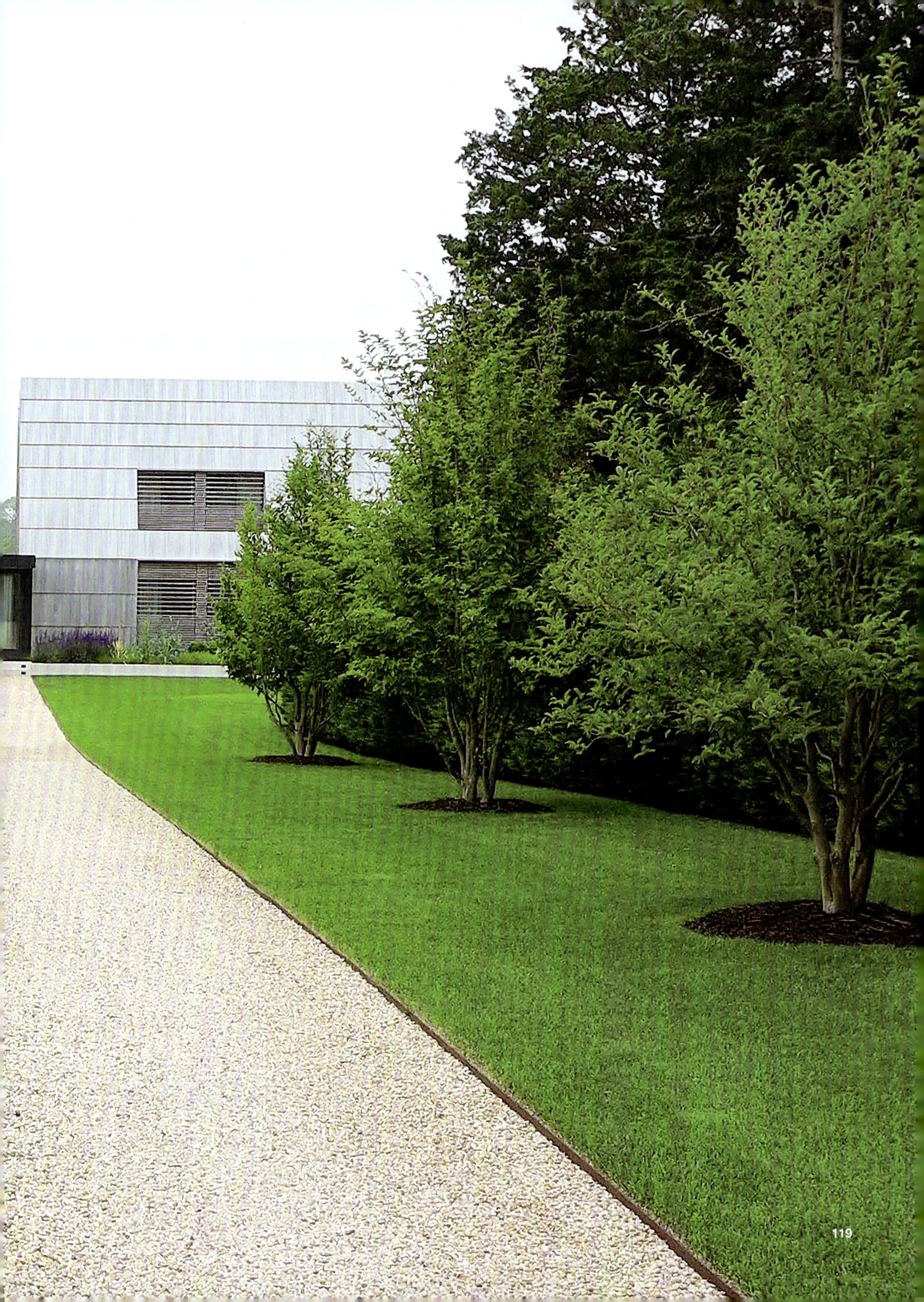

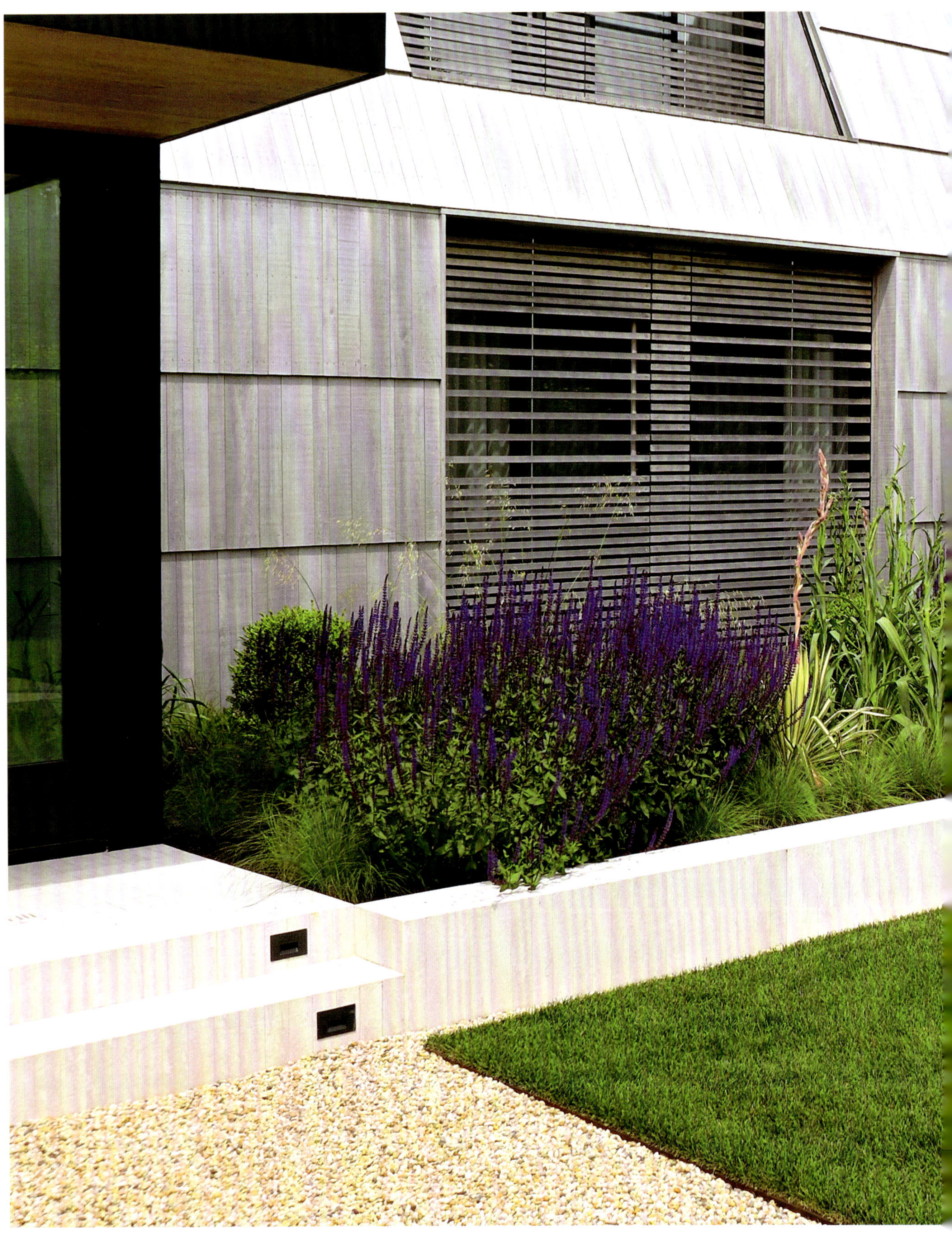

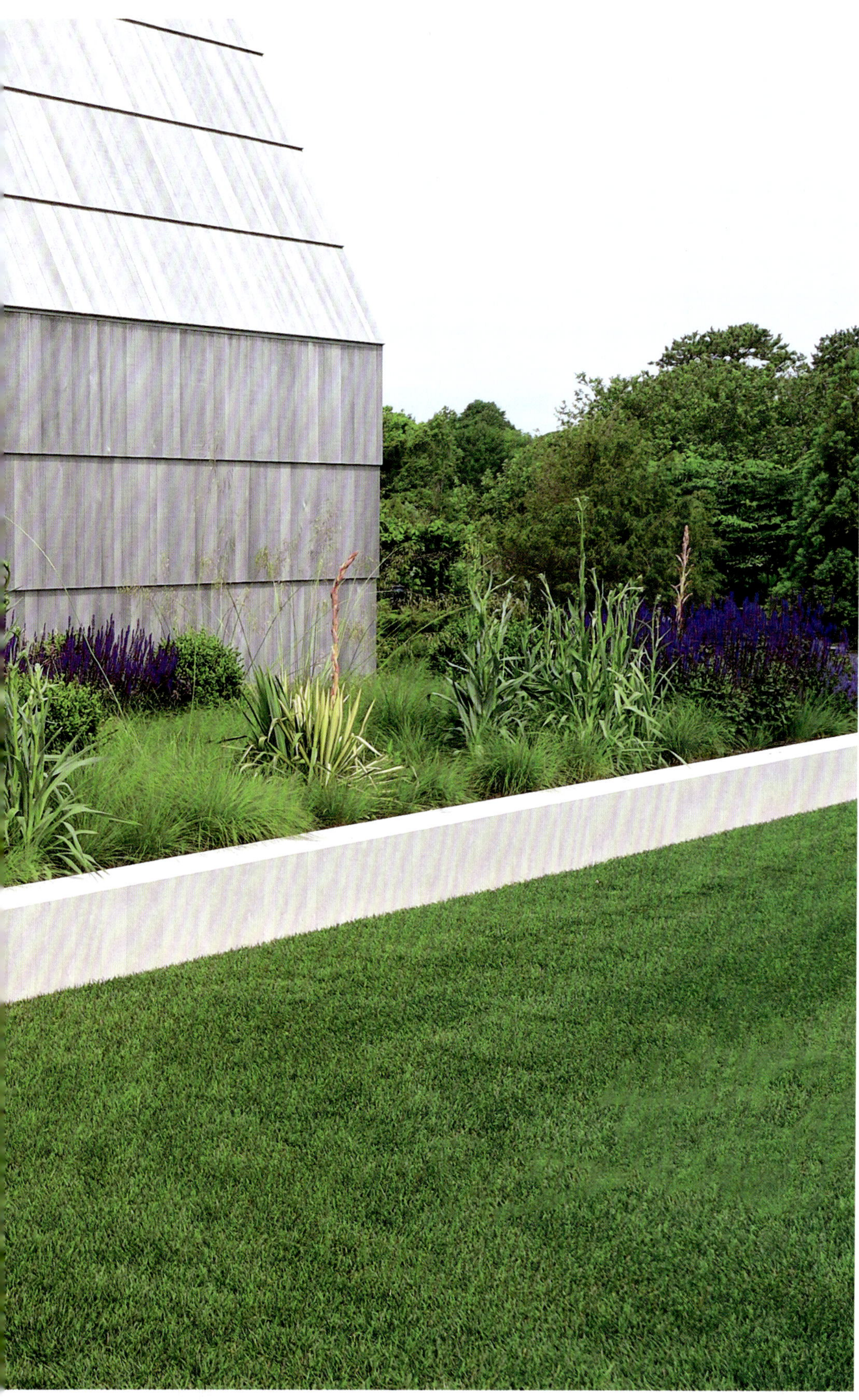

LEFT A raised bed at the entrance of the house is one of the few areas of color on the property. In the early summer, purple and yellow hues dominate the composition. Caradonna meadow sage *Salvia nemerosa 'Caradonna'* and Golden sword yucca *Yucca filamentosa 'Gold Sword'* are repeated in a mass of prairie dropseed *Sporobolus heterolepsis*. Rattlesnake master *Eryngium yuccifolium* and boxwood add a secondary interest to the composition.

OVERLEAF The interior courtyard garden is visible through the glass door of the entrance. To the right of the door, Caradonna meadow sage is in full bloom.

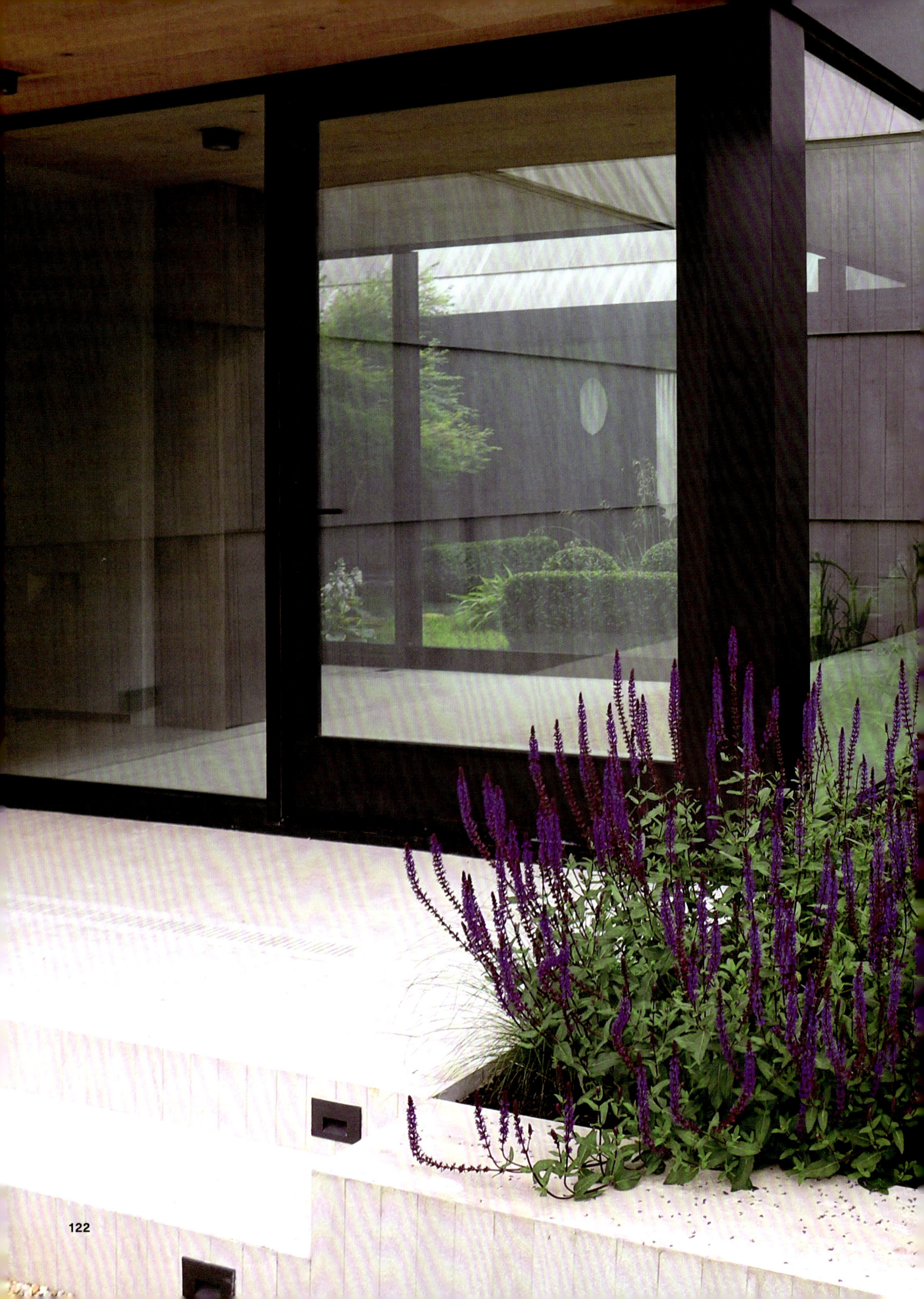

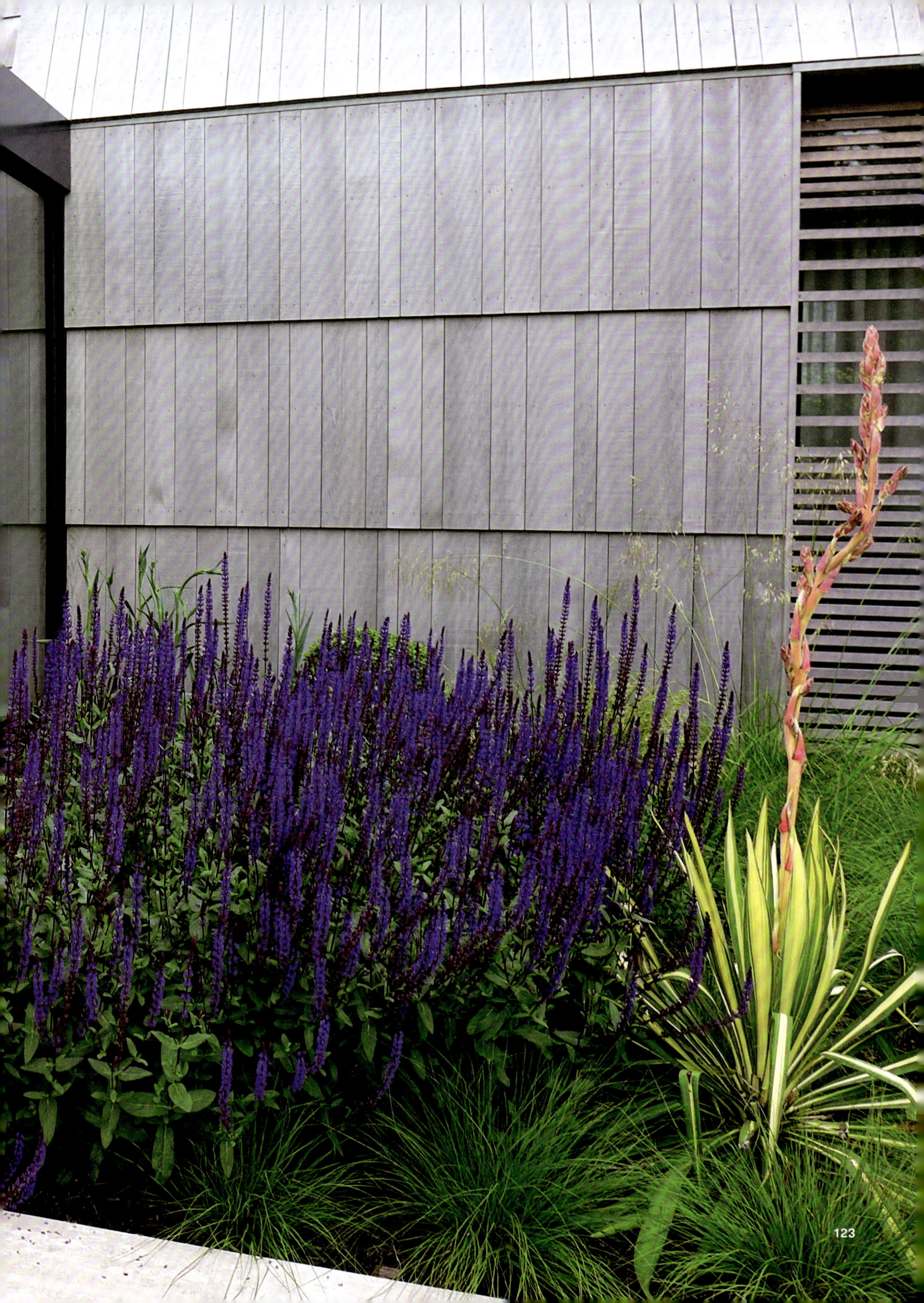

RIGHT From the living room, the interior courtyard is open to the elements and designed as a small, quiet landscape of its own. A single Japanese maple *Acer palmatum dissectum 'Seiryu'* has been planted amid a mass of dark green dwarf mondo grass *Ophiopogon japonicus 'Nanus.'* Separated by a graceful "S" curve, a second area of rupturewort *Hernaria glabra* complements the mondo grass with its light green color. Stepping stones through the grass and clipped boxwoods add visual interest to the composition.

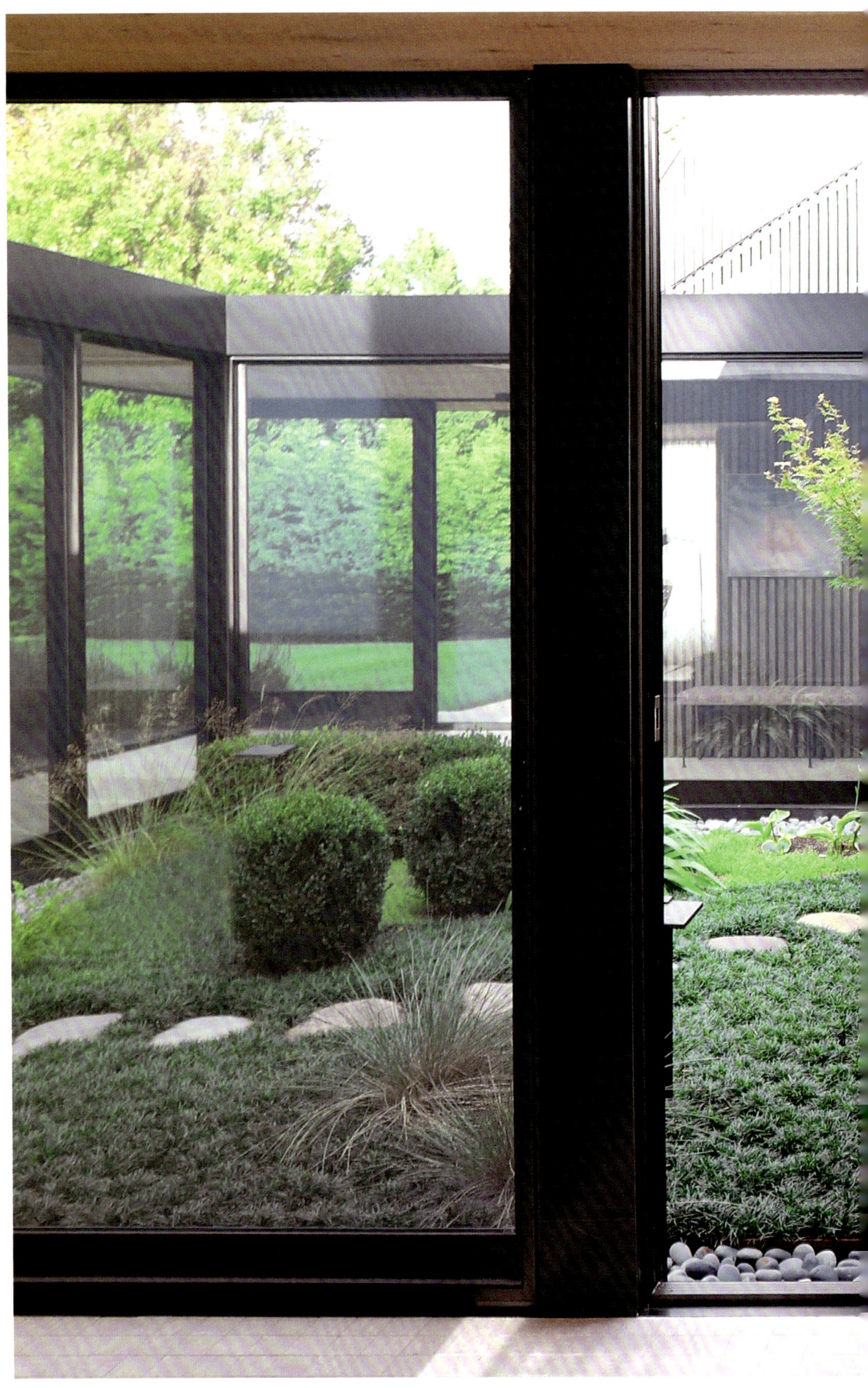

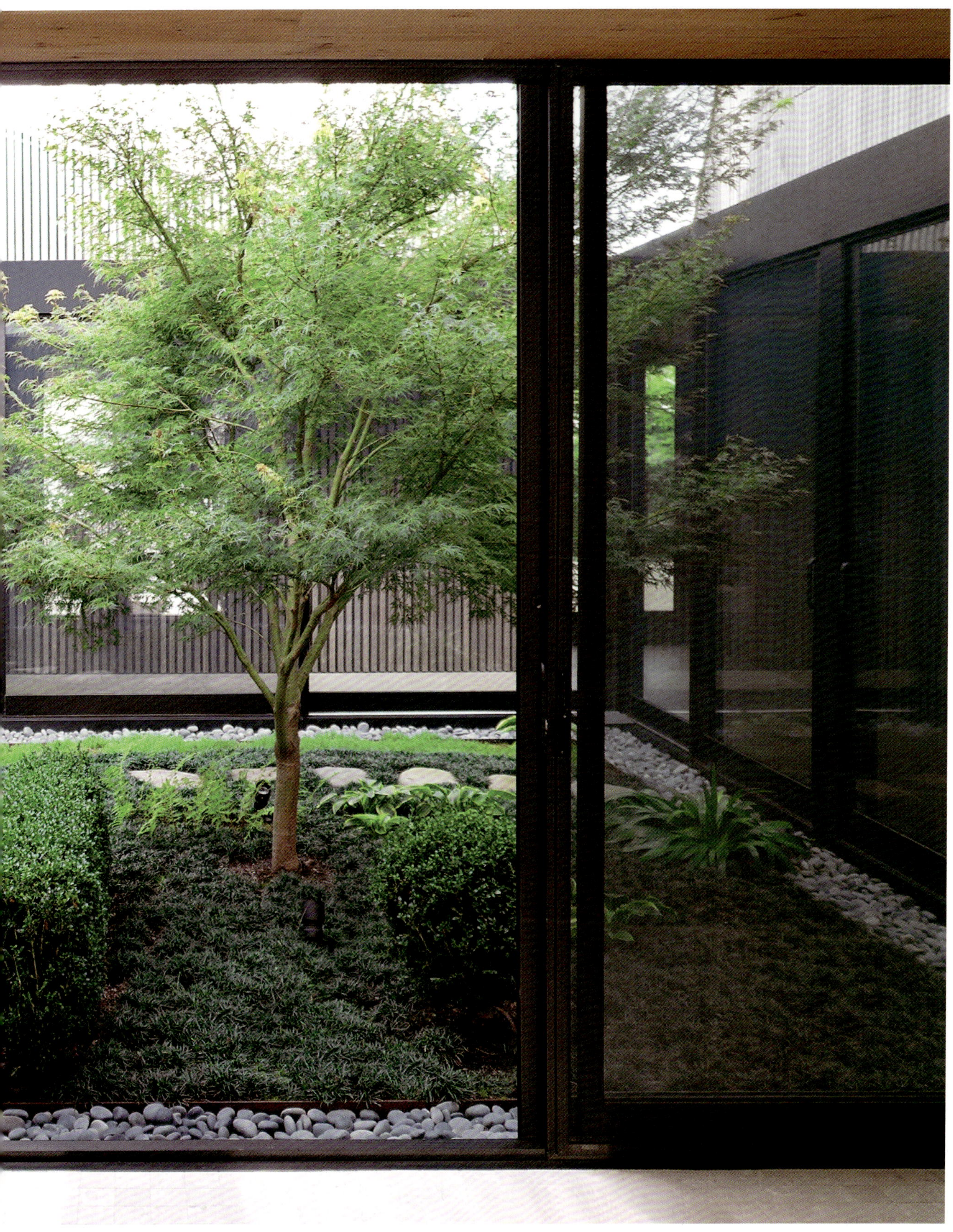

RIGHT A raised bed off the living room has been filled with flowering fountain grass *Pennisetum alopecuroides*. The field of switchgrass *Panicum virgatum* is also in bloom.

OVERLEAF At the north end of the pool, the boxwood hedge intersects the mass of grass, providing a contrast with the soft, airy grass beyond. The pool is approached by a curved path through the grass.

PAGES 130–131 After the reed *Phragmites australis* was removed, the wetlands were re-vegetated with selected wetland plants, revealing the water's calm beauty.

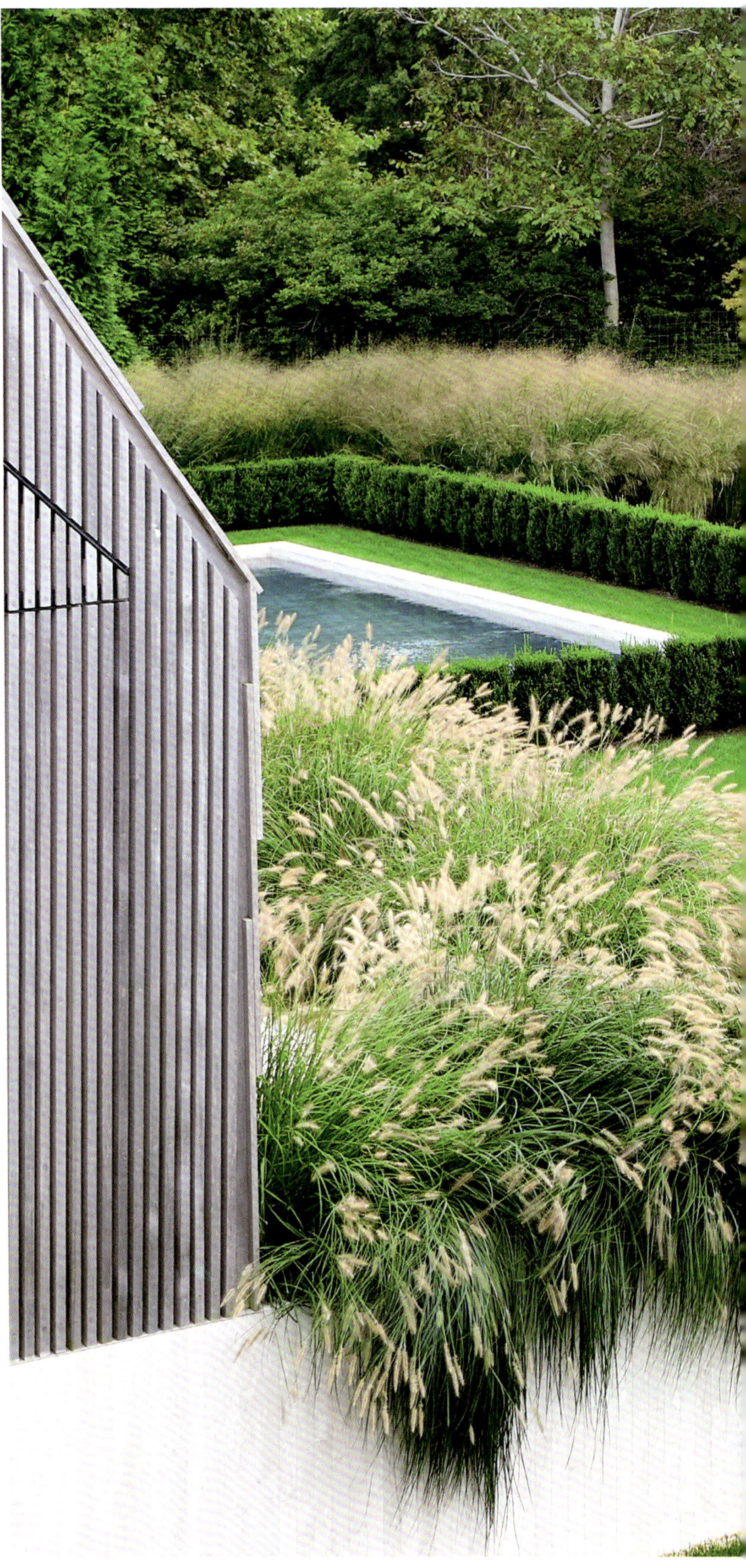

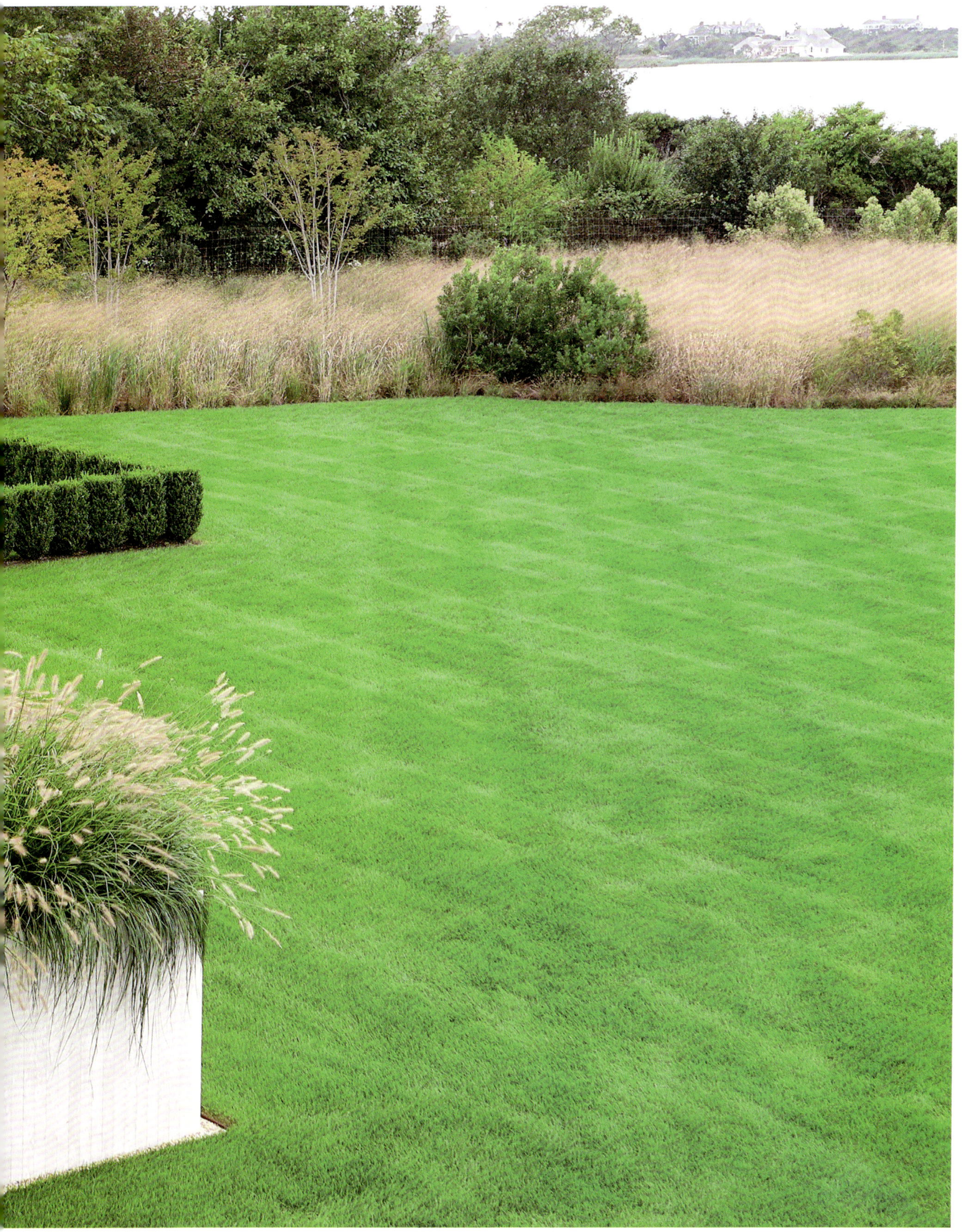

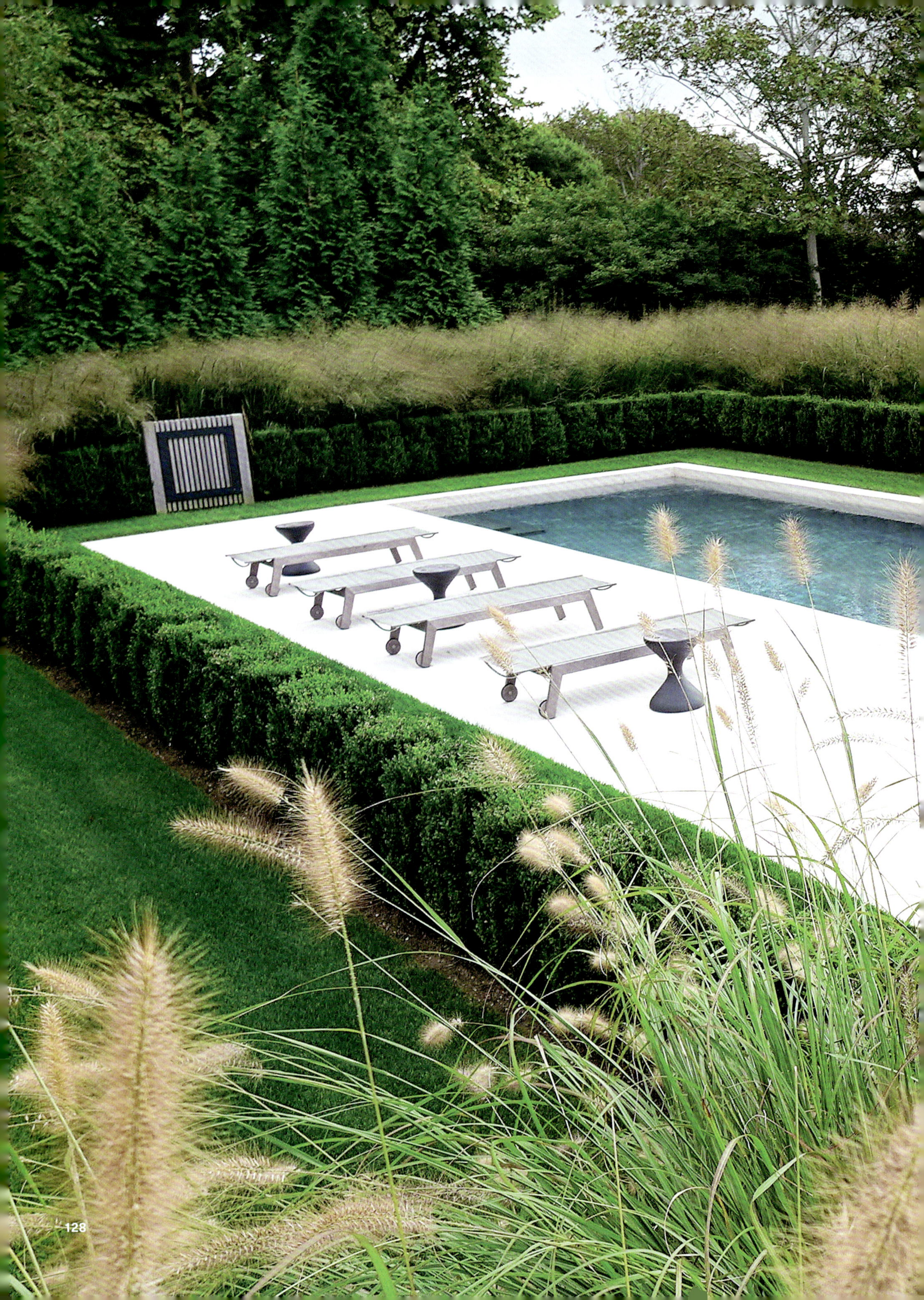

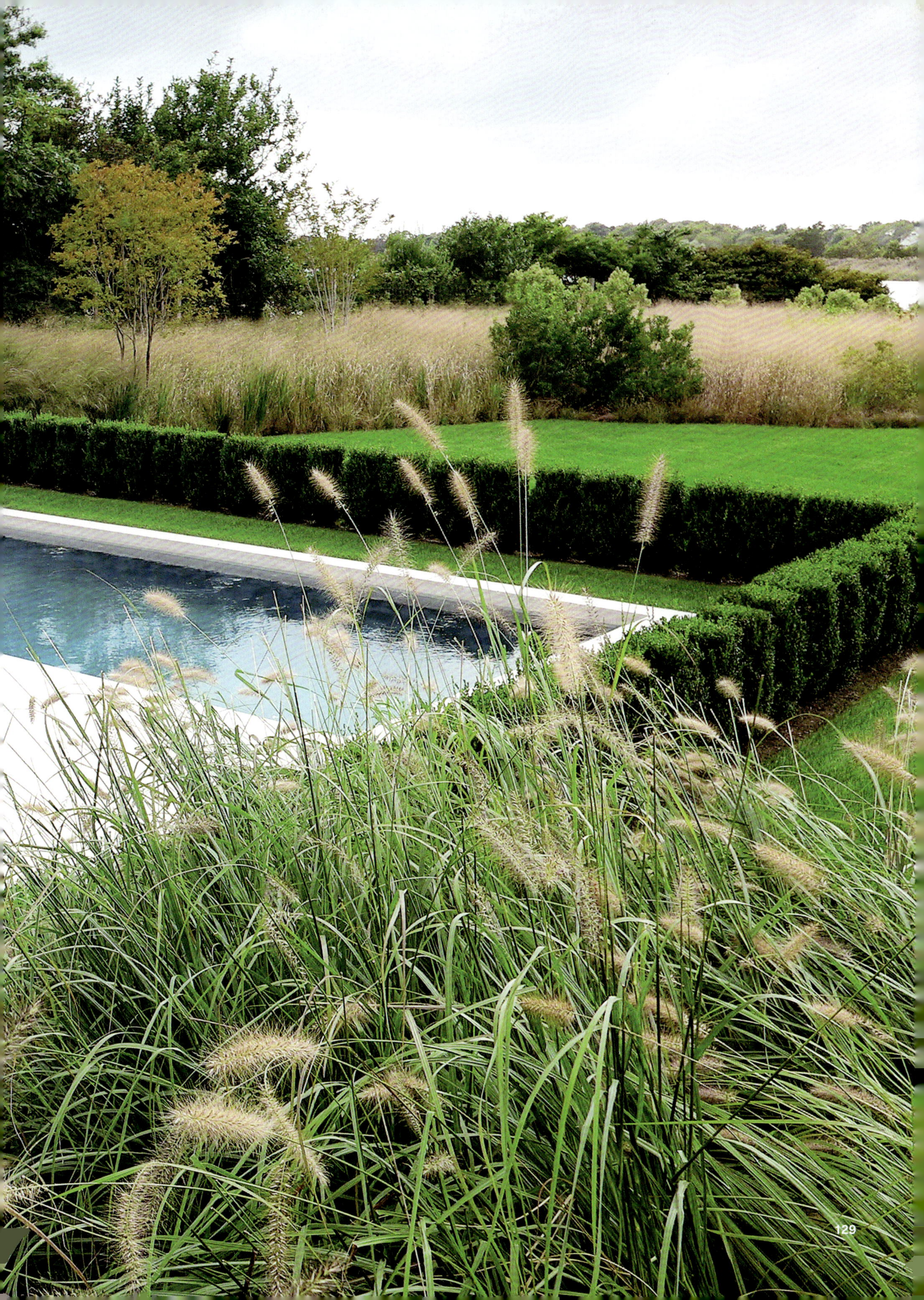

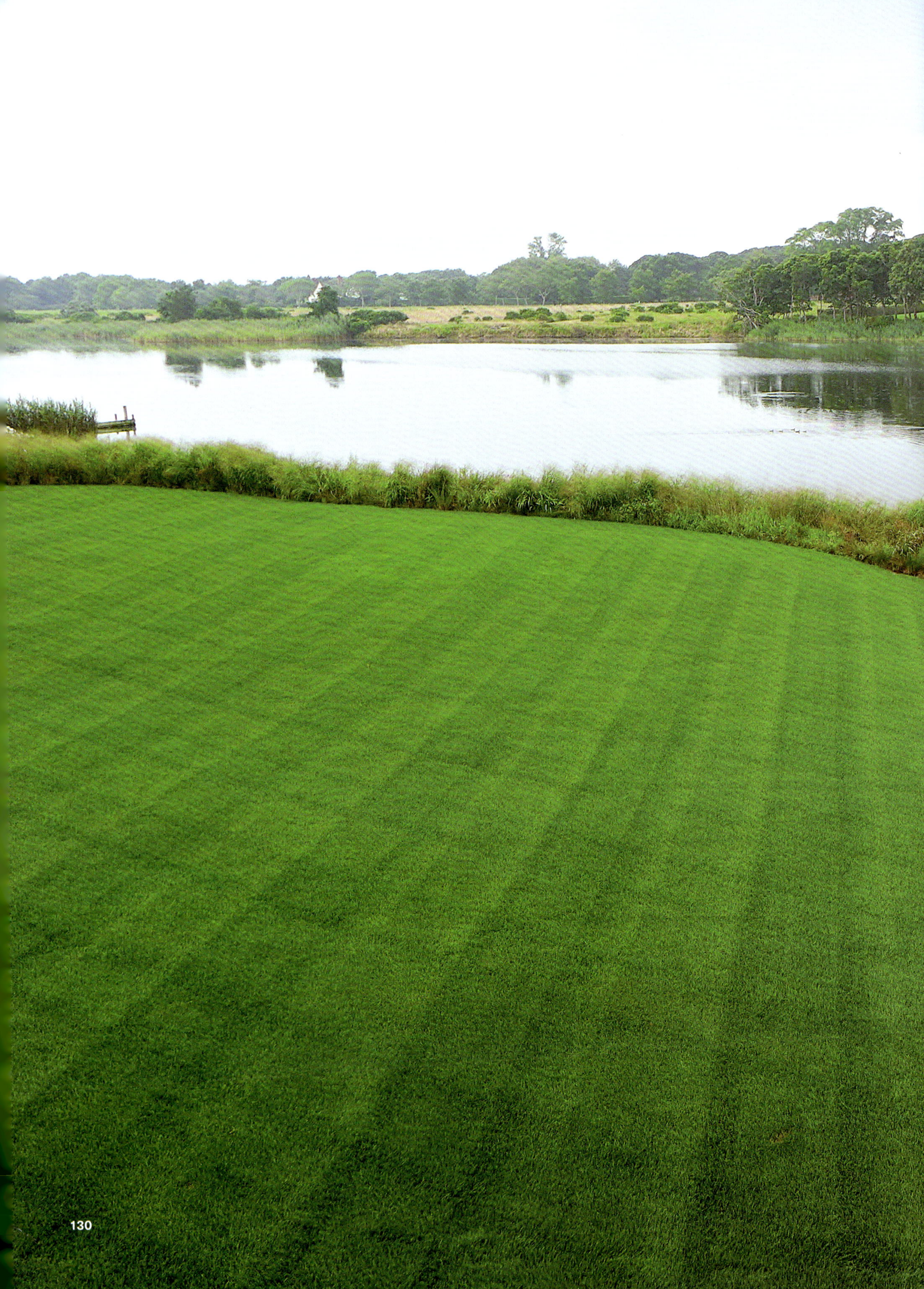

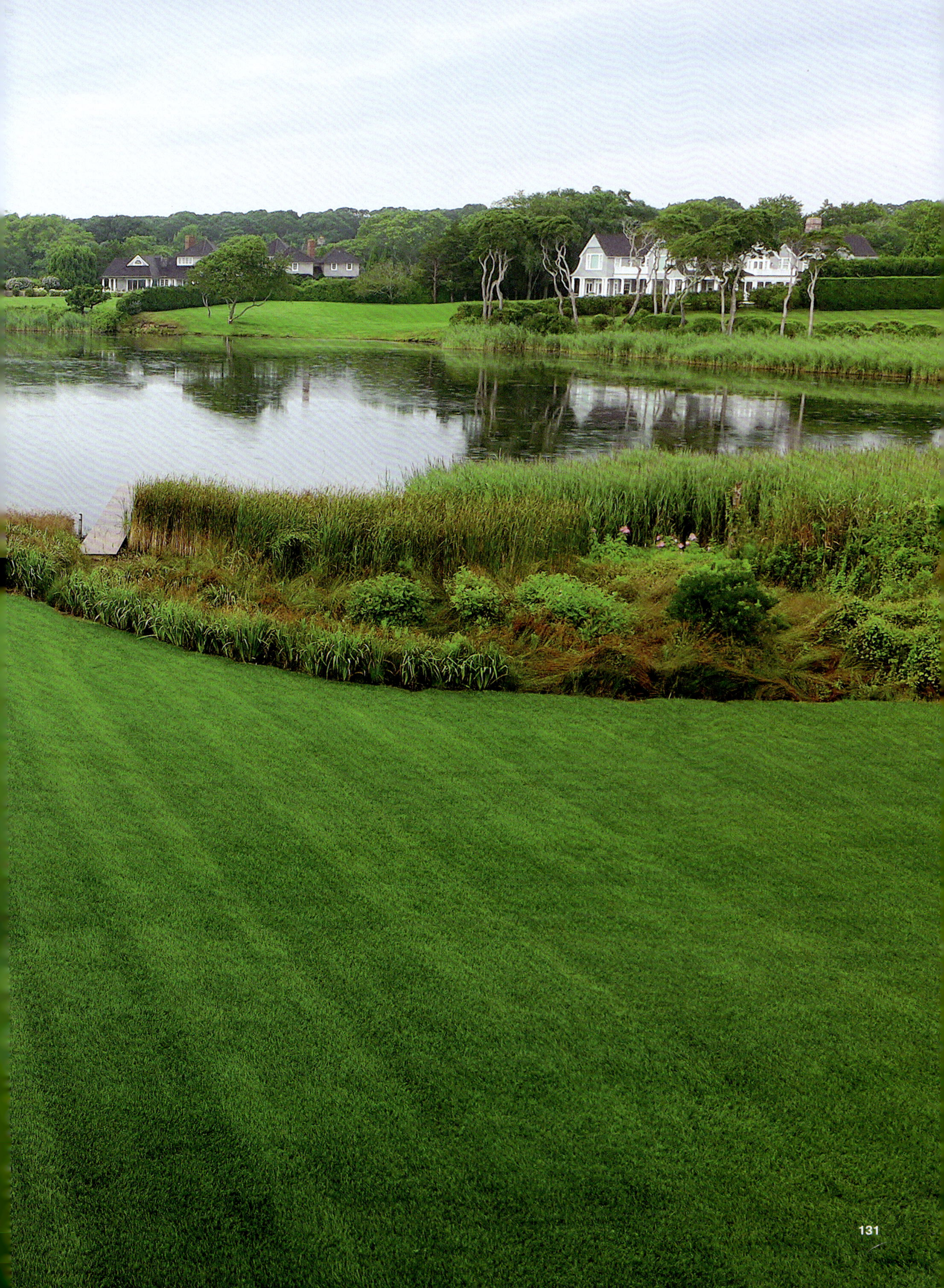

TO MY HUSBAND,
CHUCK SKLAR,
FOR HIS UNWAVERING
SUPPORT AND
ENCOURAGEMENT
OF THIS BOOK,
AND SO MUCH MORE

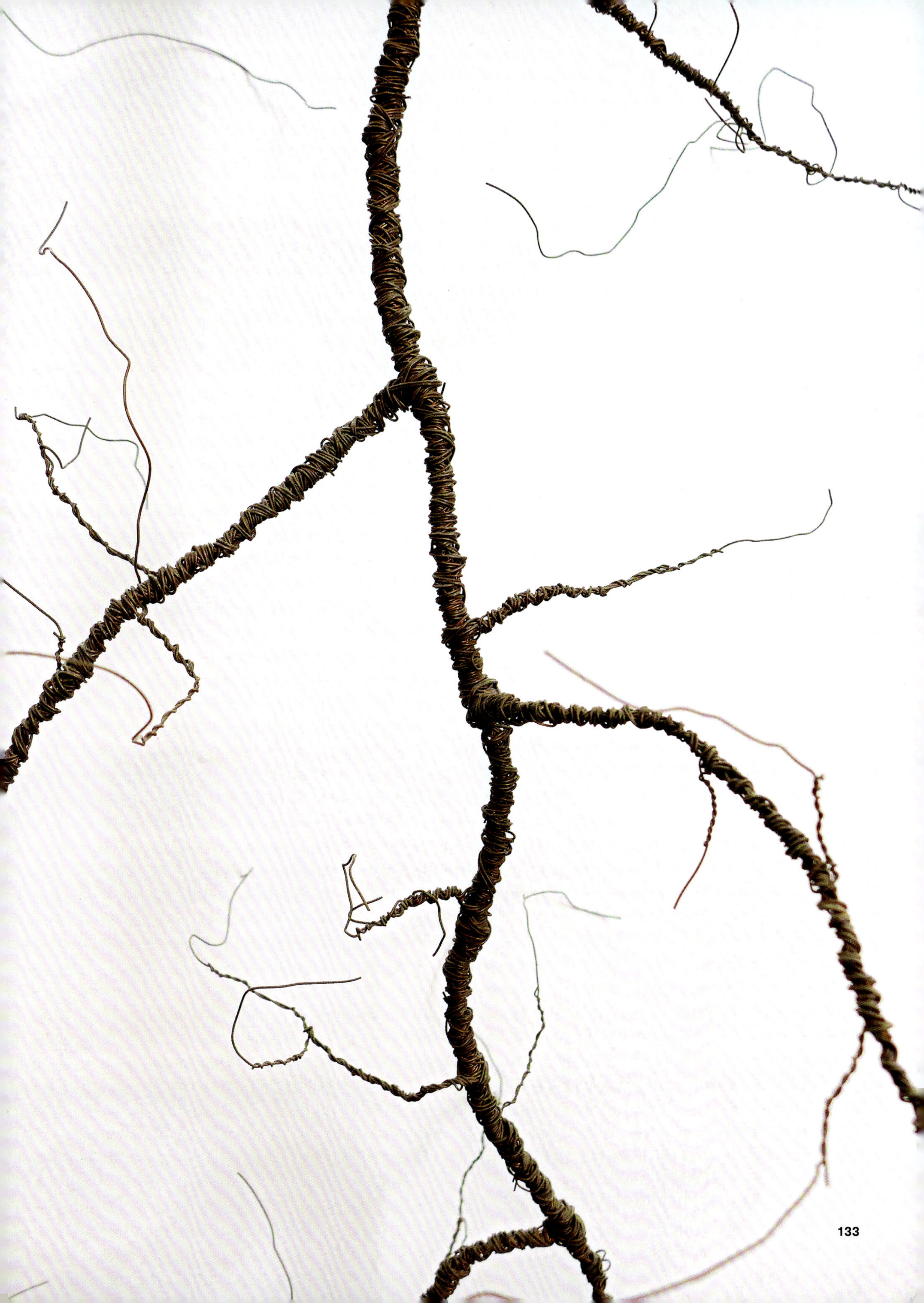

ACKNOWLEDGMENTS

None of my gardens would have existed without the trust and support of my clients, many of whom I worked with over many decades.

I've known my friend Judith Russi Kirshner for almost 50 years. We met when I lived in Chicago, and she has followed my art and garden designs over the years.

Barbara Toll is a client who trusted me with development of her property in Sag Harbor, New York, for three long decades. During this period, the gardens grew and so did our friendship.

Without the help of a talented and dedicated staff of landscape architects and designers, these projects could not have come to fruition. I want to thank: Greg Gill, Robert Monteleone, Mike Ouchakof, Seth Ruggiero, Sam Jimenez, and David Mendelson. A special thanks to Jack Henning, Paul Herkovic, and Lelsie Baglio for their inspiring plantsmanship and devotion to horticulture.

In addition to staff, I want to thank Ben Krell for his beautifully crafted carpentry, Chris Staeger of SwissScapes for his detailed attention to the issues of lighting and irrigation, Frank Tabanga of Fenix for his precise metalwork, and Stuart Cook and Bob Pucci of Whitmores Landscaping in East Hampton, New York, for their attentive installation of my landscape designs.

I also want to thank Suzanne Slesin, the publisher and editorial director of Pointed Leaf Press, for her patience, intelligence, and guidance through the making of this book; creative director Frederico Farina for his sensitive interpretation of my work and its translation into the book layouts; and managing editor Kelly Koester, for carefully keeping track of my endless emails and photographs.

—Jeff Mendoza, March 2019

INDEX

CAPTIONS

COVER The swimming pool on a property in East Hampton, New York, has been tucked into a field of switchgrass.
ENDPAPERS The linear complexity of grass was a challenge to draw. In 1978, I was home recovering from an illness, and, to occupy my time, I decided to try to draw grass, using a pen on 8 x 11-inch paper.
OPPOSITE HALF-TITLE Because of the serious weight restrictions on most rooftops and terraces, taking advantage of the floor plane for visual interest is something I like to explore. In 2000, I was working on a design for a 2,000-square-foot terrace and realized that by removing tiles and filling the empty spaces with beach pebbles of the same weight as the tiles, I was able to add visual interest to a large area without extra weight.
PAGES 2–3 Trees, which signify strength and endurance, are one of nature's most noble creations. The oldest living organism on earth is a bristlecone pine *Pinus longaeva* in California called *Methusalah*, which is estimated to be 4,848 years old. In 1986–1987 I cast a series of twigs in iron. This 25-inch-long twig humbly suggested a connection to that long lineage.
PAGES 4–5 I was hired in 1992 to create a series of gardens—an area of about 2,000-square-feet—for a Shelter Island, New York, property that would connect the pool to the main house. I sheared the top of the existing privet hedge that surrounded the pool into waves as a nod to the island's setting.
PAGES 6–7 The complexity of leaf forms and color with their endless varieties fascinate me. In 1981, using colored pencils on sketchpad paper, I started a series of drawings of leaves that focused on shape and color. This leaf was the first in the series.
I find the tactile and sculptural qualities of tree bark seductive. I created this Bark Study in 1983 by building up layers of Japan paper on a curved board, then coloring the work with acrylic paint.
PAGE 8 In 1985, I found this 22 ¾ x 15 ¼-inch Japanese bark paper at my art supply store. Using oil stick on its rough textured surface produced the illusion of bark on this drawing, entitled *Tree*.
PAGES 10–11 As New York City terraces are often long and narrow, they create numerous design challenges. This 830-square-foot one, on the Hudson River, also had fierce winds to contend with. In 2013, I created removable metal covers for the six davit pedestals—used to lower scaffolding for window washers—with shallow planters on top for sedums and thymes, to incorporate them into the garden design.
PAGES 12 AND 133 In 1980, I began a series of root sculptures made of wire. This copper wire 69 x 29 x 16-inch piece, entitled *Root #5*, has multiple associations for me, such as roots, rivers, and veins.
BACK OF BACK ENDPAPERS A copper tubing stem and a Japan paper leaf were painted in acrylic in this 4 x 1 x 5-foot *Waterlily* from the 1981 *Leaf* series. When installed on a wall, the piece projects five feet into the space with the lily pad floating about seven feet off the ground. The viewer looks up at the bottom of the leaf as if he, or she, were underwater.

All the photographs in this book are by Jeff Mendoza except for the image on pages 4–5, which is credited to Matthew Benson Foto.

PUBLISHER SUZANNE SLESIN

CREATIVE DIRECTOR FREDERICO FARINA

MANAGING EDITOR KELLY KOESTER

ISBN: 978-1-938461-89-7 Library of Congress number: 2018966462 Printed in China / First Edition

POINTED LEAF PRESS, LLC., 136 BAXTER STREET, SUITE 1C, NEW YORK, NY 10013. WWW.POINTEDLEAFPRESS.COM

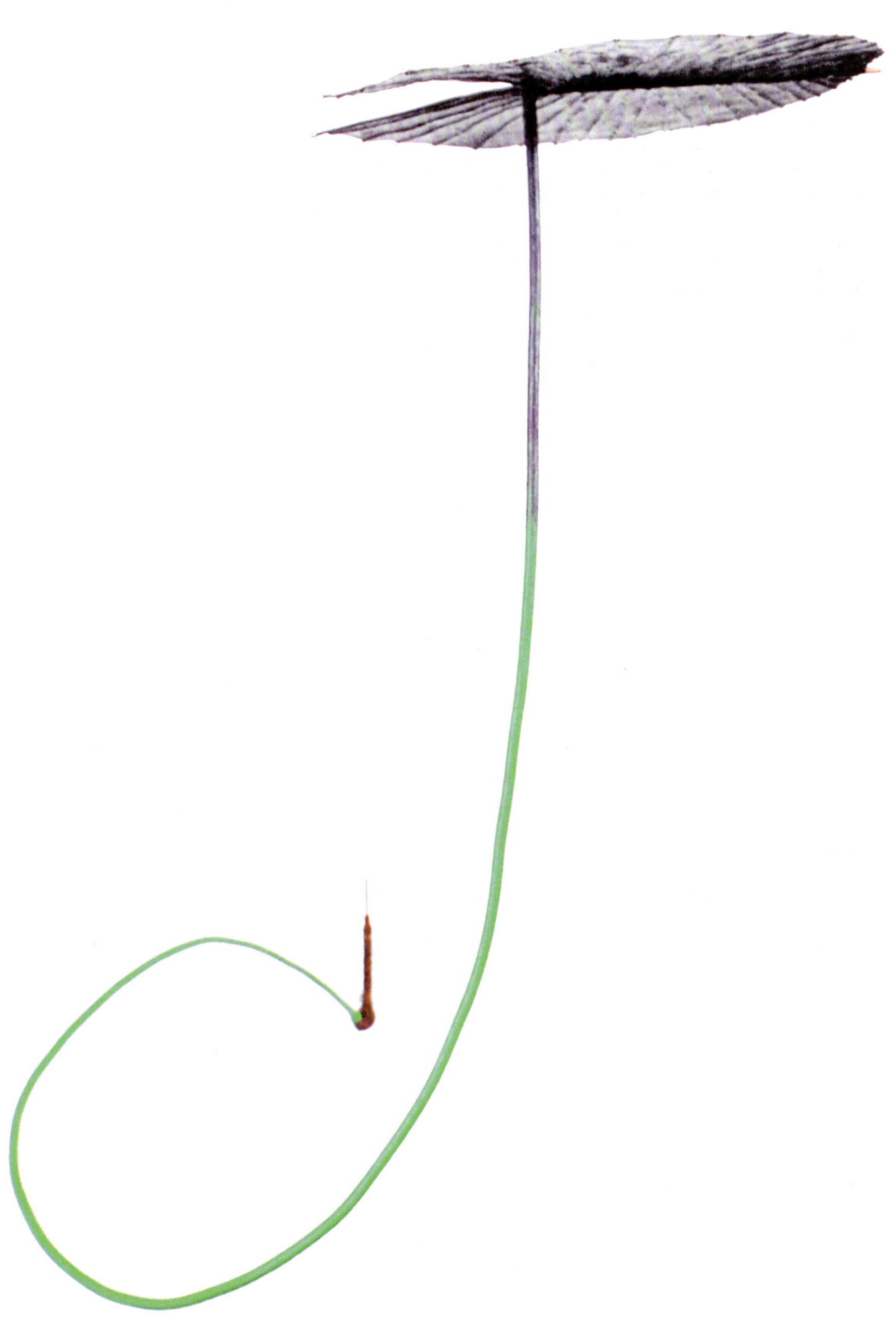

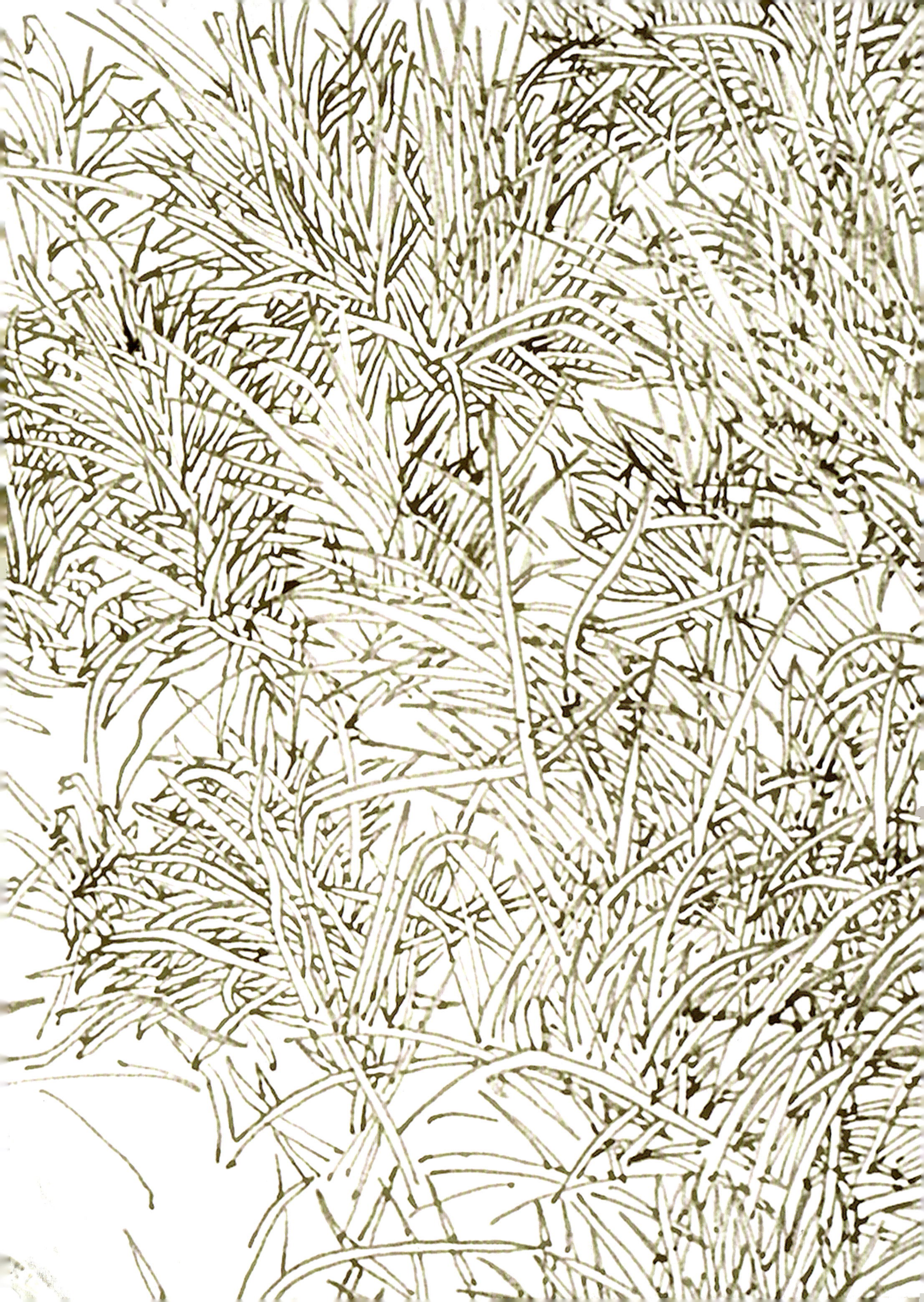